# 21st Century South Asia

# 21st Century South Asia

*Edited by*

**Sanghamitra Sarker**

**Manas Publications**
**(We Convert Fighters into Writers)**
**New Delhi - 110 002 (INDIA)**

MANAS PUBLICATIONS
**(Publishers for Defence, IAS, IPS, IFS, IRS, Judges Press etc)**
(Publishers, Library Suppliers, Importers & Exporters)
4402/5-A, Ansari Road (Opp. HDFC Bank)
Darya Ganj, New Delhi - 110 002 (India)
Phones: Off.: 011-23260783, 23265523, Res.: 011-23842660
Fax: 011-23272766
E-mail: manaspublications@gmail.com
manaspublications@yahoo.com
Website: www.manaspublications.in



**ISBN 978-81-7049-494-2**
**₹ 995/-**



*Designed at*
Manas Publications

*Printed in India at*
RK Print Services, Delhi
and published by Mrs Suman Lata for
Manas Publications, 4402/5-A,
Ansari Road, (Opp HDFC Bank),
Darya Ganj, New Delhi - 110002 (INDIA)

# Preface

National security is the requirement and pre-requisite to maintain and preserve the survival of a state through the use of economic power, diplomacy, power projection and political power.

While studying all these articles for publication, I came across a significant diversity in the perception of security within a unified aim of safeguarding security in the South Asian region. In the essay by Sanjay Bhardwaj, there is a description of attempts of the small states to survive in the international system rather than to play a dominant role. In the essay, he has studied the 'Bengali' and 'Muslim' nationalistic tendencies in Bangladesh vis-à-vis India, which helps to create a definite understanding of the history and the nationalist affinities of the people of the region. His work also stresses on the bilateral and cooperative ties between India and Bangladesh which plays a significant role in the Indian sub-continent. In the paper by Alok Bansal, the turbulent political conditions that Pakistan has faced in the recent past have been highlighted. It deals with faultlines that have affected Pakistan, such as, the growing sectarian divide, resurgence of ethno-national identities, continuing economic meltdown and growing radicalisation or Talibanisation of society. While progressing through the work, I came across the essay by Somali Mukherjee which is a theoretical study that seeks to apply the Democratic Peace Proposition (DPP) or thesis to study the role played by different regime types in constructing relations with India. There is no systematic work yet on the subject that applies the DPP to study the orientations, practices, institutional basis, power struggles, and related aspects of Pakistan's myriad regimes in their relations with India. There is no published work in the public domain which has applied DPP to India-Pakistan relations and this proposed paper is an attempt to fill in this gap. When I went through the essay written by the honourable Governor of West Bengal, MK Narayanan, I found he had mentioned the different security threats that India faces in the 21st century. Biswanath Chakraborty deals with the ethnic problems and national security issues in Nepal. His work briefly highlights the ethnic issues that the country has faced and also the history of the various ethnic groups and their movements. The paper also hints at proposals for ethnic autonomy which was close to what is defined as an ethnic federal system. Shubhodeep Chakrabarti has studied the China-Pakistan strategic axis that has been a determining factor in the evolution of India's strategic doctrines ever since the border conflict with China (1962) and the subsequent engagement of Pakistan by China. He also points out the various financial and military engagements that have strengthened the bilateral ties between the two neighbours of India. This essay also urges the policy-makers to re-assess and modify the bilateral relations with China and Pakistan, alongside other 'potential' allies. Foreign policy plays an extremely crucial role in determining security of any region and any country. In his essay, Pratyay Dutta has stressed upon the contributions of Rammanohar Lohia, who did remarkable work in laying the foundation of the foreign policy of the Indian National Congress (INC). The paper aims at presenting the multi-dimensional aspects of Lohia's ideas on Indo-Pak unity through co-existence with approximation. Quite importantly, the sea links play a significant role in international politics. In his article, Shounak Set deals with the serious issue of maritime security. Recognising the illustrative historical and contemporary trends, the paper analyses the diverse aspects and attempt to investigate and introspect on this increasingly salient but marginally realised phenomenon; fundamental for anticipating the direction of South Asian security in this century. The article by Shakti Sinha highlights the earlier-than-expected withdrawal of the US troops from Afghanistan that opens up the whole argument about the efficacy of the War on Terror, thereby stressing on the power dynamics of the South Asian region revolving around US's war strategy and the consequent role of the volatile and dubious Afghan state and Pakistan. Partha Pratim Basu, in his essay echoes the point that Pakistan is perhaps one of those few states of the world which appear to be in a state of perpetual turmoil, and the 21st century seems to be no exception to this proposition and seeks in general to emphasise two critical sources of turmoil in Pakistan: failure to establish a working balance among the three major political institutions, i e, the executive, the army and the judiciary, the latest entrant into the race; and the penchant of the powers used by radical Islamists as a foreign policy instrument since the 1980s in particular.

Unity is a crucial factor in a volatile region like South Asia. Likewise, Anindya Jyoti Majumdar has explained in his paper that in South Asia, the states are yet to come to terms with their own abilities and identities in global or regional hierarchy while steadfastly seeking to protect the outward expressions of sovereignty, thereby referring to the split personalities and the failure to comprehend each other's legitimate windows of vulnerability that lead to problems of accommodation and germinate insecurity in the region. Suranjan Das quite specifically highlights that South Asian unity today is very important if the region has to take advantage of the current decline of the traditional great powers. Further, Pradip Bhattacharjee mentions that for South Asia's security, democratisation in this region is very vital and only through this, political permanence of this area can be assured. Krishnan Srinivasan speaks about a unique concept of united South Asia, where he asserts that India has to play a distinct and crucial role in the development and progress of the entire neighbourhood. Concomitant to the idea of united South Asia, I came across quite a similar essay. Amartya Ray mentions about India's attitude towards its smaller neighbours. In his article, he argues that India is again getting back to a position to assert its pivotal role in the region and that South Asia is best secured when India maintains good ties with its smaller neighbours, while keeping its western front quiet.

While going through the papers, I had observed the concept of security being understood through a more unconventional medium. Shankhamala Ray's essay comes up as a unique piece of study which analyses the security scenario of Afghanistan and Pakistan by means of the broad array of media. She also indicates the development of fascist tendencies combined with staunch religious support that threatens an ominous future for women in Pakistan, highlighting the regressive stance of a male-dominated society that offers no liberty to women in any spheres of life. Sharmita Bhattacharya, in her paper deals with the complex and complicated phenomenon of food security in the developing countries of South Asia. The purpose of this paper is to examine the current state of food security and its future in the South Asian countries of Bangladesh, India, China, Pakistan, Nepal, Sri Lanka and Bhutan. Following the same lines, Satabdi Das has highlighted that the environmental dimension of geopolitics in general and the effects of climate change and its consequences for India's national security in particular discern different dimensions of the threat and the politics involved in India's climate policy both in domestic and international sphere.

Security also encompasses the human factor. A very unique side of this human factor is health security; on which Dr Ranjit Chakrabarti has very emphatically stressed. He has defined the concept of security from a medical practitioner's perspective and the paper deals with the challenges and possible remedies in the rural and urban health sector in India, Nepal, Bhutan and Bangladesh, on the basis of his first-hand experience. Subarna Bhattacharya's article highlights the extent to which human security in the Indo-Bangladesh border area is at stake. The paper attempts to find out avenues to curb this glaring political and social issue and recommends certain ideas for both the governments to assess upon for establishing better bilateral ties between India and Bangladesh. Talking about the human side of security, one very engaging paper has been written by Saswati Ghosh. Her paper deeply looks into existing gender inequality leading to migration decisions, greater feminisation of migration, migration associated with human poverty issues and social exclusion. It also focusses on gender-based discrimination as well as human rights and international law violation in the process of migration, and the poverty-migration-trafficking nexus. However, my paper deals with a host of security challenges in South Asia. The paper stresses on security of common people vis-à-vis security as perceived by traditional state power. Aloke Sen in his essay explains that security that hampers development, in turn fosters insecurity, which is a classic vicious cycle, of which the North-East of India can be a key example.

I also came across a different perspective of security scenario while reading these papers. The essay by Deeplekha Sengupta and Devarati Mandal deals with the security issues in the Maldives and the fact that climate change has direct bearings on its economy affecting marine eco-system, tourism, fishery and also youth employment, and therefore, the Maldives might turn into a breeding ground of terrorism and future terrorist activities. Kashmir, like always has been a key area of discussion and debate. Aswini K Ray talks about the Indo-Pak tension over the Kashmir dispute and the consequent security concerns in the region. Against the backdrop of an integrated approach to the idea of security in Post-Cold-War scenario, Moutusi Paul Choudhury (Naskar) tries to analyse the various non-traditional security threats facing the South Asian countries, in the light of the challenges posed by the process of globalisation. Water has been a crucial factor in the security management of any region. India and Bangladesh, despite sharing a common colonial heritage, have many bones of contention. Among the most complicated problems that resulted in a deadlock situation between the two countries, is the sharing of the waters of the Ganges and the Farakka Barrage constructed by India. In this paper, Utsa Sarmin stresses on the various political manifestations that have had occurred in both the countries revolving around the question of water sharing.

Hence, one could say security is an umbrella term which covers many dimensions that has direct or indirect implications to the environment, society, state, continent and the world.

Sanghamitra Sarker

# Acknowledgements

*"The facts of the world seen clearly*
*are seen through tears;*
*Why tell me then*
*there is something wrong with my eyes?"**

I am acknowledging the sacrifices of all commoners' of this region who witness and bear insecurities in each breath of their lives. The distress of these common people has been the unit of motivation for me to initiate this work.

I am obliged to many individuals and institutions for helping in the publication of this book. I gratefully acknowledge the support of Surendranath College for Women, University Grants Commission (Eastern Regional Office), West Bengal Political Science Association and fellow colleagues of Surendranath College for Women. I am especially thankful to Professor Enakshi Chowdhury, former Teacher-in-Charge of Surendranath College for Women; Dr Papia Mitra, Teacher-in-Charge of Surendranath College for Women; Dr Dilip Basu Ray, Former Secretary of West Bengal Political Science Association and all students of the Department of Political Science, Surendranath College for Women. I also express my thanks to Tarakeshwar Pandey, Amartya Ray, Shankhamala Ray, Subarna Bhattacharya, Lina Raha and Mohammad Mudassar.

*Margaret Atwood: 'Notes towards a poem that can never be written'.

The editing work was greatly facilitated by Anuja Saha. I am also thankful to Mr Vivek Garg of Manas Publications who patiently endured my inadequacies.

Sanghamitra Sarker

# Contents

# Section I

# Traditional Security

- Tenets of the 21st Century Traditional Security in South Asia: An Overview
- Af-Pak Strategy and the War on Terror
- Towards a United South Asia
- Aggravation of Pakistani Faultlines: Implications for India
- Bangladesh Small State Imperatives vis-à-vis India: Components and Constraints
- Ethnic Problem and National Security in Nepal
- Sources of Insecurity and State's Conduct in South Asia
- Pakistan: Roots of Turmoil in the 21st Century
- When the Sea Is the Key: An Analysis of the Maritime Dimension of South Asian Security
- Reminiscing Rammanohar Lohia's Post-Independence writings on South-Asian Unity: A Brief Assessment
- Sino-Pakistan Strategic Partnership: India's Countervailing Options
- India's Policy towards the Smaller Neighbours and South Asian Security in 21st Century
- Rethinking the Indo-Pak Ties in the Context of Democratic Peace Thesis

*Chapter 1*

# Tenets of the 21st Century Traditional Security in South Asia: An Overview

*MK Narayanan*
Governor, West Bengal

The disproportionate attention bestowed on West Asia during the latter half of the 20th Century, primarily due to the politics of oil, is beginning to shift as the locus of economic power and growth moves steadily to the East. South Asia, South East Asia and East Asia are now coming in for closer attention. Together, they contain more population, and have become far more central to the global economy.

Let's highlight on the wider security concerns before turning to South Asian security. Some of the factors enhance the prevailing sense of insecurity casting a large shadow over South Asia.

- *First,* the growth and spread of fundamentalist, extremist and radical ideas and ideologies. The strengthening of fundamentalist and other extremist trends in recent decades has made the world far less secure in the 21st Century.
- *Secondly,* terrorism having mutated into a global franchise has become one of the greatest scourges the world has ever known. Experts anticipate that technology upgradation and opportunities to employ even more sinister weapons—

nuclear, biological, chemical or radiological—will increase the terrorist threat multifold.

- *Thirdly,* cyber warfare though still evolving, already has the capability to cripple key functions of a State. The intangible nature of Cyber Warfare, involving unseen armies makes this threat even more frightening.
- *Fourthly* and finally, maritime security, security of outer space and problems connected with energy deficit and climate change issues are all beginning to take a heavy toll, and will impact adversely on security related matters.

Coming specifically to South Asia's security concerns, I would like to emphasize at the outset, that India does not face any form of existential threat—real or potential. Internally, we do have problems such as:

- Left Wing Extremism, which is a major concern is affecting as it does about a dozen heartland states of India. Essentially an indigenous movement it has successfully exploited perceptions of alienation, deprivation and exploitation, which have been further compounded by poor strategy on the part of the authorities of the different States and the Centre.
- The situation in Jammu and Kashmir which is far from comfortable, appears to be gradually coming under control.
- Insurgencies in the North East, but these are beginning to flag and losing their steam.
- Emergence of mezzanine forces which are, however, as yet not threatening.

The greater threat to our security is the instability prevailing in our immediate neighbourhood. Breakdowns in systems of governance have given rise to the spectre of 'failed States' in our neighbourhood. The latter provides incentives to non-State actors, who have already become today's ubiquitous global warriors. Our external vulnerabilities are hence increasing.

Also, many strategic experts are predicting that South Asia, together with China, currently possesses the highest potential for conflict, mainly over regional hegemony and leadership within the region. This is, perhaps, a gross overstatement, for while regional rivalries of a fairly serious magnitude cannot be ignored, they do not necessarily translate into conflicts.

The two major rivalries in the region are that of China-India and India-Pakistan. Yet this does not necessarily lead to confrontation. The China-India rivalry is an old one, primarily reflecting a contention over regional pre-eminence, in addition to the more common rivalry of two adjacent States over local desiderata. The India-Pakistan rivalry is a legacy of partition of the Indian sub-continent. Neither signals that a stage is being set for a conflict or conflicts.

## China and Pakistan

Of the two great rivalries that could potentially derail the security situation in South Asia, that of China-India, is the more complex. China and India are destined by geography to be rivals: neighbours with immense populations, rich and venerable cultures, and disputes with regard to their borders. Both have risen to positions of economic importance within the same timeframe.

India is not oblivious to China's vaulting strategic ambitions, nor to the fact that Chinese diplomacy in the neighbourhood has become very aggressive of late. At the same time China's political and economic relations with India have been on an upswing during the past decade and more. Many building blocks have been constructed to strengthen their friendship and the two countries currently enjoy a strategic and cooperative partnership.

Overblown scenarios of what might happen were China to 'flex its muscles', hence need be avoided. It is more realistic to view the challenge that China poses to India as primarily geographic, and incidentally strategic. There is nothing to indicate that Chinese political-military strategists see India as a geographic wedge in China's zone of influence. Neither China nor India has any incentive to go to war or engineer a conflict. The possibility of this happening through miscalculation or misperception appears remote at present.

Relations with Pakistan have remained troubled for years and do contain potential for miscalculation. Apart from the historical legacy of the formation of Pakistan, the tilt towards Islamic revivalism (even though the 1993 Constitution makes out that Pakistan is a modern state based on democratic principles), and the dominance of the military in the affairs of Pakistan, the real problem is that. Pakistan perceives an existential threat from India, however misguided this may be.

Resurfacing of ethnic identities and aspirations complicates this situation. Internal developments in Pakistan, and ascendancy of fundamentalist and extremist groups, are a threat not merely to Pakistan, but are also a danger as far as India is concerned.

Meanwhile, the military threat from Pakistan remains fairly daunting. Its gross spending on Defence remains high; China has now become a major source of support, especially with regard to acquisition of new weapon systems and in nuclear-related matters.

A more immediate threat that Pakistan poses to India and South Asian security is its continuing emphasis on asymmetric warfare methods which it embarked upon in the late 1970s. The use of ISI-mentored terrorist outfits—such as the Lashkar-e-Taiyyaba, the Jaish-e-Mohammad, the Harkat-ul-Mujahideen and the Hizbul Mujahideen run by fundamentalist leaders—with the Pakistani military providing training, strategic planning, protection, logistic and supplies, enables Pakistan to continue with its proxy war. The insidious nature of the threat remains high. Infiltration and insurgency across the Line of Control is also continuing.

## Nuclear Issues

The salience of nuclear weapons in the context of South Asian security is something which must not be ignored while discussing South Asia's security. Notions of deterrence dominate the nuclear debate in South Asia and in its extended neighbourhood. Pakistan sees nuclearization as a means to thwart any conventional threat from India, and views nuclearization of South Asia as ensuring strategic stability in the region.

Located between two nuclear armed countries, Pakistan and China, India with its 'no first use' doctrine only sees nuclear weapons as a deterrent which is essential for its protection—with no offensive intentions. India plans to have a nuclear triad—comprising land-based nuclear weapons, aircraft-borne nuclear missiles, and a submarine-based nuclear missile system. Two of the three wings of the triad are in place; the sea based system will become operational by 2013/2014. India's nuclear arsenal is however clearly dwarfed by China's, which has the third or the fourth largest nuclear arsenal today.

## Other South Asian Countries

India has close historical, cultural and other ties to every other country of South Asia. It has often demonstrated sensitivity to the needs of smaller countries in the region and accommodated their demands.

This is best reflected in our relations with Bhutan and the Maldives. Bhutan is our closest friend and ally today. India has consistently offered support and security assurances to the Maldives without infringing on its sovereignty.

India-Nepal relations remain tranquil, but the political churn in Nepal—following elections to the Constituent Assembly in 2008, and the inability of political parties in the elected Constituent Assembly to frame a Constitution—has created a void. Democratic transformation in Nepal thus remains in difficulty; while non-Maoist parties and groups co-exist, they are unable to effectively combine to achieve results.

India's relations with Bangladesh improved dramatically, following the advent of an Awami League Government led by Sheikh Hasina Wajed. The return to democratic ways, the improvement in economic relations between the two countries following the granting of market access to Bangladeshi garments and goods, the dismantling of many fundamentalist structures within Bangladesh—all have helped transform India-Bangladesh relations.

The internal security situation in Bangladesh is a matter of concern for India. Opponents of the regime are seeking to destabilize the present dispensation charging the Awami League Government of being anti-Islamic and pro-India. Hence, the urgency to utilize the present interregnum to secure more substantial benefits from India—including a mutually acceptable Teesta Water Sharing Agreement.

The end of the armed conflict in Sri Lanka has brought a tenuous peace to the country. This has made it possible for India and Sri Lanka to address most, if not all, outstanding issues, but Sri Lanka still needs to demonstrate a willingness to put in place a proper devolution package, as far as its Tamil minority is concerned. This is not evident as yet. Sri Lanka also needs to display greater sensitivity to India's concerns on the issue of China's presence in Sri Lanka, close to the Indian mainland.

The security situation inside Afghanistan is a matter of grave concern to India and the region. Any further deterioration, following a US withdrawal, could have a domino effect and could lead to further ascendancy of the Taliban and fundamentalist forces. India's excellent relations with the Karzai regime and its stellar role as far as development programmes in Afghanistan would then prove to be of little avail. India is out of the loop as far as decisions on the future of Afghanistan, post-US, are concerned, and if the security situation remains uncertain, it can realistically be anticipated that an eclipse of India's influence would follow and possibly a fundamentalist upsurge in the region as a whole.

India is feeling its way in regard to the new civilian regime in Myanmar. The internal situation is still rather indeterminate, and while India has an equation with the new civilian Government headed by President U Thein Sein it is still uncertain how matters might develop. Till recently, the Myanmar Junta was inclined towards China to the exclusion of other nations, though there are signs of late to the contrary. Myanmar's isolation is, however, likely to end and the unfolding situation will require to be carefully assessed.

## Conclusion

The security dynamics of the region are both complex and complicated. On the whole, however, I would say that prospects of peace outweigh factors that work against peace. While rivalries are endemic, prospects of confrontation appear to be under check, at least for the moment.

*Chapter 2*

# Af-Pak Strategy and the War on Terror

*Shakti Sinha*
Former Chief Secretary
Andaman and Nicobar Administration

Since Barack Obama became the President of the United States on January 2011, the entire debate on Afghanistan has changed its course, dominated by two phrases, 'Af-Pak' and 'Exit Strategy'. The first rightly sites the conflict in the larger geographical theatre encompassing both Afghanistan and Pakistan; it is difficult to see any resolution of the conflict without Pakistani complicity in one form or the other. The issue is not whether we like it or not, or whether this is a desirable state of affairs. The fact of the matter is that Pakistan remains the source from where the conflict is generated and sustained, so to pretend otherwise would be unrealistic.

The second phrase, 'exit strategy', is a more ambiguous one since it has never been defined precisely what 'exit' means. Will the US Army withdraw completely and by when? Will they leave behind a number of garrisons with adequate troop levels for counter-terrorism actions and/or in support of training? What will happen to Afghanistan in the event the US troop withdrawal is complete? If there are residual US troops stationed in Afghanistan, what sort of legal cover would the US insist upon to ensure immunity from domestic laws? These and other questions are basically premised around the issue of stability in Afghanistan, and the implications, if any, for the outside world in case Afghanistan reverts to the 1992-1996 civil war scenario that led to the rise of the Taliban.

The former US Ambassador to India and distinguished commentator of developments in the region, Robert Blackwill, sees stability in Afghanistan coming *"from improved capabilities of Afghan security forces and economic development...these crucial projects will take several years at the minimum to accomplish and therefore, Washington should stop talking about an exit strategy from Afghanistan."* However, he recognised that this would not be politically acceptable when he adds that *"But for how long will the US public support a longer and longer war in Afghanistan with no end in sight."*

These two very contradictory realities best explain the dilemma in waging the 'War on Terror' and why its resolution would be messy at best. Something that we in India must accept much as we would like the US and its allies to sort out the mess that Afghanistan now seems headed for with the real risks of the country becoming a sanctuary and launching pad for all kinds of terrorist groups that would target India. This outcome should not have been unexpected if one looks at what this 'War on Terror' is all about.

This war is not a conventional war with defined battlefields and a known enemy or enemies who can be fought with conventional weapons. There is no contested territory, except in a very negative way—"Kafirs get out of Muslim lands", but with a fluctuating definition of Muslim lands to include all territories that were once under the rule of rulers who were Muslim. The enemy is a nebulous one, with no headquarters, no army and even no State. The war is as much psychological as physical, if not more so.

It is unclear if the protagonists themselves know who they are fighting for. Is it the al-Qaeda? Or their erstwhile hosts, the Taliban? Or is it the different Wahabi endowments in Saudi Arabia and the Gulf States that have been, and continue to be, the patrons of al-Qaeda-Taliban? What about the Pakistani army and its various elements that have facilitated the creation of these outfits in order to consider them as 'strategic assets'? This lack of clarity has not helped the fight as it has meant a lack of focus, changing goal-posts and the inability to build a broad societal coalition that could have acted as the bulwark against extremist ideologies that is used by the al-Qaeda-Taliban to rally support.

This lack of clarity has hobbled the US war efforts from the beginning. The Bush Administration was clear that its efforts would be concentrated against the al-Qaeda-Taliban combination; unfortunately it was against what it called nation-building—more appropriately state-building—and so did not invest enough and appropriately on creating conditions that would deny extremist host's population and territory on which to survive. The Bush administration saw itself as too dependent on Pakistan to really focus on what was feeding the Taliban resurgence, post-2005. In fact, in the initial years after the ousting of the Taliban, the entire effort was al-Qaeda-centric, with extremely light security footprint in the Afghan countryside.

The Bush administration got a key aspect right when it sited the war in Af-Pak, and not Afghanistan exclusively. For the record, President Karzai has been saying it for years that there were no terrorists in Afghanistan and that they were all safely ensconced in Pakistan. Obama's aims were clearly to prevent al-Qaeda re-grouping and threatening the USA. Realising the need for Afghanistan to have a minimum modicum of stability, he referred to the need for a minimum level of governance in Afghanistan, and also wanted to make the Pakistani army accountable. While the first was not really followed up, purse-strings to the Pakistani army was sought to be controlled through the Kerry-Lugar Act. Unfortunately, the political situation in Pakistan with a democratically-elected government unable to bring the army in line, largely for extraneous reasons, has meant that the army is able to still ride both horses at the same time—lend support to the Americans and also to their own protégés who the Americans are fighting.

The continued insecurity in Afghanistan is something that continues to puzzle observers, who offer various theories in support of their contentions. Some suggest that the country has never been at peace; caricaturing that Afghans are at peace only when they fight. Others say that Afghanistan is ungovernable and whosoever tries to bring a semblance of order would face stiff resistance. Building on it further, it is often suggested that *"Afghanistan is the graveyard of empires."* Not of all these are myths and many have grains of truth in them, but these are episodic and not systemic. And tend to build theories on these isolated 'facts'. It is another story altogether that the Afghanistan as a country is a colonial construct, a creation of the British who wanted a buffer separating the expanding Russian Empire and the prized British colony, India. Afghanistan's boundaries were determined by Britain and Russia, with the Afghans having no role to play in its determination. And the country served the purpose for which it was created. For the British, the annual subsidy paid to the King of Afghanistan was very minimal, but it enabled the King of take control of his country, effectively seal it off from the world outside, carry out 'internal colonisation' to prevent any challenge to the State and prevent direct foreign interference in internal affairs.

During the 20th century, Afghanistan was mostly peaceful till 1979, when President Daud was overthrown. The earlier violent overthrow of King Amanullah in 1929 was resolved pretty easily and ultimately quite peaceably. Other transitions may not have been smooth but the country was overall peaceful. The present insecurity has two dimensions, internal and external.

Key factors behind the internal causes of insecurity can be traced back to the Bonn Conference of 2001 which was premised on wrong presumptions. Inevitably it led to perverse solutions. Its first key assumption was that there was ethnic conflict that had to be resolved. In fact, there was no such issue, and while the Talibans were largely Pashtuns, arrayed across them was a cross-section of Afghan society, including Pashtuns. Needless attempts at ethnic balancing only led to a fractured polity. The second key assumption is that in Afghanistan, only personalities matter and not systems. Hence, no attempt was made to build inclusionary systems that people could identify with and which would deliver justice and fair play. The third assumption, and this is a take-off from the second, is that the allies must get the key persons involved and decide on the way forward. And the 'key persons' were selected by the US and its allies and not by the Afghans.

In fact, the standard criticism about the Bonn Conference, particularly in Pakistan and increasingly in the West, is misguided. These critics accuse Bonn of ignoring the Taliban, as if in that milieu, barely a few months after 9/11 it would have been possible for the USA and others to sit down with the Taliban. Not that there were any Taliban to sit down with; that had to wait for 2003, when the ISI under General Kayani was able to raise, in effect, a new Taliban, quite different from the antediluvians who existed before 2001.

The end result of Bonn was that the victors made extraordinary efforts to ensure 'ethnic balancing', rather in 're-balancing' in government formation and specifically in setting up the Afghan National Army (ANA). Unfortunately almost no thought was given to the core of democratic governance—in setting up inclusionary systems, establishing merit-based selection, access to justice, etc. These miss-steps have meant that over the years, even as aspirations have increased, the results on the ground have been disappointing. The increased insecurity arising from corruption, extortion, rent seeking behaviour and state capture has meant that there are increased numbers of disaffected groups and individuals, who can be persuaded and/or cajoled to pick up the gun against the government and its international supporters.

If this is not reason enough to keep Afghanistan on the boil, Pakistan's role in sustaining the Taliban has been an extremely dubious one. The new Taliban that has emerged, primarily from the Pashtun dominated areas of North Quetta, and other Pashtun-dominated districts of North Balochistan, could not have done so without the active support of the Pakistani army. The latter's role has generally been under-played, and at best, they have been accused of sins of omission, not of commission, when the reality suggests otherwise. In fact, the behaviour of the different protagonists at critical junctures leads one to the conclusion that, in fact, the relationship between the two is very close, with the Pakistani army controlling the strings. Two examples would suffice to show the close and intricate nature of the relationship.

One, when Mullah Omar's deputy, Mullah Baradar, opened negotiations with Kabul directly, he was picked up by the Pakistani army from Karachi, and proudly went on to announce his capture. The message was clear and unambiguous—Kabul, or that matter the USA, could only negotiate with the Taliban through the Pakistani army. Two, earlier when relations deteriorated between Baitullah Mehsud's Tehreek-e-Taliban Pakistan (TTP) and the Pakistani army, with the former calling for the clearing of the latter from its areas, Mullah Omar appealed to the TTP not to attack the Pakistani army who was, in fact, their friend.

The conclusion is clear that it is the Pakistani establishment—not the effete Pakistani state—that is both the problem, and in that sense, has to be part of any effective solution that would arise.

Afghanistan, at present, faces a paradoxical position as it has a Government that is legitimate and strangely effective in many ways, but which is extremely low in credibility. And even more paradoxically the two phenomena are inter-linked. It is the government appointees in the provinces and districts, who have bought their offices at and are at the beck and call of Kabul, who are responsible for the massive surge in extortion and other corrupt practices that have so alienated the people, who are otherwise fearful of the Taliban. The net result is that the Government is seen by many Afghans as one that has been captured by groups of self-seekers. It is seen as an entity that cannot provide security or good governance, but which has encouraged corrupt practices across the country that has worked to the detriment of the common people. All the surveys conducted across the country, by NGOs, the Asia Society, the United Nations Office on Drugs and Crimes (UNODC), etc, at different points of time have brought out common trends, though actual numbers have varied. These are that for the people, insecurity and rising corruption are the key concerns and that the government's credibility is low because it has not delivered on these two variables. Other important questions also, where the numbers have varied but trends are more or less uniform, are the high expectations from the government, President Karzai's popularity, support for the continued presence of foreign troops and low support for the Taliban.

This credibility crisis of the Government can be compared, unfavourably, with the past when this was not so. In the late 1960s and early 1970s, groups of disaffected Afghans led by Mullah Rabbani, and comprising future legendary commanders like Massoud, Hekmatyar and Khalis, under the banner of Jawanan Muslimeen, had attempted to stir up insurrection in different Afghan provinces with the support of Pakistan, which trained them and supplied weapons, but the whole effort was doomed as people in the villages caught them and handed them over to the government. But this local support for the government did not happen post the PDPA coup in 1987, and is not happening now because of lack of faith in the government, particularly its ability to protect the people.

The net result of all these development is that most of the country is now insecure. This does not mean that the Taliban is in control, but simply that the country is unsafe. The Taliban actually do not so much control territory, as are able to harass the international military by launching suicide attacks, make them insecure by laying remote-controlled Improvised Explosive Devices (IEDs), but rarely engage them in direct conflict. Government functionaries and supporters are threatened through night letters, subject to assassinations, etc. The basic idea is to frighten the inhabitants of insecure localities into 'cooperating' with the Taliban, rendering them logistical and other assistance and lose faith in the ability of the government and its international backers to protect them.

The Afghan National Army (ANA) now has substantial

numbers but its ability to hold off against the Taliban and assorted insurgent groups after the withdrawal of the US army is a big question mark. It takes decades to build up an army, develop its spirit de corps and have a viable officer cadre at different levels, the luxury which the ANA has not had. It is being created as a war is being fought on its own territory, and the result is high desertion rates and an inability to conduct independent operations. The ANA is further handicapped by being poorly trained and extremely ill-equipped.

It is in the context of the 'exit strategy' and the inability of the ANA to really set the conditions under which the US could do so that the surge should be seen—a short-term measure that would change the situation on the ground so that the US could then declare 'Mission Accomplished' and withdraw from Afghanistan. Those who saw the surge as meant to defeat the Taliban were completely off the mark, so were those who feared that Obama wanted to get deeper in the war, committing the US to a long-drawn out involvement. Paradoxically, though it did not appear so at first light, Obama bought the Biden line that the US should get out of counter-insurgency and concentrate on counter-terrorism. The accompanying escalation in targeted strikes within Pakistani territory of terrorist targets, culminating in the daring killing of Osama bin Laden, substantiated this line of thought. The aim was clear. The USA would cripple al-Qaeda and its affiliates for the ground situation in Afghanistan to be sufficiently reversed putting the Taliban on the back-foot so that a negotiated solution could take place.

Unfortunately, this is not how the situation has developed. In retrospect, this should have been expected for it was unrealistic to expect the Taliban to negotiate, knowing that it could always temporarily withdraw to its sanctuaries in Pakistan and wait out the American withdrawal. In fact the surge was ill-fated as it came with an expiry date. Obama had to announce a withdrawal time-table to satisfy American public opinion, and this doomed it from the start. Its most pernicious aspect was that it substantially weakened President Karzai and others like him in Afghanistan who thought that the USA would enable Afghanistan to emerge as a nation that could resist the manipulations of the Pakistani army. In effect, it made them re-think their attitude to the latter, which emerged as the supreme arbiter on Afghan matters. An intended consequence of this was that it weakened the elected dispensation in Pakistan, which tried to bring the army somewhat under control but saw the ground slip underneath their feet.

One should end this analysis by reflecting on why the Pakistani army is so fixated on controlling the destiny of its western neighbour. Historically, because of the unsettled nature of the Pak-Afghan border that left more Pashtuns in Pakistan than Afghanistan, and the latter's refusal to accept the historical injustice done to it by the British by the Treaty of 1893, Pakistan felt this unsettled question to be an existential threat to its existence. Hence it's a continuous, and ultimately successful effort to supplant Pashtun nationalism with Islam as a political identity. This culminated in the Taliban takeover of Afghanistan in 1996. The overthrow of the Taliban and the efforts to create a plural, democratic Afghanistan then posed a far greater threat to the 'garrison state' that the army had managed to impose on Pakistan. This had to be resisted at all costs as the 'garrison state' would have become an unsustainable proposition if it were bordered on both its eastern and western frontiers by two vibrant democratic states, one of which would be an Islamic one. The absence of any security threat to Pakistan from its neighbours would simply force the Pakistani State and society to reassess the army's stranglehold over the country. The US-led War on Terror, that could have ensured this, does seem to be failing as it was based on false assumptions that lead to the evolution of the exit strategy that has doomed it from its inception. Ultimately it left the Afghans short-changed, with little hope for a peaceful, sustainable, plural democratic state in the near future.

*Chapter 3*

# Towards a United South Asia

*Krishnan Srinivasan*
Former Foreign Secretary
Government of India

Some people claim that 'South Asia' as a geographical expression was devised first by the American military, which likes to designate theatres for its various military commands. Though, not happy with the expression; the term 'Indian sub-continent' is more accurate, but perhaps we bend over backwards to accommodate Pakistani sensitivities, and be politically correct, by dropping the name India. It is doubted if the Lodhis, the Moghuls, Nadir Shah or the British Empire thought in terms of South Asia; they thought of India, as did Herodotus and Alexander. If we want to propagate the similarly misleading term West Asia, we have to accept being paid back in the same coin by having South Asia foisted on us.

Last year a Club in Calcutta had a debate on a united South Asia, to which they facetiously gave the acronym USA. And they posed discussion points like "a possible future visa for a united South Asia". This was ironic because one of the star participants, the Pakistani Ambassador to the UN in New York, was not given a visa by India to attend the conference. That seems to me symptomatic of a lot that is giving wrong in our sub-continent.

No big country is loved by its neighbours. India is a big country and we have no designs to become bigger. But we have no wish to become smaller, either just because it suits the agenda of some of our neighbours. India has on its land borders six countries, including the most populous and fastest growing big economy on earth, and another one that is correctly described as an international migraine. We also have several more neighbours on our maritime borders.

The northern boundary of South Asia, or rather SAARC, is putatively now supposed to be the Oxus river. But the boundary between Afghanistan and Pakistan, the Durand Line, is in dispute. Even so of course is the border between India and Pakistan, and India and China. With some neighbours, both our territorial and maritime borders are yet to be mutually settled. We live in a very dangerous neighbourhood—the least integrated region in the whole world.

The three major river basins flowing to and through the Indian sub-continent, far from being waters of cooperation, have been waters of acrimony and discord, whether India is the upper or lower riparian. The lack of an agreement on the Teesta and Feni rivers, courtesy, the current government in West Bengal, jeopardizes our friendly relationship with Bangladesh, which is essential for the security of our Northeast and in India as a whole; and also for our transit links to the Northeast via Bangladeshi ports and through Bangladesh proper. The final outcome of this is incalculable.

Much has been made in SAARC rhetoric about unity in diversity, and that South Asia has a civilisational unity despite its many languages, religions and races. The rhetoric is necessarily political, but I wonder if it does not mask an awkward reality. The Indian subcontinent, despite its geophysical coherence, was brought into a political entity, artificial from the outset, by colonial rulers whether from Europe or from beyond the Hindu Kush: and the natural state of the politics in the subcontinent is in fact centrifugal rather than centripetal. The Radcliffe Award only exacerbated an already pre-existing problem. India and Pakistan as the biggest entities, quite apart from Afghanistan, are finding this a daily and serious concern. Even the smallest countries in the region have also suffered from separatist tendencies, such as Bhutan and Sri Lanka.

It is pointed out that the blessing of democracy has touched all countries in the region, though flawed and fragile it may be in some. This has certainly not been enough to stimulate moves towards greater unity.

In India, democracy, Indian-style, seems at best dysfunctional. The most common adjective used for the central government nowadays is paralysis, and in our elections, appeals to sub-castes and a religious minority seem to be much more important than policies. Who even pretends nowadays to bother about a political party's manifesto?

In Bangladesh, the second most populous country in the sub-continent, the ruling party has a commanding majority but still seems hamstrung by street protests and internal maladministration and distorted priorities.

In Pakistan, there is a weak economy, the government's deteriorating finances, a hostile military, judges spoiling for a fight over corruption charges, determined militants who have proven that they can strike virtually anywhere inside the country, and worsening ties with the main source of direct and indirect financial aid—the United States. Severe flood in the past two years did considerable damage to exports of rice and cotton, undermining the country's balance of payments position. Higher electricity subsidies and renewed pressure for large financial bailouts for cash-strapped public sector enterprises (especially airlines and railways) will also limit the government's ability to mind the budgetary gap. The only thing this government has going for it is that neither the opposition nor the military wants responsibility for this mess and aren't ready to try to force the ruling party from power—at least not yet. There seems to be a fight to the finish between the party in power, the Army and the judiciary, with the untried and untested Imran Khan and his party waiting sullenly in the wings, but the finish in this case will be more of the same with the three-cornered contest continuing indefinitely until the Army again takes over front stage instead of controlling from the wings.

In Bhutan there is a guided democracy. In Nepal there is a

shamble with the parties deadlocked and the Maoists unable to decide whether they want to be a part of the political process or go back to insurgency. In Sri Lanka, the party in power is strong but there are serious questions about how it treats the 18 per cent minority of Tamils. It does not seem to believe in Churchill's dictum: *In victory, magnanimity.*

What sense of unity can there be when Pakistan denied India, even on a reciprocal basis, 'most favoured nation treatment' under GATT/WTO, which is a basic and standard facility in international trading relations? It also denies India overland transit to Afghanistan. Until the highly welcome Awami League government came into office in Dhaka, no transit was even contemplated for Indian goods to and from the Northeast. And what can we say of Pakistan, not taking action against, and denying India access to, the notorious terrorist sponsors like Hafiz Saeed, Zakiur Rehman Lakhvi and others, who publicly engage in hate campaigns and fund-raising for terrorists against India?

It is stating the obvious that there is no political or economic structure that tends towards unity in South Asia. There is no machinery for meaningful security discussions or for conflict resolution. And there cannot be, while there is such a high level of trust deficit. SAARC was set up in December 1985 at the initiative of Ziaur Rahman of Bangladesh, followed up by President Ershad. This was an obvious effort, later openly acknowledged by Bangladesh, to constrain India by the weight of numbers of the other members.

Being present at the first SAARC summit and also at the Foreign Ministers meeting to prepare the Charter of SAARC at Thimpu some months earlier; there was consternation from the other delegations at Thimpu when it was pointed out there was no exit clause for members stipulated in the Charter. The last thing the others wanted was that India should opt out of the association at some stage.

It has often been mentioned that India has a land border with all other South Asian countries, except Afghanistan, while none of the others have. India is the only country that has air connectivity to every other SAARC capital. India has to be at the heartbeat of South Asia's success. But India's very centrality can cause jealousy and resistance.

Sixty-four years ago, India, Bangladesh and Pakistan were one country and you only have to see the animosity between South and North Korea or Greek and Turkish Cyprus today, or between the two Germanies and the two Vietnams of yesterday, to understand the degree of negativity that prevails when countries are divided by political circumstances. Anti-Indian politics is a good politics and a common currency among many political parties in India's neighbourhood.

This inherent negativity in the Indian sub-continent is compounded by India's size and population, its human and material resources, and its healthy economic prospects when compared to some of the others. The main grievance of the countries in South Asia is that their concerns are ignored and neglected by India, and they resent this 'big brother' attitude.

What our South Asian neighbours would like is a non-reciprocal financial and technical aid, free ability to export whatever they produce to India, free movement into India, and the freedom to criticize India and to seek the help of other countries inside and outside the region to counterbalance India's preponderance. In other words, they want all the advantages and none of the responsibilities of being India's neighbour.

The countries of the SAARC have less than 5 per cent of their total trade among themselves, due to high tariffs, lack of a common customs union and harmonized commercial processes. This low level of commerce does not help us in fostering any spirit of mutual interdependence in the sub-continent.

Unlike China, which has been careful to have a balanced trade or deficits with its smaller neighbours, India has a credit trade balance with all its neighbours other than with China ($ 15 b exp; 50 b imp) and Burma ($ 100 exp; $ 300 m imp). This lack of symmetry only aggravates matters.

Former Prime Minister IK Gujral's 'doctrine' rests on non-reciprocal facilities to be unilaterally offered by India to its neighbours to remove their fears and suspicions, and to create an enabling environment with India. In principle, to my mind this is an unexceptionable proposition. In practice, however, Mr Gujral was much criticized in India for selling the family silver, and it was pointed out that in South Asia unilateral concessions given by India have never had the effect of blunting hostility except when there have been *a priori* conditions amenable to such a climate.

A serious problem for India is that it does not want, politically or diplomatically, to be confined to a role within the sub-continent. It seeks a world role and wants to exercise global influence. India's size gives it a global responsibility; this is not conferred on any of the others in the sub-continent. But we have to admit that in this region, India is the elephant in the drawing room. When India looks beyond the region, it is accused by other South Asians of neglect, and when it looks within the region, it is often accused of hegemony. It is a stark fact that relations with the neighbours play no part in domestic elections in India, not even in Punjab, West Bengal or Tamil Nadu.

Mrs Hillary Clinton wants India to assume a leading role, and she is right; if India is to be a global power, it must be a global player. But are our neighbours ready and willing to acquiesce in this? I think the answer to that question is: certainly not.

To reach a position of becoming a country that counts in the world, India will have to have a mutually cooperative sub-region. But India can never achieve global status unless it reaches out beyond its immediate neighbourhood to the wider world. Our former National Security Adviser Brajesh Mishra has said recently that India is diminished by being boxed into the sub-continent. But can India do otherwise with neighbours like China and Pakistan? These are the paradoxes that need to be resolved.

India's neighbours always study Indian developments with interest and mixed feelings. They have no option but to do so, with India representing more than 70 per cent of the population and more than 80 per cent of the region's GDP.

In which case, why is there any reason to feel any sense of optimism?

Despite all the turbulence and historical resentments, I have confidence, not in any mirage of eventual unity, but in the progress and stability of the region, essentially thanks to the centrality of India, the pull-effect of its economic progress, and its stable role in the Indian sub-continent.

## *Chapter 4*

# Aggravation of Pakistani Faultlines: Implications for India

*Alok Bansal*
Senior Fellow, CLAWS, New Delhi
and Visiting Professor
Jamia Millia Islamia, New Delhi

As one democratically elected government in Pakistan completes five years and for the first time in the country's history is going to be replaced by another democratically elected one, the country is far from stable. It has been going through serious tumult; in fact the whole five-year long tenure of the Pakistan People's Party (PPP) government was marked by tumultuous events. The country saw the spectre of 'Memogate', where the security establishment traded charges with the political leadership and subsequently with the involvement of judiciary; there was a conflict between the judiciary and the political leadership. One Prime Minister had to go on account of this tussle between the two major institutions of the government and the next one barely survived. The outcome of the elections is still an uncertainty, although there is bound to be a change.

The political turbulence, however, does not really affect Pakistan much as the real power is always wielded by the Army, which is the final arbiter in all cases that involve India, Afghanistan, nuclear issues and Kashmir. Irrespective of the direction that Pakistan takes, the real faultlines that have affected Pakistan do not change. These faultlines can broadly be grouped under four mutually related heads, viz, the growing sectarian divide, resurgence of ethno-national identities, continuing economic meltdown and growing radicalisation or Talibanisation of society. All the four related faultlines have their genesis in the flawed ideology of Pakistan. All have existed in some form since the creation of Pakistan, but have got aggravated in recent times and have been analysed in subsequent paragraphs.

## Sectarian Divide

Pakistan is a by-product of 'Two-Nation Theory', which was premised on the belief that the Muslims of the subcontinent were a separate nation and could not live in harmony with others in a unified India. This obviously gave pre-eminence to Islam in the affairs of state despite the avowed secular credentials of its leadership. The Objectives Resolution virtually gave *ulema* a justification to overrule some of the acts passed by the legislature and this again highlighted the doctrinal differences between various sects and sub-sects. The next logical step was to define the Muslim identity. As early as 1954, Munir Kayani Commission, a judicial commission comprising two service justices to investigate whether Ahmediyas were Muslims, could not give a ruling on the subject as no two *ulema* could agree on the basic definition of a Muslim.[1] The court inferred that "no two learned divines are agreed on this fundamental. If we attempt our own definition as each learned divine has done and that definition differs from that given by all others, we unanimously go out of the fold of Islam."[2]

After the separation of Eastern Wing, when the numbers of non-Muslims became insignificant in Pakistan, the fanatic adherents of the exclusivist 'Two-Nation Theory' turned their ire towards their co-religionists, who differed from their own version of Islam. Consequently, the violence was used to settle scores not only between Shias and Sunnis, but also between different strands of same sect. Meanwhile in 1974, the Pakistani State acquired the Right of Takfeer and declared Ahmediyas as non-Muslims by a Constitutional Amendment.[3] Since then there have been repeated demands for declaring adherents of various other sects and sub-sects as apostates.

Many extremist Sunni clerics have declared Shias as heretics. This has been followed by violence against Shias perpetrated by Sunni militant organisations. As the sectarian identities in Pakistan were not quite pronounced, the usual pattern of sectarian violence followed attacks by Sunni extremists on Shia elites, whose sectarian orientations were known because of their eminence in the society. In addition, Shia clerics and *Imambaras* were targeted. Distinctive Shia processions like Ashura and Chelhum, as well as Shia funerals were attacked. Consequent insecurities amongst Shias exacerbated their assertion of sectarian identity and resulted in the formation of armed Shia militias, which started targeting the members of Sunni radical outfits and hardline Sunni clerics.[4] Today the sectarian divide is so deep that not only Sunnis and Shias are fighting each other, even amongst Sunnis Deobandis are targeting Barelvis. Amongst the Shias, the adherents of *twelver* school of Islam consider Ismailis to be heretics. Now the Talibans are exploiting the sectarian fissures and have climbed on to the Sunni sectarian bandwagon to spread their influence outside Federally Administered Tribal Areas (FATA) and Khyber Pakhtoonkhwa.

According to Pakistan Institute for Peace Studies (PIPS), 314 persons were killed in 111 acts of sectarian violence in Pakistan in 2011. The year 2012 was even worse for sectarian minorities and 502 adherents of Shiite faith were killed in Pakistan, however, the figure for 2013 had already crossed 300 within the first ten weeks of the year. The menace is not confined to Karachi and Balochistan as is widely perceived, but has spread to every corner of Pakistan and territories controlled by it. According to ARY News, in 2012, Balochistan was the arena for a continuing pogrom of Shias, where 156 of them were killed. 146 Shias were killed in Sindh, most of them in Karachi, 99 in Gilgit-Baltistan in Pakistan occupied Kashmir, 80 in Punjab and 21 in Khyber Pakhtoonkhwa.[5] Of late even miniscule Shiite minorities like Dawoodi Bohras have been targeted in Karachi.[6] Nearly 5,000 people have been killed in over 2,000 sectarian attacks in Pakistan since 1989.[7]

## Resurgence of Ethno-National Identities

At the time of its creation, the biggest threat to nascent Pakistani nationalism emanated from the ethnic aspirations of its residents, more so from Pakhtoon nationalism, which had successfully countered the appeal of Pakistan movement during 1946 elections under the British rule. Consequentially, in order to nip this grave threat in the bud, an all-inclusive Islamic identity was promoted to subsume the ethnic identities of the citizens. The strategy paid huge dividends especially in the Pakhtoon majority regions of Pakistan, where Pakhtoon nationalism was subdued considerably. However, in due course it gave rise to a much bigger Frankenstein—the radical Islam. As the menace of Talibanisation—a manifestation of radical Islam, engulfs the entire state and threatens the very existence of the Islamic Republic, an attempt was made to play down the Islamic identity. This has given a renewed vigour to the ethno-nationalist identities. As a result, ethnic fissures have become more pronounced and ethnic fires have erupted in regions that had remained peaceful for long.

Of the various ethnic movements, Baloch nationalism poses the biggest threat to Pakistan's fragile nationalism. Since 1947, the Baloch have periodically risen up in arms demanding autonomy or even separation from Pakistan. Unlike Pakhtoon nationalism, Baloch nationalism has become more intense with the passage of time. Although, the Baloch are not a linguistically homogeneous group, they have been unified by a strong perception of suppression and exploitation by the Pakistani state.[8]

The alienation of Baloch from Pakistani state and its organs, today is complete, so much so that across Balochistan in most educational institutions, neither the Pakistani flag is flown nor is the Pakistani national anthem sung. The writ of the state does not run beyond the cities. Hundreds of Baloch activists have simply disappeared due to their kidnapping by state agencies. Despite the intervention of Pakistan's Supreme Court, the fate of most of these hapless Baloch citizens is not known. The perception amongst various sections of the society in Balochistan is that the situation there is worse than Palestine or Waziristan. Nationalists and their sympathisers are kidnapped by the intelligence agencies and their dead bodies are thrown away on roads. There is an acute shortage of doctors; medical facilities are non-existent and generally there is neither electricity nor gas. Consequently, many Baloch have been migrating from their traditional homeland.[9]

The alienation of even Sindhis, Pakhtoons, Mohajirs and even Seraikis from the federal government is increasing. There has been a perception that the Punjabis and the Mohajirs dominated the military and bureaucracy. This group rapidly became a strong in economic, political and military power centre of Pakistan. According to veteran Pakistani journalist Khaled Ahmed, "Leadership in Pakistan will always be supplied by Punjab because it controls two-thirds of the seats in the National Assembly. Smaller provinces may produce intellectually superior leaders but they will not be able to assert themselves nationally."[10] This has caused resentment in other ethnic groups like Sindhis, Baloch and Pakhtoons, who felt that the Punjabis and Mohajirs were dominating the power structure like the Hindus and Sikhs before partition.

Sindhis perceive that they are being marginalised in their traditional homeland. Already the cities are dominated by the Mohajirs and Sindhi population is less than half the population of the province. They own only about 25 per cent of the industrial units in Sindh, constitute only two per cent of Pakistan's armed forces and five per cent of federal civil servants.[11] The unprecedented floods faced by Sindh in 2010 and 2011 and the government apathy to the large scale destruction have further infuriated the them. It is widely perceived that Sindh was flooded to minimise the losses in Punjab. The preliminary report of 2011 census shows that the population of Sindh increased by 81.5 per cent between 1998 and 2011, against a national growth of 46.9 per cent.[12] The fact that there has been more than 100 per cent growth in border districts and Karachi indicates large scale migration to Sindh.[13] The growing immigration into Sindh will further marginalise the Sindhis. Increased migration of Pakhtoons to Karachi has already aggravated the ethnic fissures in the metropolis and has resulted in large scale violence. An elusive organisation called Sindhu Desh Liberation Army (SDLA) has carried out a number of blasts on the railway track. Some nationalists have even demanded independence of Sindh and Sindhi resources from "a Punjab-dominated, Punjab-ruled, and Punjab-manipulated state."[14]

Mohajirs, who were in the forefront of the struggle for Pakistan, consider themselves to be its creators and ideologues. They were also the ardent supporters of Pakistani nationalism, as opposed to the regional identities professed by various ethnic groups. They dominated the politico-bureaucratic space in the initial years of Pakistan, however, subsequent developments, like Jinnah's death, Liaqat's assassination, and creation of One Unit and shifting of capital from Karachi to Islamabad, diminished Mohajir hold on Pakistani polity.[15] Army's growing salience in national polity has enabled the Punjabis and Pakhtoons to move up at the cost of Mohajirs.[16] The growing influx of Pakhtoons in urban Sindh in general and Karachi in particular is tilting the ethnic balance against the Mohajirs.[17] To compound the problem, the birth rate amongst Mohajirs, who are better educated, has been falling consistently vis-à-vis Sindhis, Pakhtoons and Baloch. Consequently Karachi has become a hot-bed of violence, where different ethnic groups are jostling for supremacy.

There are many smaller nationalities that keep voicing their concerns from time to time. In the run up to the 2013 elections, Seraiki nationalism has gathered momentum as it has been used to reduce salience of Punjab in Pakistan's body politic. Different growth rates of various ethnic groups are likely to further aggravate the ethnic faultlines. The population of Punjab, which since 1971, was always more than half the population of Pakistan has fallen below the halfway mark and this might increase the belligerence of other ethnic groups towards Punjabi dominated federation. The population of better educated Punjabis and Mohajirs, who have been the ideologues of Pakistan is growing at a much slower rate with respect, the Baloch, Sindhis and Pakhtoons could further exacerbate ethnic tensions.[18]

## Economic Woes

Economically Pakistan has done fairly well as it received liberal aid from the Western block during the Cold War and even later during the Global War against terror. Its expenditure on defence and debt servicing has generally exceeded its total receipts and quite often in recent times it has appeared to be on the verge of economic default. However, since 2009, it seems to have tided over its immediate economic crisis, on account of liberal economic aid from the West, especially the $ 8 billion standby loan from the IMF. Another positive part has been a robust growth in remittances from abroad. During 2011-12, remittances received were $ 13.186 bn, a growth of over 20 per cent over the previous year. Remittances sent by overseas Pakistani workers during the first half of 2012-13 (Jul-Dec 12) increased by 12.51 per cent, to $ 7.11 billion.[19] The foreign exchange reserves that had shot up to $ 18.313 billion on 30 July 2011, have been coming down and were down to $ 12.3 billion as on 22 March 2013, but are still considered adequate. Of these the reserves held by the State Bank of Pakistan have fallen to $ 7.2 billion. Pakistan is slated to pay $ 1.2 billion to the IMF by June 2013 and the reserves are expected to fall to $ 6.8 billion, which can cater to about two months of import cover.[20]

Despite an apparent resemblance of normalcy, there are serious problems with the economy and long term macro-economic picture continues to be grim. The IMF has conceded that its $ 11.3 billion standby arrangement with Pakistan has failed to deliver and the international credit rating agency, Moody's downgraded Pakistan's sovereign credit rating from B3 to Caa1.[21] During the last five years the economic growth has been an average of three per cent; industrial growth has remained stagnant at near zero per cent and agriculture growing at 2.2 per cent per annum, less than the country's population growth. More significantly, the investment rate has consistently declined over the last five years and has reached a 50-year low of 12.5 per cent of GDP.[22]

Large-scale manufacturing has remained stagnant and has shown marginal growth of 2.13 per cent during the first half of

2012-13 (July-Dec 2012) over the corresponding period of the last year.[23] Public Sector Units (PSUs) are piling up losses, the Pakistan Electric Power Company (PEPCO) is losing one billion rupees daily; Pakistan International Airlines (PIA) is losing ₹70 million daily and the Pakistan Railways is losing ₹50 million per day.[24] Private sector has been shrinking. There is a flight of capital from Pakistan to countries like Bangladesh and Malaysia. During the first seven months of 2012-13 (July 12-Jan 13), Foreign Direct Investment (FDI) slumped by 11.6 per cent to $ 525.1 million over the same period in 2011-12.[25] The FDI has been declining consistently for past five years and is at an all-time low.

Fiscal deficit averaged almost seven per cent of GDP over the last five years (2008-13), but reached as high as 8.5 per cent in 2012. The persistence of a large fiscal deficit coupled with sharp depreciation of exchange rate has more than doubled the country's public debt. By December 2012, the public debt stood over ₹13 trillion.[26] High fiscal deficit has contributed to the inflationary pressures. High budgetary deficit and current account deficits have forced the government to borrow from State Bank of Pakistan and print currency, thereby exacerbating the inflationary trends. The inflation has been high and between 2003 and 2012, at an average 10.6 per cent, hitting an all-time high of 25.3 per cent in August 2008 and a record low of 1.4 per cent in July 2003.[27] Tax collection rates continue to be abysmally low and at 9.2 per cent, Pakistan has one of the lowest tax to GDP ratios in the world. Acute power shortage continues to stymie the industrial production. Although additional generation capacities have been added since 2007, the actual power generation has not increased due to problems of circular debt.[28] Exports have been declining, while oil import bill has been rising, thereby increasing the trade deficit. The government debt has been rising consistently. More significantly, Karachi, the financial hub of Pakistan has seen endemic violence, which has seen migration of industries and closures affecting production.

Pakistan, since the early 1970s barring a short interval in the 1980s, has been on life support through continuous lending arrangement with the IMF. Since 1988, the country received 11 loan programmes from the IMF and spent 14 years in an intensive care unit. Only four of these programmes could be termed as 'successful' and that too, merely in terms of fund disbursements and not on the basis of outcomes.[29] Pakistan needs large FDI to kick start the economy as well as to bring areas on the economic periphery into the mainstream. It was hoped that the mega projects planned in Balochistan will help it to attain the twin objectives, unfortunately, it has not happened. There are 72.9 million people below poverty line and in the absence of increased investment the economic situation will only worsen as the FDI is unlikely to come till the situation on the law and order front dependent on other faultlines, improves.

## Talibanisation

Radicalisation of the society was a natural outcome of the exclusivist 'Two-Nation Theory' that led to the creation of Pakistan. According to popular belief in Pakistan radicalisation is a result of Zia's policies of Islamisation to legitimise his regime and subsequent involvement in American instigated, Saudi funded and ISI operated 'jihad' in Afghanistan. However, a careful analysis will indicate that the seeds of Talibanisation were sown in 1947 itself. Right from the time of its inception; the state of Pakistan used radical Islam to counter ethnic nationalism. An all-inclusive Islamic identity was promoted to subsume the ethnic identities of its citizens. The all-powerful security establishment promoted the religious parties to counter the Pakhtoon nationalists. Federally Administered Tribal Areas (FATA) was not incorporated into the North Western Frontier Province (NWFP) and was kept outside the political and economic mainstream with an avowed objective of preventing Pakhtoon consolidation. Subsequently, absence of any development and promotion of fundamentalist thought in Pakhtoon belt subsequently facilitated and provided an ideal atmosphere for the growth of Taliban movement in Pakhtoon belt.

Taliban as an entity as we know it, emerged in 1994, when Gulbuddin Hekmatyar, Pakistan's chosen proxy to lord over

Afghanistan failed to capture Kabul after the fall of Nazibullah government. Consequent to US attack on Afghanistan in October 2001, the Taliban and al-Qaeda elements from Afghanistan fled to the inaccessible and mountainous regions of FATA.[30] Initially Pakistani forces largely avoided interfering with them, intending to use them in Afghanistan after the US withdrawal. However, this policy had to change under sustained US pressure and the Pakistani troops were forced to enter South Waziristan Agency in FATA and directed the local Talibans to surrender the foreign militants. The aim was to create a distinction between the local Talibans and al-Qaeda led foreign militants.[31]

In February 2004, after immense US pressure, Pakistan was forced to use its military against the militants in South Waziristan.[32] From 2004 onwards the operations intensified in the region and the involvement of Pakistan Army increased in the tribal areas.[33] Since then, Pakistan government unsuccessfully tried different strategies to control the militants in the region. Despite using disproportionately large force, the Army failed to establish the writ of the state and sued peace. The Army operations resulted in a large number of civilian casualties and further increased the alienation of the population. The Army also tried to buy out the loyalties of the militants by paying them huge sums of money but it failed to herald peace in the region. It appeared as if the security forces neither had a will nor an expertise to fight an insurgency of this magnitude. The government therefore announced suspension of operations in North Waziristan Agency in February 2006 to seek accommodation with the militants.[34]

Despite failure of the peace deals in South Waziristan, the Pakistani government again tried the same policy of accommodation with the militants in North Waziristan. It accordingly signed another peace deal with the militants, with Maulana Fazlur Rehman's assistance, called Miramshah Agreement on September 5, 2006.[35] But like previous such attempts in South Waziristan it failed to usher in peace. By 2006, the violence had also spread to Bajaur and Mohmand agencies in FATA and the adjoining regions in NWFP and Balochistan. The year 2007 saw a sharp geographical expansion of the areas affected by Islamic radicalism and militancy in NWFP. In the aftermath of Lal Masjid operations in Islamabad, Tehreek-e-Nafaz-e-Shariat-e-Mohammadi (TNSM) led by Maulana Fazlullah, which had allied with Taliban virtually took over the entire Swat Valley between October 25, 2007 and November 7, 2007. Despite the presence of over 3,000 troops, the Taliban not only captured the region but also appointed its own administrators. A large number of troops and policemen surrendered and a large number were captured by the militants. All these personnel were released after being disarmed. It is at this stage that the elections were announced in Pakistan, which after the assassination of Benazir Bhutto was eventually slated for February 2008.

In the run up to the elections, the caretaker provincial government of NWFP, in a desperate bid to buy peace, agreed to implement the Sharia regulations in the entire Malakand Division. The proposal intended to take away from people, their right to submit a writ in the High Court and the Supreme Court, instead a Sharia court at the division level was to be set up as the final arbiter of justice.[36] However, the opposition from lawyers and sections of judiciary prevented the law from coming into force. The ANP government, which came to power in NWFP after the elections found it besieged by all-round violence and sued for peace with Talibans and agreed to implement Sharia laws in over half the territory of the province. The *Nizam-e-Adl* Regulation, introducing Sharia laws was formally promulgated in the region only after the approval of the Parliament and Presidential ascent on April 13, 2009. However, the *qazi* courts had started functioning in Swat Valley from March 17, 2009.[37] After consolidating their position in Swat consequent to the peace deal, the Taliban fighters, who had become unemployed, moved to the adjoining Dir and Buner districts. This eastward expansion of Talibans brought it virtually on the door steps of Islamabad and resulted in Pakistan Army launching Operation Rah-e-Rast to dislodge them.

After consolidating its position in the Pakhtoon belt, the Talibans have made incursions into the Punjabi heartland of Pakistan and Pakistan's commercial hub Karachi. As pressure increased on the Taliban in FATA and NWFP, they moved eastwards to increase their influence. Feudal elements in Punjab, who dominate the politics, did nothing to check the advance of the Talibans. In some cases they even contributed to the process of Talibanisation by making liberal contributions to madaris propagating Taliban's view of Islam.[38] The Talibans also made deep incursions into Karachi, Pakistan's largest metropolis. Altaf Hussain, the leader of MQM had repeatedly warned about the dangers of creeping Talibanisation in Karachi. Many co-educational institutions in parts of Karachi had been visited by the Talibans and threatened with dire consequences if they refused to change; some others had received letters with similar messages.[39] The situation had come to such a pass that on March 21, 2013, a girls' school in Karachi was attacked in daylight by the Talibans. Attacks on Sufi shrines in Lahore, Peshawar and Karachi, as well as sectarian attacks across length and breadth of Pakistan had been claimed by Tehrik-e-Taliban Pakistan.

With the passage of time, Talibanisation has permeated across social and ethnic barriers to engulf the entire Pakistani society. Most significant pointer to the alarming levels of Talibanisation in Pakistani society was the assassination of Punjab's governor Salman Taseer by his own body guard, Mumtaz Qadri. The incident demonstrated the level to which the radical elements had usurped the sole authority of the state to use violence. The fact that Qadri could fire two magazines, without any other guard either firing at him or attempting to protect the Governor, showed their tacit approval to the assassin's action. The treatment meted out to Qadri after the assassination even by the lawyers exhibited the extent of radicalisation. Subsequent assassination of Pakistani minority minister Shahbaz Bhatti in Islamabad showed the level of rot. What was even more galling was the complete silence of most political parties, army and judiciary, which has otherwise been quite active. The situation has come to such a pass that on March 21, 2013, a girls' school in

Karachi was attacked in broad daylight by Taliban. Attacks on Sufi shrines in Lahore, Peshawar and Karachi, as well as sectarian attacks across length and breadth of Pakistan have been claimed by Tehrik-e-Taliban Pakistan.

The most dangerous trend has been numerous instances of security personnel collaborating with the Talibans.[40] Many officers have preferred being court-martialled to fight the Talibans. Every single attack on the armed force establishments has been facilitated by the collusion of insiders. All security forces have been infiltrated by the Taliban sympathisers. The attack on PNS Mehran like almost every other attack on defence establishment bore clear signs of insider collusion and possible participation. Journalist Saleem Shehzad was eliminated for openly stating that a number of al-Qaeda and Taliban sympathisers were present within the Pakistani Armed Forces. The arrest of Brigadier Ali Khan of Pakistani Army, who was posted at the General Headquarters (GHQ) for links with Pan-Islamic radical outfit Hizb-ut-Tahrir, once again brought to fore the existence of radical Islamist elements within Pakistan's Armed Forces. The fact that Brigadier Khan is a third generation army officer, with a brother, son and son-in-law in the Army, shows the gravity of the situation.

## Implications for India

The Pakistani faultlines aggravate that the state's monopoly on instruments of power will weaken and in due course strengthen the fissiparous forces. Pakistan appears to be losing its internal sovereignty to radical elements. The instruments that were created during the Afghan war against Soviet Union have begun to haunt Pakistan. It is ironical that the *jihadi* outfits that were created by the Pakistani state are posing both a material as well as an ideological threat to the state. There is a tendency amongst the Pakistani elite to blame the fringe extremist elements and Mullahs for the menace of religious extremism, without acknowledging that it is enshrined in the Constitution and in the doctored history that is taught in its schools. Sections of Pakistan Constitution, such as those relating to the Objective Resolution, the text of oaths of high offices, the notorious Eighth Amendment, the council of Islamic ideology and the Sharia court go a long way in promoting religious extremism. While the *jihadi* outfits could serve certain perceived tactical and strategic objectives of the state, in the long run they are part of the Pan-Islamic agenda that aim to capture the Pakistani state. Even today the Pakistani security establishment is loath to disassociate itself completely from these outfits and to condemn them unequivocally.

For the first time since 1947, there is a credible threat to the cohesion of Pakistani army. This in Pakistan's case could be catastrophic as Pakistani Army is believed to be the only functioning institution in the country. According to Stephen Cohen, most States have an army but in Pakistan's case it is the Pakistan's army, which has got a State. The erosion of Pakistani army could lead to 'Lebanonisation of Pakistan'[41] and that could be catastrophic for India. If Taliban transforms into Pakistan's Hezbollah it could pose serious threats to Indian security. There have been firings by non-state actors on Indian territory from across the international borders, India did not respond militarily then, but India would have to evolve its reaction, if it becomes the norm.

Growing Talibanisation, if unchecked would eventually lead to emergence of Pakistan as a citadel of radical Islam, with liberal elements either pushed out or silenced. Such a state would start exporting its ideology across the world. Already almost all the Islamic militants from across the world—from the Philippines to Chechnya, including Indonesians, the Maldivians, Bangladeshi, Tajiks, Uzbeks, Arabs and Uighurs come to Pakistan for indoctrination. This would cause a conflict that would transcend regional boundaries. It needs to be understood that Talibans and other such outfits are closely aligned with global Islamic movement including al-Qaeda.

Their eventual aim is to create a global Islamic Ummah. Al-Qaeda cadres believe that they are fighting 'End of Times' battle in Khurasan,[42] which will be followed by Ghazwa-e-Hind (a term used in Prophet's saying and means battle for India).[43] The rise of these elements in Pakistan thus poses a direct threat to Indian security as the current phase will be followed by attacks on India. The possession of nuclear weapons by such a state would further aggravate the situation and pose the most serious challenge to Global Peace.

There is a distinct possibility that with the withering of Pakistani state, its nuclear stockpile could fall into the hands of these radical non-state actors, who could use it to make crude radiological bombs. This could pose a serious threat to India and other states in the region. Moreover, if the state weakens and the faultlines aggravate, the state structure might crumble leading to internecine war and large-scale bloodshed. This may result in huge exodus of population, especially those unwilling to live in a Talibanised state. Most of them will head to the only country, which is culturally familiar to them, namely India. Indian state is in no position to deal with millions of refugees on its soil. This influx of millions of refugees would pose a serious problem of governance and could impose serious economic and social strain on Indian state.

Thus to sum up it would not be wrong to infer that the crumbling state structures and 'Lebanonisation of Pakistan' do pose a potent threat to India, both ideologically as well as materially. It has been India's strategy to minimise its adverse impact. It has accordingly been collaborating with the international community to facilitate Pakistan's transformation into a multi-ethnic democratic and liberal society.[44]

## Notes

1. Report of the Court of Inquiry constituted under Punjab Act II of 1954 to enquire into the Punjab Disturbances of 1953, Lahore, 1954, pp 215-218.
2. Ibid, p 218.
3. Ziad Haider, "Ideologically Adrift" in Maleeha Lodhi (ed), *Pakistan: Beyond the 'Crisis State'*, New Delhi: Rupa & Co, 2011, p 117.
4. Khaled Ahmed, *Sectarian War: Pakistan's Sunni-Shia Violence and its Links to the Middle East*, Oxford: Oxford University Press, 2011, p xxii.
5. "Khara Sach" with Mubashir Lucman Show on ARY News on 18 February 2013.

6. Kamila Hyat, "The Curse of Sectarianism", *The News*, September 21, 2012, p 7.
7. Zeeshan Haider, "Sectarian Violence", *The News*, September 10, 2012, p 7.
8. Mary Anne Weaver, *Pakistan in the Shadow of Jihad and Afghanistan,* (New York: Farrar, Straus and Giroux, 2002), p 93.
9. "Conditions in Balochistan worse than that in Palestine or Waziristan: JI", *The News*, March 7, 2013, p 2.
10. Khaled Ahmed, *Pakistan: Behind the Ideological Mask*, Lahore: Vanguard Books Pvt Ltd, 2004, p 302.
11. Mary Anne Weaver, n 8, p 73.
12. "Population shoots up by 47 per cent since 1998", *The News*, March 29, 2012, pp 1-4.
13. "Sindh population surges by 81.5 per cent, households by 83.9 per cent", *The News*, April 2, 2012.
14. "JSQM holds 'march against slavery'", *The News*, March 24, 2012, p 12.
15. Owen Bennett Jones, *Pakistan: Eye of the Storm,* New Delhi: Penguin Books India, 2002, pp 114-15.
16. Ibid, pp 116-117.
17. Gulmina Bilal Ahmed, "No IDPs, Please", *Newsline*, June 2009, p 34.
18. Note 12 ante.
19. "Remittances climb to $ 7.11 billion in first half", *The News*, January 11, 2013, p 15.
20. Erum Zaidi, "Pakistan repays $ 143.8 m to IMF", *The News*, March 29, 2013, p. 15.
21. Ashfaque H Khan, "More Bad News", *The News*, July 17, 2012, p 6.
22. Ashfaque H Khan, "Down the Drain", *The News*, March 18, 2013, Money Matters Supplement, p I.
23. Israr Khan, "LSM grows by 2.13 per cent in July-Dec", *The News*, February 13, 2013, p 15.
24. Ihtasham ul Haque, "Bleeding to Death", *The News*, July 2, 2012, Money Matters Supplement, p I.
25. Erum Zaidi, "FDI falls by 11.6 per cent in Seven Months", *The News*, February 15, 2013, p 15.
26. Ashfaque H Khan, n 22.
27. Ihtasham ul Haque, "Galloping Inflation", *The News*, August 20, 2012, Money Matters Supplement, p I.
28. Ashfaque H Khan, "The Power Sector Crisis", *The News*, August 7, 2012, p 6.
29. Ihtasham ul Haque, "Begging and Borrowing", *The News*, October 1, 2012, Money Matters, p IV.
30. Christian Wagner, "Peace in Waziristan", *German Institute for International and Security Affairs SWP Comments* 25, October 2006, p 2.

31. Frederic Grare, "Pakistan-Afghanistan Relations in the Post-9/11 Era", *Carnegie Papers,* No 72, October 2006, pp 6-7.
32. Rahimullah Yusufzai, "No End in Sight", *Newsline,* April 2006, p 27.
33. Christian Wagner, n 30, p 2.
34. Christian Wagner, n 30, pp 2-3.
35. "Pakistan's Tribal Areas: Appeasing the Militants", International Crisis Group, Asia Report No 125 dated December 11, 2006, p 19.
36. Delawar Jan Banori, "Shariah Regulation Draft for Malakand sent to President", *The News,* January 30, 2008.
37. "Qazi courts start functioning in Swat", *The News,* March 18, 2009.
38. Sabrina Tavernise, Richard A Oppel Jr and Eric Schmitt, "United Militants Threaten Pakistan's Populous Heart", *The New York Times,* New York Edition, April 14, 2009, p A1.
39. Ardeshir Cowasjee, "The Price of Moral Cowardice", *Dawn,* April 19, 2009.
40. VN Sharma, "The Talibanisation of Pakistan", *USI Journal,* October-December 2009, p 491.
41. 'Lebanonization' has come to refer to a process of national disintegration, where central authority erodes to a level that different power groups start acting independent of the central authority not only as far as their interactions with one another is concerned but also with entities outside the geographical frontiers of the state. It is distinct from 'Balkanisation' as the process of disintegration does not create clear cut smaller states as in the case of later. In recent times the term has been used extensively for Somalia and Iraq before its recent stabilization.
42. Khurasan refers to parts of Iran, the Central Asian Republics, Afghanistan and parts of Pakistan.
43. Syed Saleem Shahzad, *Inside Al-Qaeda and the Taliban: Beyond Bin Laden and 9/11*, London: Pluto Press, 2011, p xvi.
44. AK Verma, "India's Trajectory to Regional and Global Power: Risks, Obstacles and Strengths", *Synergy*, May 2009, p 86.

*Chapter 5*

# Bangladesh Small State Imperatives vis-à-vis India: Components and Constraints

*Sanjay Bhardwaj*
Assistant Professor, Jawaharlal Nehru University, New Delhi

While dealing with other states in the international sphere, a small state is always guided by the constraint of inefficiency. This constraint has meticulous implications for its foreign policy behaviour, policy options and perceptions towards big and immediate neighbours. Frustration, out of comparative inferiority mould a small state to vociferously look forward for reliable options to enhance strength and to gain comprehensive bargaining edge while dealing with more powerful state or any 'international crisis'. (Snyder and Diesing, 1977) A small state attempts to survive in the international system rather than to play a dominant role. The behavioural pattern of a small state revolves around its own real potentiality to survive. If the potentiality falls inadequate, it generates insecurity syndrome and mistrust; and accordingly influences the behavioural pattern. In this background, this study is an attempt to develop an insight about Bangladesh Small State Insecurity Syndrome vis-à-vis India in particular and their behaviour pattern towards outstanding bilateral issues in general.

India and Bangladesh have common cultural, linguistic and racial affinities (Bengali) which evolve within a common historical legacy and geographical proximity. However, the perceptional religious difference (Muslim), regional dominance and the physical asymmetry of India have continued to evoke a sense of apprehension among Bangladesh (small state). In the context of Indo-Bangladesh relations, a section of the people of Bangladesh perceives India as another colonial master with hegemonic tendencies due to its emerging economic and military strength. India's dealing with Bangladesh is often taken with a sense of mistrust and suspicion. Even the Indian contribution to the formation of Bangladesh is viewed as pre-meditated ideas. The post-independence political discourse in Bangladesh society describes that the vital role of India in the liberation war was primarily designed with the intention of establishing India's supremacy in South Asia. However, the liberal-rationalist has perceived India as an inevitable friend of Bangladesh in the region. Both, perceptions and misperceptions have shaped the nature of Indo-Bangladesh relations over the years. This paper is an attempt to understand the bilateral relationship in the above context.

Many questions arise for an innocent observer, even experienced analysts of the subject. What made Bangladesh to become so suspicious to India? Why they tend to overlook India's role in their independence, when entire Islamic and western world was against Indian intervention in the erstwhile East Pakistan? How do they negate the fact about the economic and other assistance that was provided by India soon after the independence of Bangladesh? Instead of being thankful to India why have they become so antagonistic? Is the idea of Pakistan[1] still relevant in Bangladesh society? A proper investigation was essential to answer these questions. This paper explores that the reasons are widespread, manifold and in fact, intermingled. Prior to a close scrutiny of discontents and exploring small state insecurity perception, the paper had a cursory look on 'Bengali' and 'Muslim' nationalistic tendencies in Bangladesh vis-à-vis India.

## 'Bengali' or 'Muslim' Antecedents

India and Bangladesh relations require a firm understanding of socio-cultural antecedents of their unique Bengali cultural identity. India and Bangladesh have very close socio-cultural, linguistic and racial affinities which evolve from a common historical legacy and geographical proximity. This distinguished society has a large influence of syncretism that evolved through the religious intermingling, sharing of linguistic heritage and cultural commonality. However, the Partition of India in 1947 has divided these socio-cultural affinities of this eastern land without considering ground realities.[2]

In the pre modern history, Bengal was pre-dominantly inhabited by indigenous social groups. This vast majority of the Bengali linguistic community today represents present or former inhabitants of the previously uncultivated and culturally unassimilated tracts of Bengal. (Baxter 1997) The Brahmins and Mullahs were instrumental in teaching the methods of agriculture linked with eastward expansion of two distinct religious faiths and worship, ie 'the Hindu culture' patronized within Brahmanical hierarchical social order and 'the Islamic culture' patronized by mosque or *Dargah* mostly in rural Bengal. The Islamic culture pre-dominantly was influenced by Sufism, which had also developed inclusive in the cultural values of Bengal. (Bose and Jalal 2004) Hence, the culture and society in Bengal has historically evolved within the syncretic socio-cultural values where their religious inclination and devotion have been all-inclusive in nature. The people of this region had been enough tolerant and almost invited all sorts of ideals and streams of different socio-religious and cultural antecedents, viz, Buddhism, Hinduism, Islamism, Sufism, Tantrik, English and accommodated within their Bengali culture. There was a co-existence and concurrent practice of these varying faiths. (Anisuzzaman 2002)

Indeed, the growth of political consciousness in Muslims is the product of the British colonial patronages. At first, the British (after Battle of Plassey in 1757) took over revenue administration and the Hindu trading class developed a cosy relation with the company's officials. They had accumulated wealth that was reinvested in the land, and became the *Zamindars*. The urban population was also primarily drawn from the professional and trading classes, consisting of high caste Hindus (*Brahmans,*

*Kayasthas* and *Baidyas*). Conversely, the British turned to this class to form the foundation of an incipient civil society and the Muslims, with exceptions, occupied the lower rungs of society, and engaged themselves in agriculture and cognate pursuits. Such communal division of labour created different socio-economic identity between Hindus and Muslims in Bengal.

Just after hundred years of their rule, the British were compelled to rethink their British India policy when they had faced a strong revolt in 1857, mostly led by the Hindu princely states and the people. The British had realized that the Muslims, whom they had defeated in 1757, are now no more threats. (Hunter 1872) With the British introduction of cash crops like jute, cotton, tobacco, etc, had strengthened the position of the peasants, now the British also found a new friend in the form of an upcoming Muslim cultivator class. This was known as *Jotedars* (rich farmers). The Act X of 1859 was enforced, and under section V of this act, the ownership of the land was ensured for those cultivators who held the land for twelve consistent years. Moreover, rent hike and unlawful eviction were also forbidden under various sections. These laws brought in a mass unrest and awareness amongst the *Jotedars* about their control and authority over the land and on rent hike by 1860 which took the form of an uprising by 1873.[3]

The Bengali Muslims, originated from the *Jotedar* category consolidated themselves as a political force in the period of socio-economic mobilization in the first quarter of the 20th century. They emerged as a vocal political force for social and economic reforms in Muslim Bengal, which were opposed by the Hindus and some of Muslim feudals. (Rahim 2007) In the later years, these Bengali speaking Muslim leaders (Fazlul Haque, HS Suhrawardy, Maulana Bhasani) were behind the ethno-cultural nationalism. (Sen 2002) The Partition of Bengal and the formation of Indian Muslim League in 1905 and 1906 respectively were the two most significant events of political consciousness among Bengali Muslims. Nawab Salimullah emerged as a leader of the Muslim community of Bengal especially of East Bengal, who supported the partition scheme and organized a movement in its favour.[4] In the later years, the Muslims of Bengal industriously supported the cause of Pakistan in 1947.

## Political Frontiers

In a short span of 25 years, Bangladesh has the distinction of having undergone two national movements. One in 1947 which was carried out on the wheels of the 'Two-Nation Theory' (Hindu-Muslim divide) and created Pakistan. And other, the language movement in the erstwhile East Pakistan which busted the myth of religion as a sufficient glue capable of uniting the two wings of Pakistan, which resulted in the birth of Bangladesh in 1971 and put forth the secularist resistance of discrimination under the garb of religious hegemony. Having been put to mutilation twice has impacted upon the fashioning of national identities in a peculiar way—perhaps it was the confusing situation of the old being dead and the new not yet being born, and, in the interregnum the national space had been occupied by military dictatorships coupled with a strident Islamic hegemony and anti-Indianism.

The birth of Bangladesh symbolised a socio-political revolution in terms of rising expectations among a large segment of the people for self-identity, liberal democracy and a progressive society. Ironically, within a short span of time, the ideals of freedom struggle[5] have not found a clear expression in the political systems of Bangladesh. The dictum of separation of religion from politics was absent in the political discourse, and the tryst with secularism and friendship with India was short-lived. Soon after the assassination of Sheikh Mujibur Rahman, the process of Islamisation and anti-Indianism gradually began with the military dictators taking recourse to religion so as to gain legitimacy. As a result, the ruling political elites of Bangladesh have shaped the identities within 'liberal-secular Bengali' and 'Bangladeshi nationalistic hegemony with Islam at its core' tendencies either to attain the right to self-determination or to ease the ruling objective over the years.

Indeed, the genesis of Bangladesh originated in successive

conflicts related to different sets of nationalism. The first of these conflicts, associated with religious identity, led to separation from the body polity of India and associated with the state of Pakistan (the spirit of 1947). The second conflict, associated with East Pakistan's political, linguistic and secular identity, culminated in the division of Pakistan and the creation of Bangladesh (the spirit of 1971). These two distinct national identities are products of the pursuit for self-rule or ruling objective by the socio-political elites of Bangladesh.

## Bangladesh as a Small State

There are vast geographical, economic and military disparity between India and Bangladesh, where the former has a regional domination and the latter considered in the milieu of a small state fear-psychosis. Bangladesh small state insecurity syndrome vis-à-vis India has been substantiated with the above religious-cultural construct. Hence, it is essential to understand the definition of small state in international system, and to what extent Bangladesh fits into this definition.

Designation of small state is a relative observation of size, capability, resources and global influence of a particular state in comparison to other states. Generally, if the geographical size of a state is comparatively small, it can be called a small state. The smaller size works as a barricade to the satisfactory availability of natural resources and promotes unreasonable steps to meet the diverse demands of the populace. This situation weakens the potentiality and compels the small state to develop external dependency. On the other way dependency undermines the 'independent international role'[6] of a small state. This compulsion often made small state a pawn or satellite in the hands of big and powerful states. However, Rothstein (1968) has defined a small power through psychological and material perspectives.

> "A Small Power is a state which recognises that it cannot obtain security primarily by use of its own capabilities, and that it must rely fundamentally on the aid of other states, institutions, processes, or developments to do so; the Small

> Power's belief in its inability to rely on its own means must also be recognised by the other states involved in international politics."

Relying on this definition most of the states will be designated as small power, because most of the states in one way or other are dependent on some other states. Only the superpowers are out of the rubric of Rothstein's small power definition.

While categorizing and defining various states Keohane (1969) has examined their behaviour in accordance with the 'System Theory'. He has classified four kinds of states: "'System-Determining States', 'System-Influencing States', 'System-Affecting States', and 'System-Ineffectual States', who can do little to influence the system-wide forces that effect them, except in groups which are so large that each state has minimal influence and which may themselves be dominated by large powers." Thus, in the opinion of Keohane these four of states can be called small state.

However, there are significant conceptual differentiations of small state with weak state and pawn state or satellite state. If the size is the sole denominator of a small state then all small states are not weak states, but most of the weak states are smaller in size. Weakness denotes a comparative inferiority in the economic independence and self-military deterrence along with limited international role. The guided or influenced behaviour of a pawn state is an outcome of its heavy dependence on a particular or some selected states. In case of Bangladesh, it always looks beyond the national boundary for economic development and military security and behaves like a weak state or pawn state in many instances.

Physically, Bangladesh is surrounded by more than 90 per cent of its international border with India alone. It has also a common border with Myanmar in the Southeast, but is very limited and insignificant. It is this physical geography, which makes Bangladesh to feel 'India Locked'. (Hussain 1989) However in the southern part, Bangladesh is also exposed to the Bay of Bengal. Nevertheless, Bangladesh also suffers from higher population density and limited natural resources. In fact, Bangladesh is one of the most densely populated countries of the world. According to the 2011 census, Bangladesh's population density is 964 people per sq. km. As per the 2011 government estimate, Bangladesh's population is 142.32 million. The area of the country is 1,47,570 square kilometres. (Bangladesh Bureau of Statistic, 2011)

It is also one of the most disaster prone countries in the world. Increased frequency of natural disaster, such as cyclone and floods, lean season crisis and drought, is likely to undermine poverty (31.5 per cent) reduction efforts. Thus, the country is considered to be one of the most vulnerable countries to climate change, which is composed largely of low-lying lands less than 6 meters above sea level. About 80 per cent of its land is floodplain. These frequent extreme climatic events are causing damage to life, property, and the economy.

Thus, being a small state in terms of size, population, resources, state of economy and military capability, Bangladesh somehow behaves differently from the economically and militarily stronger countries, particularly India in pursuit of its foreign policy objectives. Its potential mismatch with India has generated small state fear psychosis of the dominance of a big neighbour.

## Insecurity Syndrome

India, being a dominant military power in South Asia develops a threat perception among small neighbouring states. The Indian initiatives in the name of domestic stability of neighbouring states have created serious mistrust and suspicion. This has substituted anti-Indian feelings in the region. Being a self-appointed custodian of peace and stability in South Asia, India's relations with her neighbours deteriorated as the neighbours considered Indian hegemony in the region. This was reflected clearly by the comments made by K Subrahmanyam in 1971, "there is not the same risk of the Chinese cutting off Assam as there was in 1962, since in the course of hostilities, the northern Bangladeshis likely to be overrun by the Indian forces and the communication lines with Assam will be broadened rather then narrowed down or closed." The problem was compounded with the signing of India-Bangladesh Friendship Treaty of 1972. Article 10 of this treaty stipulates that in case of an attack and threat of an attack the "high contracting parties shall immediately enter into mutual consultation in order to take appropriate effective measures to eliminate the threat." (Hussain, 1989) In view of Indian relationship with China, it could ask the right of passage through Bangladesh territory in case of Chinese attack. On the other hand, since Bangladesh had earned the friendship of China in post-August 1975, it would not have been in its national interest to help India against China. Thus, Bangladesh became sceptical of the Indian domination and major political stakeholders had declined to renew the treaty after its expiry in 1997. However, a simple answer of this sceptical posture of Bangladesh is that in spite of taking advantage, the ever strong leadership of India, and the then Prime Minster Indira Gandhi had helped Bangladeshis when it was at the verge of extinction in 1971. In this age of information and technology as well, this fear psychosis posture seems merely inspired for political discourse in Bangladesh. Nevertheless, this perception is recently melting through an invitation to Indian soldiers to visit Bangladesh after 37 years; they had fought for Bangladesh's liberation against West Pakistan.

## Extra-Regional Alliance Strategy

If a small state unevenly placed in a regional security complex with insecurity syndrome and bilateral hostility towards a big neighbour, that state looks beyond the region for self-protection. On the other way, an extra-regional power uses the small state to grip its strategic hold upon that region in general and against a comparatively strong state of that region, with which that extra-regional power does not share trustworthy bilateral relations. Thus, a small-state relation with an extra-regional power always generates security concern in the region, particularly for the dominant power of the region. Regional power imbalance and fear of the domination of a much stronger neighbour have provoked the small states of South Asia to develop strategic relations with extra-regional powers.

Bangladesh's liberation war involved all the prominent Cold War actors with the South Asian region. From the liberation war period to the military coups, Bangladesh's strategic relation was limited to India and the USSR. The assassination of Mujibur Rahman opened the gate for the anti-Indian powers to grip their strategic hold over the region. At this point of time Bangladesh's strategic relations with China touched its zenith. Guided by the objective to counter India, China started giving military aid and assistance to Bangladesh. During the military regimes Bangladesh also developed dynamic relations with the US. However, its relation with the US was limited to the aid donor-receiver relations.

There is also always scope for the altercation of the nature of the relationship in case of any improvement nudged between the extra-regional power and the dominating power of the region. However, a relation with extra-regional power presents small state more options to deal with states of its immediate vicinity. Bangladesh's perception to protect its sovereignty, territorial integrity and co-existence with India has compelled her to nudge strategic relation with the extra-regional powers. Thus, its strategic relation with China and the USA can be viewed as a small state's desperate attempt to counter-balance a big neighbour through the collaboration with extra-regional powers.

Generally, a small state is a congregation of five basic elements—territoriality, population, sovereignty, legitimate government and international recognition. In reality, India has been instrumental in endorsing or protecting all of the above elements of Bangladesh since its war of independence. Nevertheless, way back in 1972, framing the foreign policy of Bangladesh, Mujib told the newly independent nation, "Friendship with India is a cornerstone of the foreign policy of Bangladesh." Even in India, the same mood prevailed then, which could be well understood from Indira Gandhi's speech in

Lok Sabha in 1972 as she stated "In future, the governments and people of India and Bangladesh, who share common ideals and sacrifices, would forge a relationship based on the principles of mutual respect for each other's sovereignty, territorial integrity, non-interference in the internal affairs, equality and mutual benefit."[7] However, there is an asymmetry in the real powers of the states which created an air of mistrust and differentiating threat perceptions between the neighbours.

## Political Vulnerability

Most of the small states' political set-up in South Asia is struggling to nurture the norms of real democracy. The society is heterogeneous, uneducated and economically underdeveloped which further leads to the legitimacy crisis.[8] The real challenge before these states is to sustain institutional democracy and attract participatory political culture. In such types of political system, military directly or indirectly influences the political decision-making process. Many a time military or undemocratic regimes toppled an elected civilian government with an elusion of speedy economic development. Similarly, in the case of Bangladesh, the political environment is volatile and less democratic.

Soon after the assassination of Mujib, democracy was totally toppled by the military regimes. The process of anti-Indianism had gradually begun with military dictators taking recourse to sensitive bilateral socio-economics and territorial issues to attain legitimacy and divert attention from the pressing problems of mass poverty and tottering economy. The ideals of the freedom struggle were slowly buried under the new construction of anti-Indianism and Islamic brand of nationalism. In this deliberation, the religious difference[9] had been inflamed by the crucial and sensitive issues, viz, water sharing, border, migration which have vital socio-economic implications for the country. The military regimes built a hostile perception towards India. Particularly, the construction of Farakka barrage across the Ganges river was the epicentre of the entire subject of mistrust and anti-Indianism.

Attempts at unilateral exploitation of the trans-boundary water resources annoyed the people of Bangladesh. However, internationalization of the issue by the military regimes had deepened the inter-state conflicts that spilled over to other areas of bilateral relations between India and Bangladesh.

Over the years the ruling political elites have shaped Bangladesh's policies towards India in a way that secure their domestic power base. In fact, the perceptional patterns in domestic political discourse are based along the Bengali nationalistic (pro-India) and Islamic nationalistic (anti-India) identity constructions of Bangladesh. Subsequently, the country has been ruled by these liberal-rationalist and the radical-rationalist forces particularly after the restoration of democracy in 1991.

## Evolution of Bilateral Relations

Indeed, just after the independence, India and Bangladesh enjoyed extensive and wide-ranging relations covering a number of areas of mutual interest. In the initial period, both countries followed a policy of expanding and deepening their friendly ties on the basis of respect for each other's sovereignty and mutual benefits. The reasons were two fold: first, India's role in the liberation war of Bangladesh, where India intervened and saved Bangladeshi people from the verge of extinction by Pakistan Army. Secondly, India and Bangladesh believed in common ideals and sacrifices, principles of mutual respect for each other's sovereignty, non interference in the internal affairs, policies of anti-imperialism, anti-colonialism and non-alignment at international level. The regular exchange of high level visits took place between the two countries, which underscored a number of agreements and treaties, viz, Peace and Friendship Treaty of 1972, Trade Agreement of 1972, Land Boundary Agreement of 1974, etc.

After the assassination of Mujib, the military regimes formulated a policy based on anti-Mujib and anti-India. The process of Islamisation of Bangladesh had distanced the two countries. Meanwhile, who? Mujib or Zia? had also signed a Water Accord of 1977. HM Ershad's government took little initiatives to resolve the issue and the two Memoranda of Understanding on the issue of the Ganges Water sharing were signed in 1982 and 1985. (Partha, 1982) However, it is clear that these military regimes maintained anti-Mujib and anti-Indian plank for political discourse since both leaders did not have political legitimacy at home. They have constantly accused India's lack of political will to implement the Land Boundary Agreements of 1974 and the unilateral approach in dealing with trans-boundary rivers water sharing. This had grounded mistrust among Bangladeshi people and provided an opportunity to legitimise their undemocratic rules in the shake of dealing with India. Thus, the power sobering gesture of these rulers had distanced two neighbours for many years.

Since 1991, the two major political parties—Bangladesh Nationalist Party (BNP) and Awami League (AL) have ruled the nation under the leadership of Khaleda Zia and Sheikh Hasina respectively for two alternative tenures. A careful examination of Indo-Bangladesh relation in the last twenty years reveals that it has significantly progressed under the AL governments whereas the BNP government had differed virtually on all bilateral issues. In other words, on the question of dealing with India, indeed, AL followed the path of Mujibur Rahman whereas BNP had carried out the legacy of military regimes.

During the first tenure of BNP government (1991-96), Indo-Bangladesh relations marked the lack of high level contacts. There were no serious attempts from either of the sides to resolve any of the outstanding problems between the two countries except an agreement on the issue of Tin Bigha Corridor in 1992. Although in the changed world scenario, Khaleda Zia moved towards the policies of liberalization, globalization and privatization to enhance the trade and investment for the economic development and added extensive economic contents in the foreign policy of Bangladesh. However, until the mid-1990s, the Indian foreign policy stances were also very negligent towards the small neighbours in South Asia. With the introduction of Gujral Doctrine, (based on non-reciprocity) and the AL coming into power, all the major agreements and cooperative attempts were taken place between the two countries.

BNP's second tenure (2001-06) progressed in strengthening ties between Bangladesh-Southeast and East Asian countries under the Look East policy particularly with China on the issues of military and economic cooperation. As usual, Indo-Bangladesh relations were marked with anguish and disappointment. The BNP always used the anti-Indian stand for domestic political discourse particularly appeasing their radical political alliance. On the line of military regimes, it has also given top priority to Islamisation and emphasised special relations with Islamic world. Even it could not realise that in the present circumstances and given the geographical and economic realities, maintaining good relations with India and resolving outstanding bilateral issues has become pre-conditions for the development of Bangladesh.

Sheikh Hasina's governments (1996-2001 and 2008 to till date) have well understood the need of the time and revived the gesture what Father of the Nation wanted to maintain with India. In her tenures, India and Bangladesh has been constructively active in bilateral cooperation for the development of both the neighbours and reached on understating to resolved the crucial issues, viz, Indo-Bangladesh Ganges Water Sharing Treaty of 1996, CHTs Accords of 1997, Protocols for operation of passenger bus service between Dhaka and Kolkata, and Dhaka and Agartala, bilateral trade promotion agreement, agreements Haat/ Bazar at border areas and most importantly addressing the security concerns of neighbours.

High-level exchanges, visits and meetings are taking place regularly alongside the wide ranging people-to-people interaction in recent years. The exchange of visits by the head of the governments of both the countries has strengthened the bilateral relations and opened many areas of cooperation between India and Bangladesh in the recent past. India has extended a line of credit of US $1 billion to Bangladesh for a range of projects, including railway infrastructure, supply of BG locomotives and passenger coaches, procurement of buses, and dredging projects. India has also stood by Bangladesh in its hour of need with aid worth over Taka 250 crore to help it cope with natural disasters and floods in 2007-08. The visit of Indian Prime Minister Manmohan Singh in 2011 has signed historic accords which include Framework Agreement on Cooperation for Development, Protocol to the Agreement Concerning the Demarcation of the Land Boundary and Related Matters, viz, exchange of enclaves and adverse possessed lands. An addendum to the Memorandum of Understanding (MoU) between India and Bangladesh to Facilitate Overland Transit Traffic between Bangladesh and Nepal, Renewable Energy Cooperation, further the academic objectives between two premium universities were also signed.

The efforts were in progress to reach on agreement point on water sharing of the Teesta river. But at the last moment, Chief Minister Mamata Banerjee, rejected the deal, and cancelled her plan travel to Bangladesh, saying the agreement would hurt farmers in Paschim Banga. The nature of federal structure of Indian political system and the on-going coalition politics of the country had impacted on the process of making a neighbour as a partner in development. On other side, India has recently proposed the construction of the Tipaimuki Barrage in its territory which may bring bitterness if lower riparian is not taken in confidence. In fact, a wider opinion in Bangladesh concerns about Tipaimukh project because they claim that it will adversely affect the greater economy, environment and river morphology of the Sylhet district of Bangladesh.

The Awami League government not only approved the passage of Anti-Terrorism Ordinance, but also initiated several measures to address the menace of terror faced by Bangladesh and its neighbour in the last few years. The government has also led to arrests of some Indian terrorists operating from Bangladesh. India also found ways and means to address some of Bangladesh's long standing demands. Its readiness to dilute trade barriers, its willingness to consider Bangladesh's fears on border conflicts as well as agreeing to Bangladesh's demand for transit to Nepal and Bhutan, reflect a constructive shift.

The seven integrated check post and eight land custom stationed along the border would also be upgraded. These programmes will help in filling critical gaps in the social and physical infrastructure within Bangladesh. In totality, this will help in inculcating a sense of security and integration among the population of eastern South Asian sub-region. The present tenure of AL government wants to reinstate the spirit of 1971, which will bring a new height in the relationship between the two countries.

However, the leader of opposition Begum Khaleda Zia, is still busy with her old discourse maintaining anti-India political discourse. She has criticised granting US $ 1 billion Indian loan to Bangladesh and said it would facilitate to India and the rate of interest is also high. Above all, she has declared the high level visits of Prime Ministers were total failure and blamed that there are a secret deal between India and Bangladesh on the cost of national interest. The Anti-India plank is still maintained by her to consolidate her power base. In short, throughout the entire discussion, one can point out that the ups and downs in Indo-Bangladesh relations are very much measured along the differentiating political discourse of two forces in Bangladesh led by AL alliance and BNP alliance.

## Conclusion

It is also established that the construction of a unique cultural or religious identity has impacted on the nature of Indo-Bangladesh relations. The long-standing political instability and growing military intervention in the political affairs of the country has solidified the small state perception of Bangladesh which is detrimental to India-Bangladesh relation. This perception has guided Bangladesh to collaborate with anti-Indian extra-regional power. However, a powerful neighbour can't be alienated forever and the better option is to engage with it through positive measures. In this recent upward swing, one thing is well understood that both the countries have understood that the trans-national development approaches would be the best antidote to reinstate the lost socio-economic and cultural linkages between the two countries. The recent change of mind set and a thrust for cooperation in the field of connectivity, infrastructural and economic development through bilateral and multilateral channels will bring the two countries ever closer. The political will from both the sides has become pre-requisite for an integrated economic approach for these geographically proximate countries. The study has identified that Indo-Bangladesh relations had become the hostage of confrontational politics of Bangladesh, where one or other political force has nationalised the 'India factor' for their political gains. The opposition forces have to cooperate to the recent efforts of government for the best interest of the people and the nation.

On the other side, if India genuinely wants to address the economic and security concerns of eastern South Asia sub-region particularly North-eastern states of India, it has to behave like a soft power or smart power in dealing with Bangladesh. One party relation gives an adhocism policy in bilateral relations. Thus, India must persuade Bangladesh to develop consensus policy approach towards India.

There is a correlation between an economically weaker Bangladesh and the simultaneous growth of anti-India posture and a more prosperous Bangladesh and the simultaneous increasing cooperation. Therefore, India should help the country to improve effective, efficient and good governance in Bangladesh. Hence, consolidation of democracy and emergence of a vibrant civil society is the best antidote for secular and democratic Bangladesh.

In dealing, India can expand the concept of 'Gujral Doctrine' to resolve the bilateral disputes and confidence building measures. Therefore, ensuring human security and effective Indo-Bangladesh relations, both the countries should have to adopt a cross border cooperative plan for business related infrastructure targeting the improvement of employability and developing entrepreneurship.

## References

1. Anisuzzaman, M (2002) "The Identity Question and Politics" in Rounaq Jahan (ed), *Bangladesh: Promise and Performance*, Dhaka: University Press Limited.
2. Bangladesh Bureau of Statistics (2011), Population and Housing Census Report 2011 Accessed 8 December 2011 URL:http://www.boi-gov.bd/about bangladesh at a glace
3. Baxter, Craig (1997) Bangladesh: From a Nation To A State, Boulder: Westview Press.
4. Bose, Sugata and Ayesha Jalal (2004) Modern South Asia: History, Culture, Political Economy, Oxford: Oxford University Press.
5. Hunter, William W (1872) Our Indian Mussalmans, London: Tubner.
6. Hussain, Akmal, "Geo-Politics and Bangladesh Foreign Policy", *CLIO*, June 1989, 7(2), 99-100.
7. Keohane, Robert O (1969), "Lilliputian's Dilemmas: Small States in International Politics", *International Organization*, 23(2): 291-310.
8. Partha, Sarala, (1982) Foreign Relations: At a Formative Stage. World Focus, July 3(7).
9. Rahim. A, (2007) 'Communalism and Nationalism in Bangladesh', Journal of Asian and African Studies.
10. Rothstein, Robert L (1968), Alliances and Small Powers, New York: Columbia University Press.
11. Sen, Swadhin (2002) 'Community boundary, secularized religion and imagined past in Bangladesh: archaeology and historiography of unequal encounter', World Archaeology, 34, 2, pp 346-362.
12. Snyder, Glenn H and Paul Diesing (1977), *Conflict Among Nations: Bargaining, Decision Making and System Structure in International Crises*, New Jersey: Princeton University Press.
13. Subrahmanyam K (1972), Bangladesh and India's Security. Palit and Dutt; Dehradun.

## Notes

1. 'Two-Nation Theory', on the basis Pakistan was created in 1947.
2. Carrying one culture, one language, one society and one geo-economics.
3. Against this backdrop a putative Islamic community emerged in lower Bengal (now Bangladesh). Using official statistics and data the book

(Hunter, 1872) argued cogently that the Hindu, in every branch of government, got the upper hand over the Muslim.

4. Giving a territoriality shape, a newspaper 'the Bengali' on 15th January 1904 had described it as a manifestation of the policy of divide and rule.
5. Democracy, socialism, secularism (DSS) and Bengali nationalism and centrality of India in the foreign policy of Bangladesh.
6. Because, foreign policy is primarily a projection of country's socio-economic and political compulsions in international politics.
7. Indira Gandhi, delivering her speech at Lok Sabha on December 6, 1971, granting recognition to People's Republic of Bangladesh
8. Legitimacy crisis is the incapability of a political system to engender and maintain the belief that existing political institutions are the most appropriate or proper ones for society.
9. 'Hindu India's domination over the 'Muslim Bangladesh'

*Chapter 6*

# Ethnic Problem and National Security in Nepal

*Biswanath Chakraborty*
Associate Professor
Rabindra Bharati University, Kolkata

National security essentially means the state of the health of the nation within which citizens enjoy life, liberty, property and participation in every sphere of the society. Political stability, economic well-being and equitable distribution of resources are its essential preconditions. The peacefulness of the environment of a nation is based on sound civil defense, a modicum of trust among citizens themselves and with the national institutions of governance. The sources of threat can be extra-systemic (inter-state tension, cross-border terrorism, unwanted immigration, climate change, fuel and financial crisis, refugees, etc) or intra-systemic (civil war, poverty trap, inequality and exclusion of citizens from ecological, social, economic and political resources).

Nepal occupies a central part of Asia geopolitics between two advanced technological super-states—China in the north and India in the east, west and south; each with over one billion population, leading infrastructure, software technology industries, high growth markets and highest engagement of multilateral institutions. This potentially makes it a transit corridor for increased Sino-Indian competition for trade and commerce. Its location in the geopolitical underbelly of China, Tibet and India's heartland states of Uttar Pradesh, Bihar and West Bengal constitutes its strategic geography vital to their security, stability, progress and peace. An increasingly open and democratic Nepal in the future is more likely to be swayed by the ongoing geo-strategic competition between them and the great powers for their influence.

The ruggedness of Nepal-China boundary is clearly revealed by its length which is 1,415 kilometres, while Nepal-India boundary which runs along three sides of Nepal is only 1850 kilometers, 465 kilometers longer than Nepal-China boundary. So far as Nepal-India boundary is concerned, the mountainous portions of the boundary lie in the Sikkim state and Darjeeling district of West Bengal state in the east, while rest of the boundary runs along the plains in the south and along the Mahakali river in the west. The few territorial disputes that existed between Nepal and China were resolved by the Joint Boundary Commission on October 5, 1961. On the other hand, none of the treaties between Nepal and India ever mentions the procedures for the regulation of the Nepal-India border. The trade agreement has specified the agreed routes for mutual trade, but there is no agreement regarding the movement of the people and the agreed routes for the movement of people of both countries along the border. As for trade, there are 22 agreed transit and customs posts along the Nepal-India border. The concept of open border between Nepal and India has still remained an enigma. Besides, there are several sub-customs posts. It is alleged that it is possible to have illegal movement of people and goods in collaboration with personnel deputed in those posts. There is no denying the fact that it is not unusual from the practical point of view to have illegal smuggling of goods, trafficking of girls to brothels in Indian cities, trafficking in narcotic drugs, arms and ammunition and movement of criminals and terrorists. In principle, both Nepal and India have positively agreed to control such illegal activities along the border, but there is a lack of an effective and practical approach.

The ethnic tensions that spilled across Nepal's international boundaries also posed security and foreign policy problems. In 1987 the Nepalese residing in Darjeeling district of West Bengal mounted a violent agitation demanding statehood within the Indian union for Indian citizens of Nepalese origins. As many as 6,000 ethnic Nepali refugees fled to Nepal from areas adjacent to Darjeeling in India. More than one lakh Nepalese fled from Bhutan having being forcibly evacuated by the Bhutanese Army. It further intensified not only the ethnic problem in Nepal but also created a trans-regional security problem involving all three states.

A sound civil security relation is the key to enhance national security in Nepal and may contribute to achieve three national tasks—(i) building modern state; (ii) inclusive democracy based on a new social contract and (iii) sustainable peace rooted in the realization of human security. But this requires the political leadership to remove the five defects of democracy such as:

(a) access of public to power;
(b) denial of opponent groups' claim to power;
(c) erosion of the legitimate state monopoly on power;
(d) narrow power base restricting pluralistic politics in opinion and democratic will formation; and
(e) the mode of rule violating basic democratic values.

Rectification of the defects of democracy and democratisation of security agencies must be accompanied with a formulation of national security doctrine, institutionalisation of dialogue and regular identification of sources of threat by various stakeholders of society; and strengthening of National Security Council. Mutual appreciation of each other's roles and responsibilities between civil and security forces is crucial for the construction of a post conflict Nepal and building a shared and peaceful future.

It may be pointed out here that Nepal's vulnerability to external pressure has traditionally been dealt with using various foreign policy strategies: (1) friendly isolationism; (2) conformation; (3) submissive isolationism; (4) projection of independent national contacts; (5) participation in the non-aligned movement; and (6) proposing Nepal as a Zone of Peace (ZoP).

However, those strategies did not address the problems of poverty and regional inequalities threatening national integration, which remain unfulfilled challenges. Nepal's national security and sovereignty should ultimately be addressed through internal socio-economic development. The failure of Nepal's government to address the political crisis in 1951 and 1990 and the Maoist insurgency in 1996-2006 raise questions about the capacity of Nepali state to manage its own internal security and deal with external threats effectively.

In Nepal, ethnicity has become an important variable in the politics. In fact, the issues such as the formation of various organizations on ethnic line, demand for regional and ethnic autonomy, political tensions arising due to unequal distribution of power among various communities and regions, etc, are becoming critical factors of Nepali politics. The long-standing domination of the Brahmin-Chettri-Newar trio has come under severe criticism by ethnic groups. The Hindu Tribal communities, which are undergoing fast social and political mobilization are challenging the traditional power base of the Nepali society and polity and also trying to assert for equitable redistribution of resources and goods. In fact, it can be said that various underprivileged ethnic groups have started demanding a greater share in socio-political sphere.

## About Ethnic Groups and Communities

A brief look at the various ethnic groups will help us in understanding the pluralistic nature of Nepali society. Nepal has a multi-racial, multi-lingual and multi-cultural society. Its inhabitants can be classified into three main racial stocks: The Indo-Aryans, the Mongoloids and the Austro-Asiatic. Majority of the population of the country is Hindus, followed by Buddhists, Muslims and Christians.

The people speaking various languages and dialects of Indian origin who had migrated from India to Nepal at different points of time are Indo-Aryans. They became a part of the Nepali society in due course. They are settled in both the hill areas and the Terai region of the kingdom. In the Terai region a large number of people of the Indian origin who migrated at a later stage are still awaiting citizenship of Nepal. The people of Mongoloid origin such as Rai,

Limbu, Tamang, Sunwar, Gurumg, Magar, Bhote, Sherpa, Chepang, Thakali, etc, are settled in the Himalayan and the hill regions. They are believed to have migrated to Nepal from the north. Their language, culture and lifestyle are quite similar to those of the people of Tibet. The people of Austro-Asiatic origin are Sutar, Dure, Dunwar, Rawate, Santhali, etc.

The people of the Terai region, that is constituted of the Indian migrants and the tribal groups have a regional identity. They include plain Brahmins, Rajputs, Banias, Bhumihars, Yadav, Kayastha, Kurmi, Rauyniyar and the tribals like, Tharu, Sutar Rajbansis Dhina, Jhangad, etc. There are dalit groups in the hills and the Terai. The Newar mostly dwelling in the Kathmandu valley have a separate cultural identity. There are Muslims and Christians as well. Muslims mostly dwell in the Terai region.

## Ethnic Mobilization and Identity Politics

There were indications of resurgence of pan-tribal sentiments in Nepal towards the end of the 70s. The people of Mongoloid origin had strong feelings against discrimination towards them. In September 1979, KB Gurung convened a conference of the people of Mongoloid origin. Members participated in the conference demanding proportionate representation of the Mongoloids in the public sector. Gurung questioned the validity of declaring Nepal as a Hindu state and demanded that Nepal should be declared a secular state.

The 1979 movement for democracy and the consequent referendum of 1980 did evoke tribal sentiments but it seems that the Mongoloid people failed in mobilizing themselves on ethnic lines in an organized manner largely due to systemic prohibitions.

Various ethnic identities again started surfacing in the political arena of Nepal after the establishment of democracy in the country in 1990. It has given a new dimension of ethno-politics in the country. It may be noted here that in three years time after 1990, nearly 44 ethnic associations had come into existence by the end of 1993. It clearly reflects upon the mobilization of ethnic groups after the dawn of democracy in the country.

The resurgence of Mongoloid ethnic groups took a new turn after 1990. With the beginning of the democratic process a number of tribal ethnic identities have surfaced. These organizations began to assert the promotion of their interests. On the eve of the 1991 general elections, Nepal Rashtriya Jana Jati Party demanded division of Nepal into 12 autonomous regions such as Khasan, Jadan, Magarat, Tamuan, Tamba, Saling, Khambuan, Limbuan, Kohila, Maithili, Bhojpuri and Awadhi. Thus, demands for regional autonomy on ethno-linguistic lines began to surface. The issue of language also got complicated with the use of language other than Nepali in the Parliament.

The ethnic groups are highly critical of Brahminic hold of politics. The strong reactions of the ethnic Mongoloids against undermining their religious-cultural identity and their underprivileged position against the Brahmin-Chettri-Newar domination have reflected in the expressions of the Mongoloid leaders. Bir Nembang, a Mongal leader raised voice for a separate self-ruled state in Limbuwan while Hark Raj Limbu formed a Limbuwan National Council. Rai's, on the other hand have demanded for a separate Khambuan.

Since the formation of political parties on religious and cultural basis is prohibited in the Constitution of 1990, the various ethnic groups sought alignment with one or the other political parties. The latter have tried to exploit the organized strength of their ethnic groups for their own purposes and have tried to patronage the ethnic leadership. In fact, the ethnic leadership is seeking support from their ethnic organizations as well as the political party to which they have sought affiliation.

The Maoists seem to be more concerned to ethnic demands. Some of the demands of ethnic groups and the Maoists are similar. Therefore, there has been a convergence of interest of the two. It was for this reason as well, that the young people of some of the Mongolian communities joined the Maoist movement. If the ethnic groups are politicized further it may pose new challenges to the internal security of Nepali State.

## Identity Politics in Terai

Historically, the people of Terai region have been discriminated in Nepal. The hill people and the ruling elite did not trust them ever. Hence, they had strong resentments against the state. After 1950 people of the Terai region began to assert against the domination of the hill people. The major discontent of the Madhesias was against their under representation in the political structures, bureaucracy and army. During the 50s, the people of Terai also tried to assert their linguistic identity and demanded status and recognition to Hindi, which was a lingua-Franca among all the communities of the Terai. A 'Save Hindi Movement' was launched in the Terai during the 50s. But not only that the discrimination against people of Terai continued, the citizenship rules were framed in away making it difficult for them to obtain Nepali citizenship.

After the introduction of the Panchayat System in 1962, deliberate attempts were made to encourage Nepali language in the Terai in place of Hindi, migration of hill people in the Terai and the consolidation of citizenship rules. The people of the hill region migrating to Terai were given surplus land by introducing land reforms. The surplus land was denied to the Terai people who had been the tiller of the land for a long tine. The people of the Terai region viewed these steps as a deliberate denial of rights to them and a cultural invasion over them by the hill people. The Madhesias were considered as a second rate citizens. However, since organized political activities had been banned under the Panchayat system, the discontent among the people of the Terai region remained more or less latent. The resentment of the Terai region has surfaced in a big way in the post-1990 Nepali politics. The Nepal Sadbhavana party has come forward to protect the interest of the people of Terai. It aims at fighting against the discrimination towards the Terai people.

It clearly indicates that the Terai people are not only unhappy with their disproportionate representation in the power structure but also with cultural hegemony of the hill people. In May 1991 General Elections, Sadbhavana Party raised ethnic issues and demanded regional autonomy for the Terai, declaration of Hindi as an official language of Nepal, citizenship to all the people of Terai and 50 per cent reservations for the people of Terai in army and administration. Therefore, the emerging trends of ethnicity call for restructuring of state and the accommodation of diverse groups within a liberal democratic socio-political order.

When the Constituent Assembly was elected in 2008, it appeared as being among the most inclusive national legislatures of the world. This had been achieved through an elaborately worked-out formula of quotas that guaranteed representation to all the sections of the society. The Constituent Assembly election has broadened the social, gender and intergenerational bases of political power. The most difficult problem remains that of political and constitutional instability caused by a move of constitutional actors from consensus to competitive politics, free-riding tendency of some actors who are enjoying more power than their actual social representativeness, and extra-constitutional activities of armed non-state actors thus spoiling peace and security. Most of the political parties are faction-ridden, organised through the stabilisation of client networks and are less interested in the transformation of people into citizens.

Federal restructuring of the country will be instrumental in power sharing and peace in the long run. It is also believed that federalism will promote inclusive development by granting political autonomy to states (regions) and assuring proportional and fair representation of all ethnic or sub-cultural groups in future governments and other decision-making organs of the state. However, it is not yet clear what kind of federalism this multi-ethnic country will have. Many analysts see federal restructuring of the country as an over-ambitious and challenging task for Nepal. There is also a fear that any hurried decision in this direction may further intensify the underlying conflict and ultimately cause the disintegration of the country. Furthermore, economic issues like revenue and expenditure sharing and resource mobilization are not fully spelled out by the proponents of federalism.

In Nepal, most proposals for ethnic autonomy come close to what is defined as an ethnic federal system, where the borders between the regional units should match the boundaries of relevant ethnic or linguistic communities. Although support for federalism as a tool of ethnic conflict mitigation is generally strong among political scientists, the idea of ethnic based federalism is highly controversial. A major argument in favour of ethnicity-based federations is that the country's ethnic subdivision ensures that the various ethnic groups will form a local majority in one or more of the subunits. In this way, minorities may feel a sense of security and be enabled to promote their own culture and identity. It is assumed that when the demands of self-determination are met and the culture of the groups is assured, the source of inter-ethnic struggles may be undermined and instead intra-ethnic competition is likely to occur.

Those who are against ethnic federal subunits would counter the above argument by the exactly opposite claim. When ethnic groups have their own subunits, instability and the pressure for secession are likely to increase. When the group is endowed with resources, legitimacy and an independent power base, people's loyalty will shift to the regional subunit rather than to the federation as a whole, thus undermining the existence of the dual loyalty, which is essential to the unity of the state. There is also a practical problem in the creation of ethnically homogeneous regions, which is very relevant for Nepal. Ethnic homogeneity is hardly possible in any territory in multi-ethnic state due to the diversity and mixture of peoples across ethnic boundaries. Therefore, new minorities are likely to be created within the subunits, which are in danger of being victimized, intentionally or not. The new constitution should facilitate a deep-rooted and inclusive democracy where all minorities are protected. Irrespective of the final partition, there will be a number of ethnic minorities within all federal states. A thriving and inclusive local democracy is necessary to secure the interests of all local people.

The Constituent Assembly emerged a divisive arena rather than a place of compromise amidst diverse demands, between the political parties, classes, linguistic groups, regions, castes, and ethnicities. The Constitution surfaced the division between those who believed that provinces must be defined on the basis of economic viability and other single-minded in their demand for identity-based division of the country to counter historical marginalization by the Kathmandu valley. The Constituent Assembly State Restructuring Committee proposed, by majority vote, a 14-province federal model with eight to nine ethnicities getting their own provinces—in a country of mixed habitation with more that 100 officially recognized communities. But in the deliberations of the Constituent Assembly the political parties left the issue of federalism till the very end. By the time they came around to consider it, in late 2011, the public debate around it had become highly polarized, giving little scope for an agreement on the issue before the final deadline for agreement on the Constitution. Nepal is currently in a state of flux. The government has been declared a caretaker one by the President. The parties are debating between going for a fresh election or reviving the Constitutional Assembly, but agreement is going to be difficult.

## References

1. Lawoti, M, *Towards a Democratic Nepal: Inclusive Political Institutions for a Multicultural Society*, New Delhi: Sage Publication, 2005.
2. Richard Burghart (ed), *The Conditions of Listening: Essays on Religion, History and Politics in South Asia*, Delhi: Oxford University Press, 1996.
3. Stephen Lawrence Mikessell, Class, State and Struggle in Nepal, Manohar, New Delhi, 1999.
4. Fredrick, H Haige, Regionalism and National Unity in Nepal, California University Press, California, 1975.
5. Urmila Phadnis, Ethnicity and Nation-Building in South Asia, Sage Publication, New Delhi, 1990:123.
6. Dilli Ram Dahal, "Ethnic Calandron, Demography and Minority Politics: The Case of Nepal" in Dhrub Kumar (ed), State Leadership and Politics in Nepal, CNAS, Kathmandu, 1995.
7. Krishna B Bhattachan, "Ethno-Politics and Ethno-Development: An Emerging Paradigns in Nepal", in Dhrub Kumar (ed), State Leadership and Politics in Nepal, CNAS, Kathmandu, 1995.

8. Praya Raj Sharma, The State and Society in Nepal, Historical Foundations and Contemporary Trends, Hindu Books, Kathmandu, 2004.
9. Pancha N Maharjan, "The Maoist Insurgency and Crisis of Governability in Nepal", in Dhrub Kumar (ed), *Domestic Conflict and Crisis of Governability in Nepal*, CNAS, Kathmandu, 2000.
10. BC Upreti, Nepal Democracy At Cross Roads: Post 1990 Dynamics, Issues and Challenges Kanishka Publishers, New Delhi.
11. Kanak Mani Dixit, "The Life and Death of the Constituent Assembly of Nepal" in *Economic & Political Weekly*, Vol XLVII, No 31, August 2012.
12. Jeevan Raj Sharma, "Social Science Engagement and Political Interregnum in Nepal", in *Economic & Political Weekly*, Vol XLVII, No 31, August 4, 2012.
13. Lawoti, M, *Contention Politics and Democratization of Nepal*, Sage Publications, New Delhi, 2007.

*Chapter 7*

# Sources of Insecurity and State's Conduct in South Asia

*Anindya Jyoti Majumdar*
Associate Professor
Jadavpur University, Kolkata

There are a number of issues concerning South Asian security that have been discussed and analysed and therefore hardly one can add something new to this particular aspect, but perhaps as there are people and scholars on the different clients of analysis and various approaches to interpret to one particular problem, therefore, few observations can be made. First, of course, as we all know at a time when the context of security was synonymous with that of national security and that of the military security and that the state would be strong enough to remove the external order, territory, integrity and political sovereignty and would be able to protect national properties and life evidence, the idea was pretty simple—if the state is secure the people will be secure too. State itself becomes threat to the security and well-being of its people if the narrow concept of security is no longer, security gets its evidence and its terrible and then human security will get its predominance so far security of a state. However, one would legitimately exist to the other and generally the powerful state and secure state can neglect issues on the human security and it introduces challenges within for beautiful long-run existence for state itself, the people and the human security can hardly be protected in which existence remains honourable and interference by external agencies security has its many components traditional, non-traditional, conventional, non-conventional, external and internal politics, economic, cultural, societal, military, and in fact environmental. The idea is, it has its rational dimension. Cooperative strength offers human collectivity within geographical area combining all these aspects and therefore the very idea of security is dynamic rather it is multi-dimensional and cannot be comprehended if classified under one particular context.

The dictionary meaning of security being in a state in the absence of threat and challenges since many of these threats are perceived and misperceived and security can also be a state of mind and hence would be dependable upon the attitude of the environment involved. However, axis of wave threat and challenges confront us almost everyday and security seems to be elusive everyday with the broadening of meaning of security and in session and accession of security of necessary elements of human existence, allowing the emergence of the new form of security almost every day in actuality. Insecurity discourses that came into being that is the focus is now on the major to delay, to manage and to prevent crises of any form rather than on a re-substance of remodelling of relation that incrementally increases for security. Once again it is to be connected with the changing attitude of the actor's symbol and these are certain serious accession in the way of the political changes. One of such hindrances is of brackets.

State responds to the demand of security to secure from certain said pattern established by the brackets they follow by the major stream of existing system. The state sets the rules of law, rules of international regimes in all the support of the state. These are the agenda of international institutions, meaning privatization of issue according to preferences and thereby encouraging the middle power to control, once they decide the small state of its option forming and re-adjusting according to the decision of the major powers. Now in South Asia we have the middle power and surrounding this middle power, we have an array of small powers and the situation is known as complicated. However, in the name of security starting over the year we have developed and elaborated the security discourses and this security discourse may remain elusive in security because of a part of human existence and therefore sets of security may be absent under any circumstances. Hence the idea is perhaps absolutely different to go out of this insecurity syndrome. We are always talking about insecurity and less about security but the idea is perhaps that it is a kind of way that cannot achieve security; they must eliminate security to make the region habitable and to perpetuate human existence.

The rise of the security issue in the South Asian region is because of the sources of insecurity in the region that are many and in fact, it is a major factor that can be a difficult model for many insecure regions. Perhaps all these unmanageable sources of insecurity are preserved in one entity of the factor of the region. Now here in this region we have witnessed all the major forms of conflicts; we have the experience of inter-state war, border disputes, cross-border interference, submerceive activity, hostile propaganda, regional behaviour that always leads to frequent breakdown of communication, diplomatic tussle, military alerts, tit for tat and border starvation, movement of troops and the relation in these region from some point rises that the sources of insecurity among the people in the region also grows. It is still believed that further territorial fragmentation is possible and therefore it could lead to inter-state or infra-state conflict for territorial possession over Kashmir. It is just once again of the territories like Sri Lanka.

In India itself, basically the idea of inter-state can be interpreted as the conflict over the territorial position by protocol state which is able to say inter-state war was no longer reality. We are concerned about inter-state war, infra-state break-up. The proto-state finally working for territorial position is not in order to build up proper identity and it is very elusive but the identity with the proximity within the geographical area in a policy of explosions so called outsider is followed in the text to generate a local tension and vibration within the state and coercive measure and thereby serious undermining human security. Now since the state is not our agitator, the existence of transnational ethnic group and internal politics is with external relation. As a result the state and neighbour are free from tension in this region. You also know about this asymmetric power for structure and India as an eccentric pattern of policy in this region. The Indo-phobia among the smaller neighbours of huge countries comprehensively intensifies the smaller neighbours to transform the region as the multiple sub-standing, bringing in China into security calculus. China engaged the smaller powers and interpreted as deliberate supplement of China while India has impressive relation with China and obviously it is not interpreted as some kind of strategy. They employ these gross deficiency; this kind of suspicious tendency with each other so what it is called territorial rise disputes and as security competition in various parts and certain meaningful cooperation in this region. Now we know that one cannot ignore India in the particular region of South Asia, it eventually voices down India and Pakistan's tough competition laid on security. India is a vital factor in the domestic politics of the states in the region for nation-building at this stage to diffuse phobia in India.

We all know this India as a guidance use of skill by opposition as a suitable photos of possibility taken by the state which regarding to India as equally region has maintained the relation cooperative initiates regimes with beneficial relation during given period of time has been not sustained defensive building in its region so essentially this refer to different part of insecurity. Now in fact in South Asia create their own ability, own identity in a global regional hierarchy well the state firstly projects out word expression of sovereignty. Now therefore a number of ways has been suggested by scholars towards peace-making regimes including primitive diplomacy, application of peaceful means of settlement of disputes like arbitration, possession, mediation and political cooperation creating coordination, disputes resolution and conflict that take place. In this context people they said to have important element write to reinforce unity among the people. However, one to one relation across the border in fact is meant, but hardly it influences the general perception and behavioural pattern of the state. So, it could appear that those statse made hypothesis inter-depending towards their building a functional issue and reinforce security and stabilisation stronger to diffuse.

We can perhaps notice one is the support of democracy and democratic institution even under by compulsion has been made in the same of the Pakistan judiciary has become active arbitral the promise of the American millions has not before coming as the civilian government is toppled, in Bangladesh attempt to topple Hasina's administration has been failed, in Bhutan democrats privatization become disturbed, in Nepal monarchy has been abolished, in the Maldives changing government and democracy survive. The idea is there will be problems in front of democracy apart from beginning has been made as they matured, you know civilian government cannot understand each other better so far for the political cooperation in bringing down the differences and the other is real try for Jihad the Islamic terrorists are combining their efforts and perhaps going out of control of state agency this is another regime of cooperation.

Terrorists have been used in proxy war as an instrumental part of a state interest or as the bargaining ship. India is not a sub-continent in a new terror war, the argument is whatever of insecurity as witness so far it might felt corporism in combined neighbour initially, therefore the challenge for the terrorism. It is not need a question ISI supporting to particular groups over new Jihad you know is now grows along state are hardly control over the unless greater try to make the better and from the possessive law this under the security members lose its delivered importance and military corporation are would have been announced for the day.

Thus in term start to change its attitude within a security towards in this region South Asia will remain so far strengthening.

So basically the argument is not an economic corporation that is still a part that accepted the wisdom will have a political, military, economic corporation well it is not those is a possibility of political, military, economical corporation of all these while make South Asia somewhere secure it was difficult to get out of the scene in security syndrome.

*Chapter 8*

# Pakistan: Roots of Turmoil in the 21st Century

*Partha Pratim Basu*
Associate Professor
Jadavpur University, Kolkata

Pakistan is one state which through the decades, seemed to be perpetually in the grips of all conceivable kinds of turmoil. The manifestations were manifold: a volatile democracy, repeated military takeovers, rampant corruption charges, recurring sectarian violence, terrorism spawned by the Taliban militias, an unsecure nuclear capability, an economy in doldrums and so forth. This article, instead on commenting on this prodigious variety of issues, seeks in general to highlight two critical sources of turmoil in Pakistan: failure to establish a working balance among the three major political institutions, i e the executive, the 'A'rmy and the judiciary, the latest entrant into the race; and the penchant of the powers that be to use radical Islamists as a foreign policy implement since the 1980s in particular. It contains two sections—each introduces the major proposition at some length which is followed by case studies that led to political turbulence of various proportions. We conclude with some observations regarding the shape of things to come in future.

## Institutional Imbalance

The roots of Pakistan's institutional weakness and imbalance could be traced to the earliest days of its independent existence[1] precisely to fact that the *mohajir* leaders who had migrated from India and dominated the country's political, economic and cultural scenarios in the early 1950s had no viable support base in the provinces of West Pakistan. As a result, the Muslim League, the dominant political party already weakened by the death of its supreme leader Mohammad Ali Jinnah and the assassination of his deputy, Liaqat Ali Khan, got fractured down the middle. Thus while the *mohajirs* advocated a secular state, *laissez faire* economy and liberal politics, the leadership from North West Frontier Provinces (NWFP), Punjab, Balochistan, and Sindh favoured Islamization, state-managed economy and slow-paced land reform policy. Moreover, the East Pakistanis—mainly Bengalis constituted an overall majority which exposed less populous West to risk of permanent subordination to the Bengali fraction. These two sets of conflicts delayed the process of the framing of the Constitution; and national elections were postponed indefinitely, for instead of seeking a fresh mandate from people of Pakistan, its early governments chose to hang on to power as long as possible. On 7 October 1958, in the face of continuing domestic disorder and political disarray that resulted from the above political bottleneck, President Major General Iskander Mirza declared martial law under General Ayub Khan and dismissed the national and provincial governments. Thus began Pakistan's long experiments with military rule broken only by spells of highly personalistic and autocratic civilian governments, all carefully watched and ultimately deposed by the army.[2] The judiciary in Pakistan had a convoluted history as the courts became increasingly sensitive to political pressures to bend their rulings in favour of military or civilian government in power.[3] Judicial power began to erode in 1955 when Mohammad Munir, Chief Justice of Pakistan's Supreme Court, upheld the dissolution of the Constituent Assembly and dismissal of the Mohammad Ali Bogra government by the Governor General former civil servant Ghulam Mohammad on the plea that the Assembly was not a sovereign body. Again, when the country was placed under martial law in 1958, Munir and his court were readily available to place a judicial seal of approval on it by declaring "...that which otherwise is not lawful, necessity makes it lawful." This became known as the 'Doctrine of Necessity' and subsequently the courts retroactively cited it to endorse coups against civilian governments by Generals Zia ul Haq (1977) and Pervez Musharraf (1999) and at the same time sustained the myth of constitutionalism by pretending that their military coups were legally and constitutionally justified. This early pliability of the judges made it easier for subsequent civilian governments to break the law with impunity and the army to launch coup.

The political system of Pakistan as a result underwent something of a roller coaster ride over the decades, a history partly captured in the three successive constitutions it generated in the course of its first three decades. The first constitution produced in 1956 replaced the governor general (a legacy of Government of India Act, 1935) with a president, but effective power rested in the hands of a prime minister who was to be elected by the national parliament. This arrangement was overturned in the 1958 coup, and the 1962 constitution (popularly known as the Ayub constitution) created a stronger presidency and an elaborate system of local government based on non-party elections ostensibly to undermine the clout of the urban politicians. The parliamentary model was brought back in the post-partition 1973 constitution but with a distinct prime ministerial flavour as Zulfikar Ali Bhutto, the new unchallenged leader of the country, reduced the president to the status of a figurehead. This constitution has remained in place over the last three decades but underwent several amendments which shifted the power balance between the prime minister and the president—the latter presumably acting as the army's spokesman on several occasions. Thus, in 1985, as Zia ul Haq's martial law was being lifted, the president was virtually put in charge, who could now remove the prime minister and dissolve an elected national assembly (Eighth Amendment). Civilian government returned after Zia's death in a mysterious air crash in 1988 but the 'democratic' regimes of Benazir Bhutto (Pakistan People's Party) and Nawaz Sharif (Pakistan Muslim League) had to battle constant oversight by the army precipitating three dismissals of prime ministers by the presidents (Benazir twice, Sharif once). Sharif managed to salvage the authority of the prime minister to some extent (vide the Thirteenth amendment) because of his landslide majority during his second tenure before he was ousted in the coup by Gen. Musharraf in 1999, which constitutes our first case study of Pakistan's political turmoil in the new millennium that yet again exposed the fragile equation between the country's major political institutions.[4]

The immediate instigation to the coup was Prime Minister Sharif's decision to sack Gen. Musharraf, his army chief, in October 1999; but an inquiry into the long-term background of that event furnished interesting insights into the dispositions and motivations of both the army and the civilian politicians in Pakistan. Immediately after registering a thumping victory in the national elections held in 1997 (as well as in several provincial elections), Sharif took two momentous steps to consolidate his rule: to ensure through the Thirteenth Amendment to the Constitution that the military hereafter would have no excuse to remove him from office under the Eighth Amendment moved by the Zia regime; and to appoint his family friend Rafiq Tarar as president following the resignation of the incumbent, Farooq Leghari. These moves were followed up by a passage of two controversial legislation: one gave him direct control over the Accountability Process to investigate and convict those officials who had served in his predecessor and arch rival Benazir Bhutto's government; the other was the draconian Antiterrorism Act—gave the police sweeping powers to combat terrorism and allowed creation of special courts to conduct summary trials for those charged with such offences. In the face of growing ethnic violence and economic downturn, Sharif's relations with the military then headed by Gen. Jehangir Karamat turned tense by mid-1998, especially when in October, the latter called for the establishment of a National Security Council consisting of a team of credible advisors and think-tank experts in order to institutionalize decision-making so that Pakistan "could not afford the destabilizing effects of polarization, vendetta, and expedient policies." When Sharif expressed displeasure with his statement,

Karamat retired three months earlier rather than withdrawing his statement, to be replaced by Gen. Musharraf, a much junior officer, who Sharif felt, would be a pliant army chief. Sharif's popularity further plummeted however on account of his failure to bring about promised economic reforms, and address the issues of continued tax evasion and bank loan default by the business community (which also included his own family members), raging corruption and extravagant government expenditures which brought the country on the throes of an economic crisis. Foreign debt rose to $32 billion while foreign exchange reserves dwindled to only $1.26 billion with the World Bank, the International Monetary Fund, and the Asian Development Bank refusing to bail out the government following the country's nuclear explosion in May 1998. Meanwhile the increasing levels of violence and mounting death tolls resulting from clashes between the paramilitary forces and the members of Mohajir Quami Mahaz (MQM—Refugee Community Front) only added to the administration's dismay while the military brass was further upset by Sharif's meddling in their professional and corporate interests through transfers, firings, and promotion.[5]

But the final confrontation came over the adventurist Kargil War of May-June 1999 launched by the generals led by Gen. Musharraf in the mountain region of Kashmir-India. Although Pakistan registered early successes in this surprise attack, by mid-June Indian troops recouped their initial losses, recaptured the hilly ridges, and launched a counter attack. On the verge of defeat, Sharif met President Clinton on July 4 on 'urgent basis' and agreed to pull his troops back to the *status quo ante* on the Line of Control against the advice of the army. However, what irked the latter even more was Sharif's contention that the war was engineered by Gen. Musharraf without his approval, although the latter maintained it was a joint decision. The mutual incrimination finally prompted Sharif to get rid of Musharraf, especially after he heard that the latter was planning to oust him from power, and on October 12 when Musharaf was on a tour of Sri Lanka, he was dismissed and replaced by the prime minister's protégé Lt. General Khawaja

Ziauddin. The military commanders who considered Sharif's dismissal of their Chief of Army an affront to their honour struck a bloodless coup détente on the same afternoon of that day by seizing control of the TV and arresting Sharif at his official home in Islamabad who was later deported from Pakistan.[6] This incident, to summarize, highlighted two sets of general factors responsible for the volatility of the army-civilian relations in Pakistan: on the civilian side it involved corruption and inept handling of the economy, failure to maintain law and order, authoritarian inclinations and politics of retribution—factors which were no less pertinent for understanding the collapse of Bhutto (Sr) regime as well. Similarly, the army's action underscored their desperate refusal to compromise their manifold corporate stakes and ultimate hold over the levers of state power posing as the final guardian of Pakistan's security.

If the first case was related to the clash between the executive and the army leading to the political rise of Gen. Musharraf, the second case pertained to a collision between the army and the judiciary which paved the way for the political exit of 'President' Musharraf. Though he captured power in 1999 with the usual promise of restoring civilian rule 'within three months', what he subsequently concentrated on was to fortify his power base by civilianising his rule and 'winning' elections for which he floated his own political party Pakistan Muslim League (Q—Quaid) and also struck an opportunistic alliance with Muttahida Majlis-e-Amal (MMA—United Council of Action), a motley contingent of Islamist parties. However, his administration encountered a series of challenges[7] beginning with the suspension of Ifthikar Chaudhry, the Chief Justice of Pakistan by the president on 9 March 2007 on the charges of nepotism and corruption. It triggered off an outburst of protest by the lawyers' community under the umbrella of the *Adliya Bachao Tehreek* (Save the Judiciary Movement) demanding the reinstatement of Justice Chaudhry to the bench. Musharraf's critics pointed out that Chaudhry was sacked because the latter had issued a number of anti-government rulings including the reversal of the sale of state-owned Pakistan Steel Mills, and more importantly, he had demanded that the security agencies disclose the location of missing persons whom the security services denied having detained. They also suspected political motives behind the government's move because with Chaudhry in office, it would be difficult for Musharraf to continue to serve in the dual capacity of president and chief of the army, in violation of the constitution.

Curiously enough, the lawyers' movement brought erstwhile adversaries such as the liberals and the fundamentalist elements on the same platform which in turn could be traced to the siege of the Lal Masjid in Islamabad laid by the security forces in pursuit of Islamist militants who had issued a call for imposition of *Sharia* in Pakistan and ouster of the Musharraf regime. The storming of the mosque in early July resulted in the loss of more than 150 lives and caused an irreparable break between Musharraf and his MMA allies who intensified their clamour for the General to give up the position of the army chief—a pledge he had long reneged on—before the impending presidential elections in late 2007. Finally, Chaudhry was restored to his office on 20 July 2007 as the charges against him could not be proved, and continued to deliver anti-government verdicts including one permitting the exiled PML leader Nawaz Sharif to return to Pakistan. In the course of the year, however, the agitators more and more came to focus on the removal of the president from office, and occasional overreaction on the part of the security forces in dealing with the movement—which was perceived as a challenge not only to the government but the army too—such as curbs on the Nat geo television added further fuel to the campaign. Musharraf first sought to deal with the situation through an imposition of a national emergency in early November but by the end of that month he had to yield before mounting popular pressure and step down as the army chief handing over the baton to Gen. Pervez Ashfaq Kayani.

The fallout with the judiciary turned out to be Musharraf's political nemesis for though he managed to secure a second term for himself as president, the run-up to the parliamentary polls in the following year—especially in the context of the unfortunate assassination of PPP supremo Benazir Bhutto in December 2007 for which also the Musharraf administration was put on the dock—saw an unprecedented understanding between the two major political parties traditionally at loggerheads with each other. Following the installation of a PPP-led government in Pakistan with Yousaf Raza Gillani at its head in March 2008 ultimately forced Musharraf to demit the presidential office giving way to Asif Ali Zardari, the widower of Benazir. An analysis of this train of events sparked off by the army-judiciary confrontation draws our attention to three issues: first, the new-found assertiveness on the part of the courts vis-à-vis an army-backed government which somewhat rid of its previous image as a spineless entity staked its claim as yet another major player to reckon with—in addition to the army or the civilian executive—in the battle for the institutional space within Pakistan's polity. Secondly, though the bold stance taken by Justice Chaudhry and the accumulating grievances against the Musharraf administration remained crucial, the reincarnation of the judiciary in Pakistan was backed to the hilt by the approximation of a bestirred civil society with the belligerent lawyers' association and a vigilant private media forming its core components. Thirdly, the role played by the civilian leaders in this political saga remained perhaps the weakest—Nawaz Sharif arrived on the scene only in the final hours taking advantage of one of Justice Chaudhry's verdicts on 5 November 2007 while Benazir Bhutto returned to Pakistan in October 2007, then again following a tacit political understanding with Musharraf—though it was another story that the immediate benefits of this turbulent phase of Pakistan's struggle for restoration of democracy was reaped by the two mainstream political parties during the 2008 elections.

While the battle-ready posture adopted by the Pak judiciary remained the highlight of our second case, the third instance involving a showdown between the PPP-led government and the Supreme Court under Justice Chaudhry has been perceived by many as a display of judicial over-activism posing a veiled threat to the future of democracy in Pakistan. One of the redeeming features of the Zardari-Gillani government installed after the

2008 elections—the first civilian government to complete its tenure since the Zulfikar Ali Bhutto regime (1972-77)—was that during its tenure, the army under Gen. Kayani apparently took a step back. The word apparently needs to be underlined for the behind the scenes the army (and its Inter Services Intelligence or ISI) very much called the shots which was evident on critical moments such as the Mumbai terror strikes (2008) or the Memogate issue (2011).[8] Gen. Kayani repeatedly stressed that he had little intention of deposing the civilian government which was effectively matched by fewer public statements on his part or fewer public interferences with the affairs of the government. But the government encountered threats from unexpected quarters—the highest court of the land—which culminated in the disqualification of Gillani from holding the prime ministerial office by Justice Chaudhry since 26 April 2012. The bone of contention was the National Reconciliation Ordinance—a remnant of the Musharraf era—issued by the General in 2007 which granted amnesty to any politician or bureaucrat accused of a crime between 1986 and 1989. Indeed, this was a part of the deal (referred to above) arrived at with President Musharraf by late Benazir Bhutto who through this instrument sought to insure the political future of herself as well as her husband Asif Ali Zardari. Subsequently however the Supreme Court declared the ordinance unconstitutional and struck it down, and using this ruling Justice Chaudhry exhorted Prime Minister Gillani to write to the Swiss authorities to reopen the various cases against President Zardari but Gillani's reluctance to fall in line resulted in the premature termination of his tenure.

It is easy to see this judgement as part of the tradition of a proactive judiciary set by Chaudhry ever since his encounter with the Musharraf administration in 2007 which had subsequently won him a fierce following among lawyers, the media, the civil society and the public in general.[9] The move was welcomed by the opposition leaders and a section of the media which proclaimed that the law of the land should always receive the highest priority. However, other commentators and activists—including people like lawyer Aitzaz Ahsan and activist Asma Jehangir who had voiced their full-throated support for Chaudhry in 2007—questioned whether the judiciary was exceeding its mandate.[10] After all, the differences in the two situations were difficult to overlook: the Gillani government was democratically elected as opposed to the Musharraf regime that was initially established through a military coup. Indeed, some even contemplated if the judiciary was acting with an agenda for as the PPP and its allies scrambled to find a replacement for Gillani who would be acceptable to all parties while at the same time would remain loyal to President Zardari, aggressive actions by the Supreme Court in the interim became a source of concern for many.[11]

Commentators have sought to explain the judiciary's motivations in taking these steps from different perspectives: for some, it was the ineffectiveness of the Zardari-Gillani administration to tackle the multiple problems faced by it produced a legitimacy deficit and the judiciary simply stepped into this void;[12] for others, it was the growing proactive posture adopted by the parliament following the 2008 elections that accounted for this response from the courts.[13] Some even sensed an attempt on the part of army chief Kayani to "establish the red lines for the activist Supreme Court" when he repeatedly warned through his speeches against the adverse fallout of a clash of institutions ostensibly keeping in view the conflict between the executive and the judiciary.[14] All said and done, Pakistan's political system, like democracies in general, was supposed to have built-in checks and balances to ensure that power was not concentrated at any one branch of the government, a mechanism which was badly damaged by years of military intervention in politics. However, once the system seemed to have found its rhythm with the visible retreat of the army under Kayani from overt political intrusions allowing the PPP government to complete its tenure followed by transfer of power to the hands of a PML-led government under Nawaz Sharif in 2013, emergence of a new *fulcrum* of power under whatever pretext did not seem to bode well for the future of its democracy.

## Islamic Militancy as a Foreign Policy Tool

The Pakistani Army and the ISI have long instrumentalised Islam to prosecute Pakistan's strategic interests in Afghanistan and India, using a horde of Islamist militant groups among other means to keep the country's 'enemies' off balance.[15] Contrary to conventional narratives, Islamabad started using militants and Islamists as a tool of foreign policy not during the Soviet invasion of Afghanistan in 1979 but immediately after its independence when it initiated covert warfare in Kashmir using irregular fighters along with regular army operatives (though in disguise). Similarly, it began to clandestinely support Islamist Pashtun militant groups in Afghanistan since early 1970s against President Daoud Khan's regime though after the Soviet invasion these activities already underway were intensified with active support from the United States, Saudi Arabia and others. In addition to the huge funding and military assistance provided by the US, Islamabad also employed, in service of *jihad*, religious institutions and parties such as Jamaat-e-Islami (JI) and Jamiat Ulema-e-Islam (JUI) to mentor Pakistan-based militant groups and to train Afghan militants who had sought refuge in Pakistan. Once the *mujahideen,* with immense international support, succeeded in ousting the Soviets from Afghanistan, Pakistan redeployed many of these surplus battle-hardened *jihadis* from the Afghan theatre to the Kashmir front and established militant training camps in Pakistan and Afghanistan.

Meanwhile, following the withdrawal of the Soviet troops, Pakistan sought in the 1990s to intervene in the Afghan civil war—started by the warlords for control over the country—with a view to prop up a political dispensation positively disposed towards Islamabad. Initially it patronized Gulbuddin Hekmatyar, the Hizb-e-Islami supremo whose contacts with Islamabad went back to the mid-1980s and he was expected to secure for Pakistan a corridor to Central Asia and also recognizes the disputed international frontier, the Durand Line. When Hekmatyar failed to deliver, the army-ISI combine switched support to the Taliban and emerged as the most avid champion of this much-maligned regime though in reality the Taliban with its visceral anti-women stance, vandalisation of the Bamiyan Buddha statues and growing al-Qaeda connections was fast becoming a liability for Pakistan. After the terrorist attacks on the New York World Trade Centre on 11 September 2001 and faced with stark option of abandoning the Taliban and joining the War on Terror or becoming its target, the Musharraf government chose the first option. However, this policy reversal on Taliban remained short-lived as Islamabad recommitted it to the orthodox movement in view of the US permitting the Northern Alliance which enjoyed cosy ties with India to take Kabul contrary to assurances and failure to secure in the new dispensation adequate representation of Pashtuns with whom Pakistan shared a natural alliance for long.[16] In sum, Islamabad despite the US demands refused to give up the choice to use Islamist militants as instruments of its foreign policy in the region which we would argue with reference to three issue areas constituted a potent source of political turbulence in the new millennium.

Following the launch of Operation Enduring Freedom by the United States in Afghanistan in 2001-02, the Taliban regime was ousted from power but its top leaders along with their al-Qaeda allies escaped and found refuge in Pakistan's FATA (Federally Administered Tribal Areas) region. For one thing, this region lay immediately across Afghanistan's eastern frontier and was characterised by mountainous terrains over which, for historical reasons, Islamabad never exercised substantial control. Moreover, this was largely the land of the Pashtun tribe—to which the Taliban predominantly belonged—which straddled the Durand Line and inhabited large segments of Pakistan's western regions and Afghanistan's eastern and southeastern provinces. During the Soviet occupation of Afghanistan, it was the people from these border tribal regions who were at the forefront of mujahideen resistance efforts, providing staging posts for cross border operations against Soviet forces as well as sanctuaries from which prospective and returning mujahideen to and from the Afghan Front could be housed, trained, armed and indoctrinated. Thus, in order to deal with Taliban and al-Qaeda members fleeing across the Afghanistan-Pakistan border and also to evade the potentially negative political fallout of stationing foreign troops on Pakistani soil or of conducting large-scale, highly visible 'hot pursuit' cross-border actions, the United States was forced to enlist the assistance of the Musharraf government.[17] Meanwhile, Musharraf's decision to join the War on Terror had made him an object of the Islamists' ire which in their view amounted to turn against fellow Muslims, particularly an act of treachery against the Pashtuns. The Bush administration, on the other hand, questioned the sincerity of the Musharraf regime which it suspected was only going through motions of cracking down on the Islamist militant organizations while the Taliban and al-Qaeda elements were alive and well in Pakistan, protected by sympathetic clerics and perhaps waiting for the US departure to launch a jihad against the Hamid Karzai regime in Afghanistan.[18] Some pointed out that President Musharraf was more active against the al-Qaeda members who threatened the US but had no intention to rein in the Taliban or the Pakistan-based militant organizations active in Kashmir.[19] Sandwiched between these claims and counter-claims, in July 2002, Islamabad dispatched approximately 80,000 troops to sensitive border areas of the FATA for the first time since 1947, to flush out Taliban and al-Qaeda elements.

This military campaign met with a violent and increasingly expanding resistance which could be traced to the traditional freedom-loving spirit of the tribal population many of whom ever since British days perceived the central government (and by extension its armed forces) as an opponent to be resisted. In addition, the similar ethnic composition of populations on both sides of the Afghan-Pakistan border; Islamabad's unfulfilled development and political promises towards the region; and its oscillating policy of repression and appeasement towards militias and armed tribes all coalesced to fuel the violence that was observed following government operations in mid-2002. Two assassination attempts against President Pervez Musharraf were traced to militants in the region comprising the agencies of North and South Waziristan in 2003, while in early 2004 a general insurgency developed against the central government of Pakistan, marking the beginning of what later came to be known as the Waziristan conflict. It was estimated that in the period from 2004 to 2006, as a direct result of the 'War in Waziristan', the Pakistani army lost approximately 1,000 to 3,000 men. All this finally led the Musharraf government to agree to a ceasefire with the tribes and militants inhabiting North Waziristan in September 2006.[20]

Apart from growing restiveness within a section of the army which resented the loss of a huge number of soldiers while fighting their own countrymen, the ceasefire accord was also resulted from pressures exerted by the MMA which was originally formed in opposition to Musharraf's decision to join the War on Terror but later became the president's electoral ally holding power in the western provinces of NWFP and Balochistan. However, the accord, while bringing some temporary respite for the Pakistani army, failed to bring about a cessation of attacks. In fact, withdrawal of the army units allowed the Taliban to re-group and consolidate their position in the tribal regions, engage in extra-judicial killings of pro-government leaders, and keep on exacting an increased toll of the US and NATO forces across the border in Afghanistan.[21] The only conclusion that followed from this account is that Pakistan's strategy of nurturing and supporting and the groups and organisations of its border regions to consolidate its political footprints in Afghanistan and secure 'strategic depths' there in the event of an Indian attack virtually ended up providing strategic depth to the Taliban operatives in its own territory of which brings us to our second issue area under this head: the spawning of a Pakistani Taliban in its wake.

Since 2003-4, Pakistan witnessed development of a cluster of militant groups whose activists referred to themselves as 'Pakistani Taliban' and presumably had their origins among the Taliban-sympathisers of the Pashtun belt described above. In late 2007, largely in the wake of the Lal Masjid incident referred to above, it assumed an official identity—Tehreek-e-Taliban Pakistan (TTP—Pakistan Taliban Movement) when several

Pakistani militant commanders announced that they were operating under its banner led by Baitullah Mehsud. Baitullah was killed in a US drone strike in August 2009 and amid discord the TTP leadership announced that Hakimullah Mehsud, Baitullah's cousin, would succeed him. TTP doubtless were in contacts with its Afghan counterpart and shared their extremist ideology but its distinctiveness lay in its object and target: the Pakistani state and its military. It resented Islamabad's military alliance with the West, rejected the constitution and the democratic process and wanted the whole of Pakistan to come under the rule of *sharia*. It is not a monolithic entity nor does it have the coherent command and control structure as is often attributed to it by the media. Yet under the leadership of Hakimullah, the TTP has been surprisingly coherent and has actually intensified its suicide campaign against Pakistani security and intelligence agencies. Likewise, TTP campaigns against civilian targets have become more vicious, singling out Shia and Ahmedis, who are considered *munafiqeen* (Muslims who spread discord in the community) and *murtad* (liable to be killed), respectively.[22]

What was more worrying however was the expansion of TTP networks beyond the tribal regions and they were reportedly maintaining loose factions spread out as far as Punjab. The arrival of this 'Punjabi Taliban' was announced in 2009 which virtually took the battle into the heart of Pakistan with a series of terrorist strikes traced to this coalition: on March 3, a team of about 12 militants ambushed the Sri Lankan cricket team as it travelled to a sports stadium in Lahore leaving five policemen and two civilians killed and dozens wounded including some cricket officials; on May 27, twenty-three people, including police and officials from the Inter-Service Intelligence agency, were killed after an assault team opened fire on security personnel and stormed the ISI headquarters; on October 10, four soldiers were killed after a terrorist assault squad attempted to storm the Army General Headquarters in Rawalpindi.[23] The term Punjabi Taliban was resented by many Punjabis who preferred to attribute the threat to the 'Pashtun other' often characterized in stereotypical terms as 'violent' and 'warlike' if not 'uncivilized'. Leaders of the Pakistan Muslim League-Nawaz (PML-N) also objected to the term likely in part because of the party's ongoing support for groups such as Sipah-e-Sahaba Pakistan (SSP) and Lashkar-e-Jhangvi, driven by electoral imperatives. However knowledgeable observers of Pakistan's political scene maintained that the sites of military across Pakistan were inter-related and the movement contained both Pashtun and Punjabi components (among others including some foreign elements). Punjab-based groups such as the LeJ and Jaish-e-Mohammad (JM) were constituents of TTP and conducted attacks on its behalf on Sufi, Shia, Ahmedi and other civilian targets in Punjab.[24]

It was in this context that the Unified Command of the Pakistani Armed Forces opened the Operation Rah-e-Nijat (Path to Salvation) in South Waziristan, the TTP hideout, in June 2009 which imposed heavy casualties on the militants. However, though the army largely regained its control over the region through this campaign, the TTP leadership including Hakimullah Mehsud escaped either to North Waziristan or Afghanistan.[25] Since then a North Waziristan campaign seemed very much on the cards—the army chief Kayani repeatedly identified religious radicalization, fundamentalism, extremism and terrorism as the most potent threats confronting the state and the nation[26]—and yet the requisite consensus could not be built up even after the TTP targeted Malala Yousafzai in October 2012.[27] During the electoral campaigns of 2013, the brunt of the wanton violence let loose by the TTP had to be borne by the secular parties—especially those allied with the PPP such as the Awami National Party in the NWFP—who were prevented from running an effective campaign giving thereby an edge to the conservative parties.[28] Indeed, after returning to power in June 2013, Prime Minister Nawaz Sharif put all anti-TTP army action on hold in order to facilitate peace dialogues and his administration lambasted Washington when Hakimullah Mehsud was killed in a US drone assault in November. However, the militants it appeared utilised this breather only to reverse the losses and mounted a wave of murderous attacks on military and police targets in several major cities from Peshawar to Rawalpindi propelling the new army chief Gen. Raheel Sharif to order bombing of Taliban bases in North Waziristan.[29]

This move undoubtedly highlights a new determination on the part of the Pakistani army to fight an internal war against the Taliban under a new commander who has already communicated his policy of zero tolerance to all forms of militancy in his close circles. Still his sober intentions and programme of action might get stymied by one alarming factor if left unaddressed—the growing radicalisation of the armed forces of Pakistan—which Fareed Zakaria described as a "deep internal crisis of identity, its most serious" since 1947.[30] The founding fathers of Pakistan wanted the defence forces to remain outside the pale of religious influences, uphold the 'Sandhurst tradition' and develop as a professional and disciplined entity. However, it was in the aftermath of the defeat in the 1971 war and partition of Pakistan that a section of its officers sought to trace yet another military debacle against India to reposing blind faith in western strategic models and alienation from the indigenous religious roots. Of course it was Gen. Zia ul Haq who brought the army within the purview of his Islamization drive along with buoying up the linkages of Islamist radicals with the foreign policy establishment. The heraldic slogan of the Pak army of Jinnah's days—Unity, Faith and Discipline—was changed to *Iman, Taqwa* and *Jihad fi Sabilillah* (Faith, Obedience to God and Struggle for the Path of Allah). The army was exposed to indoctrination by Islamist groups such as Tablighi Jama'at and for the first time it began to recruit madrasah products as officers and soldiers. Though observance of religious practices within the army was of course watered down under Gen. Jehangir Karamat and later Gen. Musharraf, the policy of marrying the jihadi activities of the non-state players with the operational doctrine of the army continued shaping the religious orientation of the rank and files. Indeed, as Cohen reports, though many in Musharraf's generation of army officers oppose the army's Islamization, they use the radical Islamists as an instrument of policy.[32]

This close interaction between the two groups is bound to create a bond of empathy and no wonder several officers were found from time to time to secretly collude with Islamist hardliners. It may be recalled that at least one of the assassination attempts on President Musharraf was plotted in the Air Force barracks in Islamabad and was carried out by army-men hailing from the tribal areas. More recently, a few serving and retired military officers were arrested and court marshalled for passing on information to Shamsi airbase in Balochistan from where US drone strikes were being launched against targets in FATA and adjoining areas of Afghanistan in 2010.[33] A third generation army brigadier posted at the General Headquarters, with a brother, son and son-in-law in army, was arrested in 2011 for his connections with a Pan-Islamic radical outfit Hizb ut Tahrir. It was suspected that the militant attacks on Pakistan Navy's Aviation base at Mehran near Karachi in 2011 and the Minhas airbase at Kamra in 2012 for which responsibility was owned by TTP could not have taken place without insider collusion. But it is unclear how far the military has addressed the spread of radicalisation within its own ranks or whether it perceives it as a problem at all. While it may be too early to read in these developments an unfolding ideological war within the military, it would be difficult for the army, following Kayani's suggestion and the lead provided by the new chief, to effectively tackle the enemy within without first putting its own house in order.

## Concluding Observations

The tenure of the PPP government (2008-13), apart from the fact that it ran its full course, was marked by a couple of good auguries for the future of democracy in Pakistan. Most importantly, both the government and the opposition played by the rules of the game: there was little attempt by the opposition to unnecessarily pin down the ruling party; and no display of vindictiveness towards the party out of power on the part of the government either. This relative unity exhibited by the two premier political parties led to a major achievement in the form of the passage of the Eighteenth amendment which removed the president's arbitrary powers to dissolve the national assembly unilaterally. It also presumably sent a credible message to the armed forces which was at least partly responsible for the relatively low profile maintained by them during this regime as far as domestic affairs were concerned. The challenge before the government of course emanated from an unexpected source, the judiciary under Justice Ifthikar Chaudhry who had a big hand behind Gen. Musharraf's political eclipse. While none had any quarrel with its stand on corruption, the manner it went about fighting raised uncomfortable questions including speculations that the judiciary in cahoots with the army was deliberately trying to embarrass the government.

However, Pakistan at 2013—to use a cliché—literally stood at a new crossroads with a new prime minister, army chief and chief justice in office which provided a golden opportunity for beginning with a new slate. The new head of the judiciary was known for his mild manners and expected to maintain his focus on rights issues pursued vigorously by his predecessor but steer clear of any interference in government policies. That leaves the equation between the government and the army as an open question and brings in the issue of their respective positions on Islamist militants both on domestic and external fronts. Nawaz Sharif's project of bringing the home-grown militants into the mainstream through peace dialogues evidently clashes with the new army chief's hardline approach to TTP. Similarly, on the foreign policy front, Nawaz Sharif declared stance of settling differences with neighbours, especially India, through negotiations would require the army to give up its long-standing perception of militants as useful to pursuit of regional strategic objectives. The evolving balance between the government and the army in the years to come is likely to hover around these questions in a major way.

## Notes

1. Stephen Cohen, *The Idea of Pakistan*, New Delhi: Oxford University Press, 2005, Ch 2.

2. The Pakistan People's Party governments of 1972-77 and 2008-13 remained probably that kind of exceptions which only confirmed the rule.
3. See Cohen, n 1; also Abdus Sattar Ghazali, Hegemony of the Ruling Elites in Pakistan, ebook, 2000.
   Available at http://ghazali.net/book3/intro/intro.html
4. See Cohen, n 1.
5. Rathnam Indurthy, "Musharraf Regime in Pakistan" Indian Journal of Political Science, vol 65, no 2, 2004.
6. Indurthy; see also Barbara Crossette, "Coup in Pakistan—Man in the News; A Soldier's Soldier, Not A Political General—Pervez Musharraf", New York Times, October 13 1999.
   http://www.nytimes.com/1999/10/13/world/coup-pakistan-man-soldier-s-soldier-not-political-general-pervez-musharraf.html
7. See for details Partha Pratim Basu, "Democracy in Pakistan: An Elusive Quest?"in Basu et al Democratization in the Twenty-first Century: South Asian Experience, New Delhi: Har Anand, 2011.
8. After the Mumbai terror attacks in November 2008 the needle of suspicion pointed to the ISI and the militant organizations it sponsored. On the insistence of the Government of India, President Zardari agreed to a visit by the ISI chief Shuja Pasha to Delhi. The visit however never materialized ostensibly vetoed by the Pak army. The Memogate controversy revolved around a memorandum addressed to Admiral Mike Mullen reportedly dispatched by President Zardari in May 2011seeking assistance from the Obama administration in the wake of the killing of Osama bin Laden to avert a military takeover of the civilian government in Pakistan. Once made public, it became a major loss of face for the Zardari government which was snubbed by the army chief and lambasted by the opposition, and Hussain Haqqani, ostensibly the author of the memo, had to tender his resignation which was promptly accepted by the prime minister.
9. SeePhilip Reeves, "Pakistan's Fearless Chief Justice Challenged the Powers that were", December 12, 2013.
   http://www.npr.org/blogs/parallels/2013/12/12/250431216/pakistans-fearless-chief-justice-challenged-the-powers-that-were
10. Anumita Raj, "Exceeding the mandate: judicial activism in Pakistan", Strategic Foresight, August 2012.
    http://www.strategicforesight.com/inner-articles.php?id=293#.UubXQ9Io6Hs
11. "When PPP attempted to name Makhdoom Shahabuddin, a senior party leader from Punjab to the post of PM, a non-bailable warrant for his arrest was produced quickly by the courts. Fearing that every candidate that they produced would somehow be arrested or disqualified by the courts, PPP had to keep their hand hidden, choosing to reveal their new candidate only hours before the deadline". See Raj, n 10.

12. Raj, n 10.
13. Arif Rafiq, "The Judge, the General, and Pakistan's Evolving Balance of Power", The Diplomat, November 9 2012. http://thediplomat.com/2012/11/the-judge-the-general-and-pakistans-evolving-balance-of-power/?allpages=yes.
14. Rafiq, n 12.
15. C Christine Fair, "The militant challenge in Pakistan", Asia Policy, no 11 [January 2011]. http://relooney.fatcow.com/SI_Expeditionary/Fair_16.pdf.
16. Fair, n 15.
17. Evagoras C Leventis, "The Waziristan Accord", December 18 2007, *Global Politician*. http://www.globalpolitician.com/default.asp?23893-pakistan)
18. David Eshell, "The Afghan War After Musharraf", August 31 2008. http://www.defense-update +(Defense+Update)
19. B Raman, "The War against Terror—After Musharraf", August 20 2008. http://ramansterrorismanalysis.blogspot.com/2008/08/war-against-terror-after-musharraf.html
20. Leventis, n 17.
21. Leventis, n 17.
22. Fair, n 15.
23. Bill Roggio, "Terrorists assault Pakistani Army General Headquarters in Rawalpindi", Long War Journal, October 10 2009. http://www.longwarjournal.org/archives/2009/10/terrorists_assault_p.php
24. Fair, n 15.
25. Bill Roggio, "Taliban escapes South Waziristan Operation", Long War Journal, November 26 2009. http://www.longwarjournal.org/archives/2009/11/taliban_escapes_sout.php
26. See Baqir Sajjad Syed, "Kayani renews army's resolve to eradicate militancy", The Dawn, August 14 2012. http://www.dawn.com/news/742053/kayani-renews-armys-resolve-to-eradicate-militancy

    Centre for Research and Security Studies, "The Threat Lies Within", January 4, 2013. http://crss.pk/story/3726/the-threat-lies-within/;
27. Baqir Sajjad Syed, "North Waziristan operation put on hold again?", The Dawn, October 16, 2012. http://www.dawn.com/news/757034/n-waziristan-operation-put-on-hold-again
28. Tahir Khan, "Deadly Mandate: Liberal Parties targeted for their ideology, says TTP", *The Express Tribune*, April 29 2013.

http://tribune.com.pk/story/541944/deadly-mandate-liberal-parties-targeted-for-their-ideology-says-ttp/

29. Tom Hussain, "Pakistani Taliban, with new leader, is back on the offensive", The Miami Herald, January 27 2014.
http://www.miamiherald.com/2014/01/27/3896383/pakistani-taliban-with-new-leader.html
Arnaud de Borchgrave, "New Dawn in Pakistan?", January 28 2014.
http://www.upi.com/Top_News/Analysis/de-Borchgrave/2014/01/28/Commentary-New-dawn-in-Pakistan/UPI-76661390909410/
30. Fareed Zakaria, "The radicalization of Pakistan's Military", Washington Post, June 22, 2011.
http://www.washingtonpost.com/opinions/the-radicalization-of-pakistans military/2011/06/22/AGbCBSgH_story.html
31. PK Upadhyay, "Radicalisation of the Pakistan Army", *Journal of Defence Studies*, October 2011.
http://www.idsa.in/jds/5_4_2011_RadicalizationofthePakistanArmy
32. Cohen, n 1, 194.
33. Upadhyay, n 30.

*Chapter 9*

# When the Sea is the Key: An Analytical Survey of the Maritime Dimension of South Asian Security

*Shounak Set*
Post-Graduate Student
Department of International Relations
Jadavpur University, Kolkata

> "Whoever controls the Indian Ocean dominates Asia. This ocean is the key to the seven seas in the twenty-first century, the destiny of the world will be decided in these waters."
> —Alfred Thayer Mahan[1]

> "The most dangerous place in the world... is the Indian subcontinent."
> —President Bill Clinton[2]

In spite of their differing time and contexts these famous statements convey a message simple, subtle and powerful. Regardless of the dramatic rhetoric, the grand vision of a classical naval strategist and the jittery proclamation of a contemporary world leader acquire an enduring relevance since their underlying message has shaped the past and will impact the future in no lesser terms; as such, this paper aspires to express that hidden message and explore its aspects.

Any conventional map of South Asia portrays the Indian subcontinent bound by the Himalayan ranges at the apex and by the Indian Ocean at the bottom; yet this remains far from being flawless. For, in addition to the Himalayas and the Indian Ocean in the north and the south, it's also flanked by the Bay of Bengal in the east and the Arabian Sea in the west. As a matter of fact the general projections tend to conveniently constrict the collective perception as regards to the actual influence of the sea over the landmass; this is because geography may be natural and constant whereas cartography is but a construct of the human mind—and hence variable.

If security essentially entails an environment free from threat then less known and least understood is the fact that the environment on land has often been and continues to be influenced by threats arising from the seas. The accustomed continental outlook of South Asians notwithstanding, history offers a contrastive lesson which can only be ignored at peril. The subcontinent has witnessed a series of invasions which requires no belaboring. Nevertheless it's interesting to note that the Europeans, unlike others didn't arrive in South Asia through the Khyber Pass; neither did the 26/11 Mumbai terrorists cross the highly patrolled Radcliffe Line which marks the international land border between India and Pakistan.

Interestingly the eminent scholar-statesman KM Pannikar drew upon historical developments extensively to highlight the importance of the Indian Ocean during the early years of the modern Indian republic itself. Current Indian elites arguably following the footsteps of Pannikar, often articulate aspirations for naval pre-eminence in the region but ironically fail to interpret and connect the maritime developments in the Indian Ocean to its natural hinterland that is the Indian subcontinent.[3] However, if indications are anything to go by then South Asian security in the twenty-first century will be intertwined more than ever with the dynamics of the Indian Ocean to generate multiple challenges which coincide with a complex interplay of global and local actors that cumulatively contest the existing frameworks, both intellectual and institutional.

## Great Powers and Their Great Games

If a conventional dictum preaches influence of the land through the control over the seas, then South Asia is not entirely devoid of precedents generated by policies inspired by a similar strand of thinking. It can be argued that while both China and India are heirs to rich maritime legacies, these are arguably reappearing, as the Asian century fuels their appetite for prestige and power, resources and markets. If Indian maritime activity which can be traced back as early as to the Indus Valley civilisation, then it reached its zenith in the tenth century with the Chola expeditions to South East Asia. Likewise Chinese maritime activity in South Asia can be discerned as early as 2nd century BC and it pinnacled with the exploits of the legendary Admiral Zheng He in the early decades of the 15th century.

In recent times the geostrategic attributes of the Indian Ocean Region and the subcontinent made it an arena for great power rivalry and militarisation as the Cold War progressed. The cataclysmic 1971 Indo-Pak War didn't remain a duel between the two countries but also drew in their respective superpower supporters with the arrival of the US 7th Fleet in the Bay of Bengal (along with supplementary British deployments) which precipitated Soviet naval manoeuvres in response. The Cold War configuration of the South Asian-Indian Ocean security complex has however dissolved only to crystallise as a venue for power-play between the emerging Asian giants of China and India and the reigning global hegemon, the United States of America.[4]

Beijing has been consolidating its ubiquitous presence in the region through a series of ports and bases—from Chittagong (Bangladesh) and Sittwe (Myanmar) in the eastern flanks of the Bay of Bengal to Gwadar (Pakistan) in the far west and in Hambantota (Sri Lanka) down south—resembling a pincer around the Indian peninsula, euphemistically labelled as the 'String of Pearls'. New Delhi partly on account of its rising international profile and mostly in apprehension of these developments has focused to upgrade its capabilities. Acquisition and/or development of a wide array of advanced conventional and nuclear naval platforms by both India and China have become a consistent feature of the scene. A wide arc of bases from Mumbai up west to Vizag down towards east including Kochi and the newly built port at Karwar forms the Indian riposte. Delhi's design is underpinned further by the integrated tri-service Andaman and Nicobar Islands Command and the Indian listening posts in the islands of Seychelles, Madagascar and Mauritius.

The intricacy of the 'String of Pearls' is followed with unwavering attention and matched by a zealous intensity as testified by the series of counter naval exercises and strategic collaborations undertaken by New Delhi with the other key actors of the region—from the tiny island states like Mauritius and Seychelles to the extra-regional behemoth that is the United States. While the Maldives and Madagascar have long standing security ties with India, the advent of the Chinese has imparted a fiercely competitive dimension to the scenario. Indeed acquisition and/or development of a wide array of advanced conventional and nuclear naval platforms by both India and China have become a consistent feature of the scene as each country tries to outdo other and rushes to vaunt its prized assets.

Hence India and China have initiated and laid the foundations of a maritime Great Game in the Indian Ocean, complete with tactics of mutual encirclement, manoeuvres, military preparedness and diplomatic initiatives to win over allies and establish bases and posts in friendly foreign states, aimed to enlarge and preserve their spheres of influence. The USA as the reigning superpower aims to act as the balancer, mindful of the adverse impact on its stakes that an unbridled rivalry between the emerging Asian giants may bring about. In this context the strategically positioned US base of Diego Garcia located in the heart of the Indian Ocean Region with its extensive power projection capabilities seems to provide the USA with an unsinkable aircraft carrier permanently facing South Asia. Diego Garcia, already a significant military base therefore becomes more significant as a potential pad for hard power projection in the Indian Ocean-South Asia security complex; in a manner somewhat reminiscent of the role of Taiwan (and some other Pacific islands) facing China. As a matter of fact, the ongoing US military re-orientation from

Europe and West Asia towards Asia and the Pacific needs to be examined against this backdrop.[5]

## Asymmetric Adversaries

Security in this century can no longer be sequestered into water-tight compartments or be restricted in scope to the conventional paradigm of state agencies and military issues. The most pressing concerns of contemporary South Asia include issues like terrorism, piracy, smuggling and the like. South Asia is fringed by failing states like Afghanistan and Myanmar where any regime change or even disturbances of much lesser magnitude have the potential to transmit shockwaves throughout the globe. These will have not just ramifications for the fragile maritime security in the region by exacerbating already existing trends of piracy, smuggling and gunrunning;[6] but may even be facilitated by non-state actors and forces acting either independently or in collusion with established state actors to take advantage offered by the sprawling maritime domain, the soft underbelly of South Asian security.

The 26/11 Mumbai carnage which put the subcontinent on the brink of war and the successful activities of the Sea Tigers in the recent past,[7] the naval wing of the erstwhile LTTE (Liberation Tigers of Tamil Elam) which contributed to the longevity of the LTTE are but just two of the many cases which illustrate the centrality of the maritime dimension towards South Asian security. Further if in the eastern fringes, piracy in the Bay of Bengal and the Straits of Malacca augur of significant implications, repercussions in the subcontinent are already being felt due to the Somali conflagration in the western flank. Yet in addition to these, a multitude of other factors continue to increase the salience of maritime terrorism in South Asia in the twenty first century.

The shipping routes of the Indian Ocean and the ports of the subcontinent facilitate movement of goods and people in considerable volume and with undeniably lax regulations. Significant installations often with modest security include power projects, oil rigs and refineries and even nuclear plants which are in the coast or in its vicinity are the most vulnerable to subversive activities which emanate from the sea. These indicative trends then amplify the magnitude of maritime terrorism.[8]

Complicating these security scenarios are the problems of piracy, gunrunning and narcotics trafficking which often flourish in a symbiotic relation.[9] The region straddles major conflict zones from the Af-Pak to Kashmir and the vast areas of Myanmar which are under ethnic dissidents (like the Kachin for instance) and is dotted with centres of significant mafia activity like Karachi, Mumbai and the badlands of Myanmar. Drugs and weapons move through the same routes and similar networks; at times even along with regular merchandise. It won't be impertinent to point out that both Golden Crescent and Golden Triangle are located at the periphery of South Asia and sustaining through the waters of Indian Ocean, they are intimately interlinked with terrorist organizations to have generated a new coinage itself, ie narco-terrorism. Unknown to many the Bombay bombings of 1993 was facilitated by the smuggling of explosive materials like RDX through the seaborne routes and the couriers normally used for smuggling contraband items like drugs; and thereby they evaded the attention of the security agencies.[10]

## Environmental Security

Security in its modern and broader paradigm remains incomplete without taking cognizance of the challenges posed by non-traditional but no less significant threats like environment. Although often overlooked, the fact remains that the environment sustains life itself and hence no other form of security can be considered adequate if environmental security remains unaddressed.

While South Asia is the most densely populated region of the world with ever increasing demographic and economic pressures, which in turn puts its environment under severe stress, the Indian Ocean is also located at the intersection of the geological plates with intense seismic activity; as such, it's unfortunately the site of some of the world's most serious natural disasters. Environmental security of South Asia should thus take into cognizance the conservation of biodiversity and natural resources, the effect of climate change and the impact of natural disasters, and in each of these aspects the Indian Ocean is emerging integral to the process.

Further South Asia hosts such ecologically sensitive hotspots like the Sunderbans which is a sprawling expanse across India and Bangladesh. These call for joint cooperation and management by the concerned states through a multi-faceted approach which responds effectively not just to the wide range of the challenges but also dynamically seizes the opportunities posed by both the continental and the maritime spheres. Effective institutions, sustainable mechanisms, and adequate arrangements to cope with the challenges posed by the developments on seas which have severe ramifications for the littoral states (eg, oil spills, wreckage, preservation of flora and fauna, depleting stock of fisheries and marine pollution) range between being nominal and nil at present.

It's pertinent to take note of the relation that exists between climate change induced inundation of lowlands and the resultant migration which has a significant impact on the political, military and economic security of states in turn, as evident from the repercussions from the increasing rate of migration from Bangladesh into India. The global rise in sea level with catastrophic effect for Maldives forebodes of a similar mass exodus from the island state to neighbouring India with a potentially drastic impact on the latter's economic and political security.

While South Asian states like India, Sri Lanka, Bangladesh and others have for long faced the brunt of natural disasters; and the recent and most poignant case of Tsunami deserves a special mention. The devastating Tsunami on 26th December 2004 witnessed the largest ever relief operations in human history—Operation Unified Assistance. The need for similar efforts in the future cannot be ruled out, due to the regions fragile geographic condition where even instances of lesser magnitude like oil spills and wreckage and pollution necessitate similar pan-regional responses. This particular scenario highlights the connection between the emerging aspects of security and the conventional mechanism. As tsunami struck, the aircraft carrier USS Abraham Lincoln, which was operating in the vicinity, responded by sending aid through helicopters and planes to the affected areas—the process set in motion thus found its logical culmination in the Operation Unified Assistance.

Incidentally the role of powers in such sea-borne operations goes a long way to promote their interests as even humanitarian and rescue operations buttress their respective strategic positions. In this instance the USA and India flexed their muscles to provide aid and successfully outmanoeuvred China in their combined post-tsunami relief operations, thereby preserving their geostrategic significance. Thus the role of the powers in such scenarios is a poignant pointer to the importance of the Indian Ocean in the specific context of South Asian security in the foreseeable future.

## Securing SLOCs and Stabilising Economies

History testifies that sea routes always have a larger salience primarily because they facilitate movement of logistics with largely reduced costs with profound implications. It's oft forgotten that the Industrial Revolution generated scientific inventions and technological innovations which among other things made possible dramatic transformations in oceanic voyage; this in turn facilitated and sustained colonialism. Even globalisation has been possible largely on account of the remarkable advances in navigation which improved efficiency and safety on one hand and reduced the costs on the other hand. Therefore even in this era of information technology and supersonic jets, the importance of oceanic transport stands unrivalled; and accordingly this particular dimension impels a closer examination from the context of its impact on the region's economy.

The SLOCs (Sea Lines of Open Communication) of this region, one of the busiest in the world provide the jugular vein and arteries to the heart of the South Asian economy as the Indian Ocean facilitates the movement of imports and exports to and fro from the subcontinent. Pointedly, energy is the oxygen of modern economies and energy security shall continue to remain a critical priority for South Asia in the foreseeable future. Incidentally, a substantial portion of the world's net traffic of petroleum products pass through the Indian Ocean and cross the principal shipping lanes as well as several chokepoints: like the Gulfs of Aden and Oman, the Bab-el Mandeb; and the Straits of Hormuz and the Straits of Malacca respectively. Considering this dimension, the Indian Ocean is poised to gain even more significance in the coming decades as the South Asian energy requirement will spiral upwards on the back of ascendant Indian and emerging Bangladeshi economies. Further in the same breath, the volume of the goods from and towards the subcontinent which already pass through the same routes to their various destinations is set to increase exponentially; and thereby serve to further increase the salience of the Indian Ocean and its SLOCs to South Asia, as the regular sustenance of around a quarter of humanity becomes entangled with the developments on the high seas.

Paradoxically this strategic peril is contrasted by economic promise since the region acts as a natural bridge between the continents of Africa and Asia; as such, it connects the hydrocarbon rich Middle East to the newly industrialised economies of the Far East and is also home to a number of newly emerging economies.[11] Hence its SLOCs are simultaneously the avenue of global trade and commerce as oil from the Middle East, minerals from the African continent and manufactured goods from East Asia pass through principal shipping lanes as well as several crucial chokepoints; and quite a few of these are within the vicinity of South Asia like the Straits of Hormuz, and the Straits of Malacca. This operative force of maritime geo-economics generates a curious convergence of interest and thereby underscores the potential for cooperation among littoral states which outweighs the costs of a conflict.

However, before cooperative arrangements emerge, competitive trends are bound to characterize the actions of states in a manner resembling that of a Hobbesian state of nature—and this will determine the future pattern of South Asian security which will either give rise to an era of *suspicious peace* where all states remain apprehensive of others but cooperate minimally for their benefit, or to an era of *armed peace* where rivalry among India, China, the USA and Pakistan dominates the scene and results in a stabilisation at only the higher levels of balance after considerable expense has been incurred by all the actors over a period of time. The Bangladesh-Myanmar sea dispute reinforces this trend; dispute regarding the extent of continental shelf, EEZ (Exclusive Economic Zone) and territorial sea in the western Bay of Bengal precipitated naval standoffs and tensions between the two countries in 2008 but was finally settled peacefully in 2012 in the International Tribunal for the Law of the Seas.

## Retrospect, Prospect and Possibilities

Thus the matter in essence is that the Indian Ocean Region and the subcontinent particularly coalesce into a security framework where the traditional definitions of the local, regional and global are of diminishing utility. As the modern states of China and India, heirs to the ancient civiliations and rich cultures continue to be on an ascending trajectory, they will inevitably clash. Inheriting geographies and populations with titanic proportions, they have history and ample resources for generating a volatile strategic environment. This is then the elementary postulate for charting the course of security of this region in the future.

Against this backdrop, the variables of ecological sensitivity and non-state actors provide further dimension to the scenario. Even endeavours and enterprises with a 'soft' focus will be subsumed under the overarching canopy of a competitive strategic atmosphere in such a scenario. Thus issues like sea-bed mining and undersea oil extraction and marine fishing already vitiate the relations among littoral states like India, Sri Lanka, Pakistan and Bangladesh. Similarly building of infrastructure like ports for commercial advantages can nevertheless escalate the tension among growing powers, the classic illustration being the Chinese port facilities in Hambantota (Sri Lanka).[12] The absence of installations and utilities commonly associated with military presence has not allayed New Delhi's anxiety. It has also prompted the US to seek a greater engagement in the region which serves as the natural lever for its Asia Pivot strategy; "I would underscore that from a strategic perspective, as we continue to implement our strategic rebalance, we are acting in recognition of the emerging realities of the new Indo-Pacific world. Our commitment to the Asia-Pacific region is strong and irreversible, and we support and welcome the involvement of India and other countries of South Asia in the Asia-Pacific region as well."[13]

Intriguingly multilateralism has by and large failed to sail through the turbulent waves of the Indian Ocean and the whirlpool of South Asian politics, where ironically its success is needed the most. The most relevant forum in this regard, the BIMSTEC (Bay of Bengal Initiative for Multi-Sectoral Technical and Economic Cooperation) brings together several littoral and hinterland states dependent on the Bay of Bengal but has seen mixed success at the best. While the case of SAARC (South Asian Association for Regional Cooperation) as one of the least effective regional initiatives doesn't merit any recapitulation in this paper, the twenty-member Indian Ocean Rim Association's (IORA) most visible success in its seventeen years of history has been the several transformations in its nomenclature; it was initiated as the Indian Ocean Rim Initiative in 1997 before being christened Indian Ocean Rim Association for Regional Co-operation (IOR-ARC) till it attained its present title in 2013.

While the range of transnational threats might bring states closer towards common security architectures and arrangements, intermittent jostling within such frameworks will not be surprising. Further the number of failed or failing states which are located both within and in the vicinity of the subcontinent will merely render the situation more fragile. Disturbances in Af-Pak and Burma, the two powder-kegs on top of the Arabian Sea and the Bay of Bengal respectively will transmit shockwaves across the region and beyond. Likewise instability in democratising states like the Maldives and Bangladesh as witnessed in recent times provides severe stress on South Asian security. As the Maldives plunged into political crisis in 2013, New Delhi was forced to consider its options and although a direct intervention along the lines of 1988 Operation Cactus didn't occur, naval assets and elements from the armed forces were mobilised as per contingency planning.[14]

Against this backdrop it won't be premature to conceive of the US presence and activities in the region (whether in the form of covert drone and special operations or overt physical interventions) after the withdrawal from Afghanistan in 2014 being projected from substantial sea based assets. Drones and elements of Special Forces operating from carrier based task forces in the Indian Ocean remains a distinct possibility while the other alternative which involves stationing of ground forces shall necessitate even larger naval deployments for support. While Bin Laden's corpse was flown to USS Carl Vinson in the Persian Gulf the next such operation may very well see Special Forces taking off directly from sea based task forces as the availability of suitable bases like those of Bagram (in Afghanistan) decrease. Against this backdrop, South Asia characterized by inherent regional asymmetry, pervasive military hardware and arms proliferation, which include nuclear arsenal and delivery vehicles as well as small arms, along with the multiplicity of issues like unstable regimes and geopolitical flashpoints coalesces into a seamless cauldron with the Indian Ocean. All these portray a grim scenario which is driving policymakers and analysts to pray for the best and prepare for the worst.

## Conclusion

The crux of the matter remains that, South Asian security in the twenty-first century will be intertwined with the dynamics of the Indian Ocean to present a canvas with a complex intermesh of conventional and non-traditional security threats which coincide with the interplay of global and local forces. Yet of singular significance is the conspicuous absence of literature on these transformative trends. The dominant strand of thinking with its continental moorings is ill suited for the transforming times since it's inclined to miss the forest in search of woods as it stops short of conceptualizing the connection between the diversity of threats in the quest for overarching paradigmatic explanations. To illustrate the case, is it feasible for the nature of South Asian security to remain insulated from the increasing US naval buildup and activities in the region and its vicinities, under its ambitious 'Asia Pivot' strategy? In a similar vein the NATO intervention in Afghanistan remains impossible to analyse without accounting for the oceanic routes and naval assets, crucial for logistics as well as tactical calculations. Indeed it's better to consider Indonesia to be part of wider South Asia given its geographical proximity to India's Andaman and Nicobar Archipelago. In fact during tsunami the Indian assistance to Indonesia generated much goodwill and it was the geographical advantage that facilitated a prompt Indian response compared with other countries. Indeed, even countries like Myanmar, Thailand on the eastern flank and Iran, Oman and Yemen also deserve to be constituents of a South Asia-Indian Ocean Security complex.

It's pertinent to point out that a recent revival of interest among the academia in the Indian Ocean as a coherent zone of study has relied on geostrategic traditions of maritime genre,[15] but failed to connect the macrocosm of the Indian Ocean Region to its natural microcosm which is South Asia. Serious scholarship must study and grasp the past to predict and provide for the future; failure to do so shall be faltering its interpretation of the present with serious implications for the future. The historical and contemporary trends in aspects as disparate as the economy and the environment, piracy to power projections clarify this increasingly salient but marginally realised phenomenon—stability on land has been and will continue to be interconnected with security at sea in an unprecedented degree to fundamentally determine the contour of South Asian security in the Asian century.

Significantly most countries of South Asia are in a crucial era of political and economic transition in their history. At this episodic juncture the Indian Ocean has also emerged as a global arena of maritime commerce and security. How these states react to this dynamic setting with its confluence of evolving issues like great power competition and territorial disputes and emerging challenges like piracy, terrorism and proliferation along with managing this global commons shall mould the future of the region but also set precedents beyond the immediate context.

The logic of geography makes the Indian Ocean the bridge between the subcontinent and the world. It brings with it in equal measures significant opportunities for prosperity as well as severe challenges to peace. Hence if the sea is the indispensable key for unlocking the puzzles of South Asian security, then grasping it is the imperative of the twenty first century.

## Notes and References

1. Cdr PK Ghosh, *Maritime Security Challenges in South Asia and the Indian Ocean: Response Strategies,* paper prepared for the Centre for Strategic and International Studies—American-Pacific Sealanes Security Institute conference on "Maritime Security in Asia", January 18-20, 2004, Honolulu, Hawaii. Accessed on: 25.02.2014.
2. BBC Webpage, http://news.bbc.co.uk/2/hi/south_asia/691339.stm, Accessed on: 25.02.2014.
3. KM Pannikar, *The Strategic Problems of the Indian Ocean* (1944); *India and the Indian Ocean* (1945).
4. Author, *Transforming Geopolitics and the Indian Ocean,* E-Journal Jadavpur Association of International Relations, http://ejournaljair.blogspot.in/2010/07/indian-ocean-shounak-set-despite.html
5. Dean Cheng, *China's View of South Asia and the Indian Ocean,* Lecture 1163 (August 2010), Heritage Foundation http://www.heritage.org/research/lecture/china-s-view-of-south-asia-and-the-indian-ocean. Accessed on: 22.02.2014.
6. Subir Bhaumik, *Guns, Drugs and Rebels,* Seminar, June 2005, http://www.india-seminar.com/2005/550/550%20subir%20bhaumik.htm. Accessed on: 25.02.2014.
7. Amal Jayawardane, *Terrorism at Sea: Maritime Security Challenges in South Asia,* Regional Centre for Strategic Studies, Colombo, Sri Lanka. Accessed on: 24.02.2014.

8. B Raman, *Maritime Security and Maritime Terrorism,* South Asia Analysis Group. Accessed on: 23.02.2014.
9. Biswajit Mohapatra, *Globalization and Challenges of Maritime Security in South Asia,* SAP-DRS Seminar on India's Security Policy: Shifting Paradigms and Emerging Frontiers of Cooperation, February 6-7,2012, North-Eastern Hill University, Shillong. Accessed on: 21.02.2014.
10. Zaidi, Hussain S, *Dongri to Dubai: Six Decades of the Mumbai Mafia* (2012).
11. Vice Admiral Mihir Roy, *Maritime Security in South West Asia,* Society for Indian Ocean Studies. Accessed on: 25.02.2014.
12. Author's interaction with Vice Admiral B Guha on 26.07.2011.
13. Emphasis mine, Testimony of Joseph Yun, Acting Assistant Secretary, Bureau of East Asian and Pacific Affairs, *Statement Before the House Committee on Foreign Affairs Subcommittee on Asia and the Pacific,* Washington, DC, February 26. 2013, http://www.state.gov/p/eap/rls/rm/2013/02/205208.htm Accessed on: 24.02.2014.
14. *India readies 'contingency plan' for new scenario in Maldives,* Hindustan Times, New Delhi, February 09, 2012.http://www.hindustantimes.com/world-news/india-readies-contingency-plan-for-new-scenario-in-maldives/article1-809219.aspx Accessed on: 25.02.2014.
15. Robert Kaplan, *Center Stage for the 21st Century: Power Plays in the Indian Ocean,* Foreign Affairs, March/April 2009.

*Chapter 10*

# Reminiscing Rammanohar Lohia's Post-Independence Writings on South-Asian Unity: A Brief Assessment

*Pratyay Dutta*
Research Scholar
Department of International Relations
Jadavpur University, Kolkata

Rammanohar Lohia (1910-1967) was the main architect of India's foreign policy as perceived by the Congress Party during the freedom struggle. He was in-charge of the Foreign Department of the Congress Party when Jawaharlal Nehru (1889-1964) was its President and he had written many booklets on the subjects. It may be mentioned that Lohia had an original approach to the foreign policy or the international policy. Lohia was the sole architect of the foreign policy formulated by the Socialist Party (SP). Even during the days of freedom struggle, Lohia often spoke of the principles on which the foreign policy should be based. From April 1936 to August 1938, as secretary of the foreign department of the All India Congress Committee, Lohia did remarkable work in laying the foundation of the foreign policy of the Indian National Congress (INC). The report of the department presented at the Faizpur Session of the Congress (1947) emphasised the need of a separate foreign policy for India from that of the British foreign policy. In 1944 in a letter to Gandhi published in the *Harijan*, Lohia formulated a four-point programme for world peace. Those were:

(i) All nations will be free. Those countries which have achieved their independence just now will elect their own legislatives on the basis of adult franchise and will have their own constitution from these Assemblies.

(ii) All the establishments of the foreigners will be confiscated, and the matter will be referred to the International Forum. After the findings, the capital investment and the debt will be owned by the State and not by any individual.

(iii) There will be equality among castes or races, and no preference or privilege will be given to any one on that basis, anywhere in the world. Everybody will be entitled to settle down anywhere and there will be no political handicap.

(iv) Total disarmament.[1]

At the fourth session of the Congress Socialist Party (CSP) held at Lahore in April 1938, Lohia moved a comprehensive resolution which stated "the USSR as the only major power working for the world freedom and peace, and regarded the foreign policy of the Great Britain as Pro-Fascist and encouraging the forces of reaction and war."[2]

In 1943, in a scheme sent to Rajendra Prasad, Congress President, Lohia emphasised the need for peace and freedom for the world, and said: "We want to create such independent India as may work and sacrifice for the cause of creating peace and right for the freedom of the world."[3]

A special feature of Lohia's thought process is that his national vision and world vision have the same source of inspiration. A combined vision of freedom, equality and fraternity is reflected in his approach to national as well as international issues. His concern for the fraternity is reverberated in his programmes for restoration of the pride of individual by making him feel he is a part of the whole. His world-view is also determined by these highest values of human life, ie freedom, equality, and fraternity.

## Free India and Foreign Policy

India attained freedom on August 15, 1947, when the polarisation of a large part of the world into the Soviet and the Western Blocs had already taken place and with the Cold War in full swing. Hence keeping in view the national interest of the country, India adopted the policy of non-alignment to keep away from the power blocs. Lohia, a man of great insight, not merely criticized the foreign policy of the Indian Government, but also laid down some basic principles on which the foreign policy of free India should be based. The guiding principles should be to keep national interest and create peace in the world. Lohia mooted the idea of confederation of India and Pakistan to improve the relations between the two countries. This is also called Indo-Pak unity. Lohia urged all the socialist parties of the world to think in terms of an effective world union through world government. Lohia was a great socialist who did a vigorous thinking and inspired the Indian socialists to develop Asian outlook towards the problem of the day.

In a speech delivered in the Constituent Assembly in March 1948, Nehru said: "I have come more and more to the conclusion that the less we interfere in international conflicts the better, unless of course our own interest is involved, for simple reason that it is not in consonance with our dignity just to interfere without providing any effect."[4]

## The 'Third Camp' in World Politics

Keeping the political aspects of the by polar world situation in mind the first Prime Minister of India, Jawaharlal Nehru formulated the policy 'non-alignment with great power groups'[5] for establishing a just and equitable socio-economic in India and creating a climate of peace in the world. But Lohia with his knowledge of international relations, foresaw some serious shortcomings in Nehru's policy of non-alignment. According to him, it was not serving the interest of the nation. As an alternative to it, Lohia therefore, presented his policy of 'Third

Camp' at the Nasik conference of the socialist policy in 1948.[6]

Introducing the resolution on international situation at the conference, he said: "The need of today is a call for the third camp. Let us pitch our tents everywhere strengthen this Third Force. We must sign treaties of permanent friendship in Burma, Nepal, Ceylon, Pakistan and other independent countries of South Asia. Such treaties should lead us into a permanent federation. Once such federation comes into being to strengthen the third camp, the world can be made safe for democracy and world peace."[7] Nehru could not comprehend the importance of the ideas behind Lohia's policy of the Third Camp. He rejected it on ground that it had no relation to the realities of the time. He called it a wrong approach and said that "The moment we talked in this terms, we adopt to some extent the Cold War approach and language of hostility."[8] The subsequent events such as (a) Hostilities between India and Pakistan, (b) Sino-Indian conflict, (c) Murder of Tibet, (d) India's displacement from creative centre of the world stage, and (e) India's ineffective role in peace making,[9] later proved that Lohia's diagnosis of the pathology of international politics was more correct than what Nehru could envisage. Nehru had to face serious challenges in defending his policy of non-alignment. After his death the non-alignment, however, gained some respectability, especially after Bangladesh crisis, but the credit for it does not go to Nehru or his non-alignment, it rather goes to the present Prime minister, Indira Gandhi (1917-1984), who introduced an element of dynamism in the foreign policy of India by concluding the Indo-Soviet Treaty in 1971.[10] The necessity of such a treaty after 24 years of independence automatically proves that Lohia's analysis of foreign affairs was more realistic than that of Nehru. Lohia, however, was never in favour of concluding a treaty with any of the super-powers[11] because such an alliance may, ultimately, impel the weak partner to dance to the tune of the big power. Now, before we discuss Lohia's programme of south-Asian unity[12], it is worthwhile to examine Lohia's charges against non-alignment.

## Defects of Indian Foreign Policy

Lohia, even as early as in 1950, realised the hollowness in India's foreign policy which was neither independent nor serving the vital interest of the country. It believed in negative and passive neutrality and was based on sentimentalism, appeasement, easy fame and cheap popularity. As a Chairman of Foreign Affairs Committee, Lohia sent his famous report "The Third Camp in World Affairs"[13] to the Madras Conference of the Socialist Party (SP) in 1950. Painting out the ineffectiveness of India's foreign policy, Lohia said, "With freedom, India changed from being an object of world politics to the status of its creator. As fettered India was the prime object of international rivalries and wars, free India was reasonably imagined to be a maker of world peace and prosperity, if not it's prime creator.... India was hitherto field in this test. To the world and its warring blocs she makes little difference. All specific issues of foreign policy and free India's achievements or failures in regard to them are details of this grand disaster, that freedom of India has made no difference to the world and its ways."[14] Accepting India's weakness in armour and industry, the two main instruments of foreign policy, Lohia emphasised that "ideas are at least as potent a tool in foreign policy as steel, and the construction of a new world repose as much in man's minds as in the weapons which their hands wield."[15] Lohia who was in favour of a real and creative policy of non-alignment was of opinion that India had followed "a policy of vacillation and alternative service to the Soviet and Atlantic Camp."[16] Lohia said: "Delhi is not slaved of the Atlantic or Soviet Camp but it is certainly as servant who sometimes serves one and sometimes the other. Delhi is independent only in the choice of its temporary matters."[17] To Lohia, "nothing concrete has been achieved in the field of foreign policy. Except one or two affairs like Pakistan, Indonesia, the history of our foreign policy is a history of mere attractive words."[18] A foreign policy without having correlation with developed industrial and agricultural economy to back it, is impotent. Similarly defence capacity unrelated to resolute will of the people is baseless. To Lohia, till the country does not get strength, the foreign policy shall be of one of "impotent *Kautilyaism* for *Kautilyaism* goes with strength and not with weakness."[19] In India nothing concrete has been done in the sphere of national defence, industrial economic development and security. It remained: "idealist where the interests and security of the country is concerned, and realist in the affairs of the world."[20] On the contrary, to Lohia it should "be idealist in the matters concerning the world, and realist in the matters of country's interest."[21] Lohia called military power as 'fist' and economic power as 'arm'. To him only "idiots can say that the arm and the fist are in conflict.[22] The realist approach requires that the frontiers of the country which are like "a man's skin"[23] should be protected at every cost. Lohia pointed out: "once a war has broken or frontiers are threatened, a coloured people have no option except to hit back with all his might."[24]

In an article "Indian Armed Forces", Lohia criticised the Indian government for not keeping close relations with the neighbouring countries, and said: "...Never should a people or its government move out to attack freedom, however misguided. But a people must always be prepared to defend freedom particularly in neighbourhood and when given a free choice to integrate it so as to freedom a large whole."[25]

## Positive Policy vis-à-vis Third Camp

The Indian government has taken up the task of avoidance of war but it has neglected the more important task of creation of peace and equality would have to make a deep study of the crisis of human civilisation; for the crisis of foreign policy is a deeper crisis of human civilisation. In an article "Indian Armed Forces", Lohia pointed out the two purposes—one negative and the other positive, which India should pursue. "Negatively, it must learn not to rub either of them the wrong way, to observe normal courtesies, not to poke nose into affair that do not belong to it, and, above all, not to damage the nation's strength by strengthening inimical neighbours in the interest of some stupid leftist or rightist world illusion. Positively, it must persuade the government to pursue policies of approximation and equality that would make the people of the world sits up and takes note."[26] Lohia was fully aware that the approximation of human race would not be possible with the existing concept of international relationship, and, therefore, he favoured a new idea of people to people relationship in place of government to government relationship that dominates the international affairs now-a-days. His greatest contribution to the foreign policy is his theory of Third Camp.

The term 'Third Camp' was already in air before Lohia coined it in somewhat 1939 to plead for independence of the warring Allies and Axis. After the Second World War the configuration of the world power struggle changed. He wished free India to work for the creative third force instead of serving the two masters, the Soviet and Atlantic camps one by one.[27] Lohia's concept of 'Third Camp' is not based on active neutrality. Such idea of active neutrality was elaborated by Lohia, Chairman of the Party's Foreign Affairs Committee, in a report submitted to the English National Conference of the Party in Madras, 1950. "The Third Camp must not be an umpire but a participator in international events, because it will never be able to judge issues until it learns to play a part in their maturing."[28] The essential function of the world order is to secure peace. But peace is not only a negative aspect which means mere postponment of war. It has a positive aspect also. Lohia wanted the third camp to create something new in the international field. In the international field the post-war period was largely a continuation of the pre-war period of international rivalries. In order to snap this continuity Lohia wanted that, the Third Camp must indeed strive to do all it can to avoid a war, but it must also concern itself equally with the building up of such strength as will be adequate to open a new era in world relations.[29]

## Theory of Co-Existence with Approximation

The dominant impulse in international relationship of the modern world is conformism. 'Conformism', according to Lohia, "is the wish to achieve a single information policy all over the world.... The Atlantic Camp wants the whole world to conform to its foreign policy. So does the Soviet World."[30] The world exists today a world of evil, war, poverty and destruction. Hence Lohia rejected that impulse of conformism as cruelty which could only lead to war and hoped that "socialism, even in its great days, shall not acquire the conformist mind of the two titanic combatants of today."[31] In order to combat the cruelty of conformism, the theory of co-existence is professed. The advocates of co-existence believed that the capitalist and communist systems and their blocs can co-exist in peace. But Lohia's conception was that no nation could allow its foreign policy to flow out of such a belief. The Atlantic and the Soviet statesmen press the theory of co-existence "either as a rhetorical cover from their war drives or to buy respite when the tensions of the Cold War become unbearable and the disproportion in armed strength looks dangerous."[32] The two systems mutually contradictory, suspicious and hostile cannot co-exist unless a third system and new integration begin to get strength in order to force the two systems to co-exist. Hence a third system of growing authority is needed, which will start a process of approximation between the two warring camps in which they agree to check and remove their own excesses. The impulse of co-existence with approximation must at least be virile and experimenting. Lohia's idea of third bloc of Asian, African and Latin American countries, on which he built his dream of socialism and his idea of a world government[33] through which he wanted to realize his dream of a new world free from poverty and violence are his unique contributions to the world.

The section of the present article dealing with India and Pakistan has become very relevant today. Lohia was a great advocate of permanent friendship between India and Pakistan. He held that India's partition was unnatural and a big mistake and although it cannot be undone, the bitterness it created should not be further accentuated but every effort should be made to normalise the relations between India and Pakistan. For this, he suggested a confederation between the two countries.

This was in fact the spirit behind the famous resolution of Lahore convention of the Muslim League in 1940[34] and also the wishes of the creator of Pakistan, MA Jinnah, reflected in one of his letters written to 'The Times and Tide' of London on January 9, 1942.[35] He described his concept of Pakistan as "two countries under one motherland."[36] This arrangement was also proposed by the Cabinet Mission,[37] and accepted by the Congress and the Muslim League, but later rejected by both due to some misunderstanding created by Jawaharlal Nehru's impulsive statement in a press conference.[38] This proposal was opposed by most intellectuals of India and Pakistan but now the people and politicians are coming round to this view. Lohia was a firm believer in moral force as an important factor in international politics apart from economic and military power and he wanted that India's foreign policy should be based on moral principles as envisaged in our freedom struggle. The ultimate aim of any foreign policy, according to Lohia, should be world peace and unity of mankind and all other things including national interests of form must be subjected to that highest goal.

## Lohia Line on South-Asian Unity: Confederation of India and Pakistan

Lohia mooted the idea of confederation of India and Pakistan to improve the relations between the two countries. This is also called Indo-Pak unity. Lohia made it a major programme of his Socialist Party. To popularise this idea many seminars and conferences were organised in which representatives from Pakistan also took part. Among these, the founder of the Jiye Sindh movement GM Sayed was a prominent leader.[39] The opponents of Lohia called it an attempt to undo the partition and that was why people in Pakistan looked at it suspiciously. The Indian leaders who had accepted the partition in their eagerness to acquire power, or who saw in partition fulfilment of the dream of a 'Hindu Rashtra'[40] always made fun of this programme.

It was common among the intelligentsia and media persons to ignore Lohia during his life time. Lohia was pained at this but he was confident that people would listen to him one day, even if after his death. And truly, after 45 years of his death the politicians of both India and Pakistan are trying their best to chalk out a programme, which could culminate some kind of confederation. Opening borders, mutual cooperation in information, communication and trade, joint control system for atomic self-defence and even joint commands on borders to tackle the problem of terrorism, all are steps which if successful, can lead to a kind of confederation. The people of the two sides also have come to realise that if the European countries that fought bloody wars among themselves for hundreds of years, could join in a union, why not people of India and Pakistan who had shared their sorrows and pleasures for centuries?

In view of the increasing pressures of the powerful countries over the weaker ones, Lohia mooted the idea of friendship and cooperation between neighbouring countries so that the chances of armed struggle between them could be minimised. But this idea caught the imagination of the elite classes only when the European countries advanced towards a common market or a union. But the political parties of India are still scared of the idea of Indo-Pak confederation as if to mention it is to commit blasphemy. This mentality is due to their guilty conscience. Some people have been hiding in some inner corners of their hearts the idea of basic enmity between Hindus and Muslims and are deriving devilish pleasure from partition. For such people Indo-Pak unity is frightening. Lohia was not among them. He considered this thought as a big folly. He saw medieval Indian history not as a clash between Hindus and Muslims but a clash between fanatic and liberal sections of Hindus and Muslims.[41] He did not suffer from any complex. He also saw the Kashmir problem as a clash between the two-nation theory and pluralist single nation. He even opposed JP Narayan on this issue and called Kashmir as an indivisible part of India. He said, "whenever in future an Indo-Pak confederation will come into being, the freedom and autonomy of Kashmir shall possibly be realised within the purview of this confederation."[42] Whenever he thought over the problems of Hindus-Muslim unity or Indo-Pak relations, his attention remained focused on 700 years of shared life between Hindus and Muslims. He said, "Unless these 700 years' shared life does not culminate in psychological and cultural unity between these religious communities, the efforts for trade pacts, cultural pacts, traffic agreements or confederation, would not be successful. For this, both countries should relax the restrictions imposed on their citizens, so that the people from both sides get ample opportunities to meet, mix and marry with each other."[43]

It is worth noting that Lohia used the words country and nation in two different meanings. India was always a single country but it was perhaps never a single political unit. Despite being divided into several political units, the people of the entire country remained undivided in matters like economic, cultural and family relations. Any political arrangement, which disrupts or prohibits this aspect of shared life, is unnatural and bound to fail, thought Lohia. In his own words, "partition has not solved the problem for which it came into being. And, therefore the reunion of India and Pakistan, in whatever manner, has become necessary. It is a matter of little importance whether this reunion is called federation or confederation. Let us call it a Confederation to start with."[44] Further, no short term or piecemeal solutions will be able to ensure normalisation of Indo-Pak relations. Either these relations are allowed to go from bad to worse, despite the declarations and agreements entered into from time to time, or a new approach is made with the avowed object of liquidating the evils of the partition settlement of 1947.

In such a confederation both India and Pakistan will maintain their separate existence, but there will be a common citizenship. The Confederation will have same minimal power with regard to foreign, military and communication policies.[45] Newspapers and radio in both the countries should not only tone down their reporting and news commentary on each other's internal affairs but should try to highlight the positive aspects of various steps leading to a meaningful Indo-Pak co-operation.

There should be resumption of Indo-Pakistan trade on a more permanent basis. Finally, there should be more frequent cultural exchanges between the two countries.

Lohia wanted the adoption of a positive policy towards Pakistan. To Lohia, "a programme to end poverty pushed through speed will awaken nostalgia in Pakistan for re-union with India."[46] Lohia who remained unreconciled to the partition of India always advocated that the policy towards must be built out on the fresh promises of an honest federative approach on the one hand and a lively interest in the happenings across the unnatural frontier on the other. The people of India and Pakistan must come together thinking that for a long period they had a common history and a common language. With a view to come together they must follow a policy of creative independence from the two blocs, the policy of the Third Camp and of abstention in war time disputes of the two camps. Lohia knew that the government and the organised public opinion in both the countries might take a long time to think along the lines of his suggestions. But he begged "for an earnest consideration by individuals and such organisations as are not too heavily committed to an evil past."[47]

## Conclusion

It should however be noted in conclusion that these measures by themselves are not fully adequate to remove all the difficulties in the way of Indo-Pak amity, but a beginning has to be made somewhere. Thus we see that in foreign affairs Lohia is more realistic than Nehru or Lal Bahadur Shastri (1904-1966). As long as 20 years back, "he foresaw either the East Bengal would become a colony of West Pakistan or the break-up of Pakistan."[48] With little realism and foresight of Lohia we can certainly strengthen ourselves and improve our relations with the South-Asian countries.

## Notes and References

1. Rammanohar Lohia, *An Interval During Politics,* Nav Hind Prakashan, Hyderabad, 1965, p 111.

2. Rammanohar Lohia, *Fragments of a World Mind,* Maitrayani 19 C, Calcutta, 1970, p 49.
3. Rammanohar lohia, *China and Northern Frontiers,* Nav Hind Prakashan, Hyderabad, 1963, p 117.
4. Rammanohar Lohia, *Wheel of History,* Nav Hind Prakashan, Second Edition, Hyderabad, 1963, p 101.
5. Rammanohar Lohia, *Will to Power,* Nav Hind Prakashan, Hyderabad, 1956, Introduction, p III.
6. Rammanohar Lohia, *Note and Comments,* Vol I and II, Rammmanohar Lohia Samta Vidhyalaya Nyas, Hyderabad, 1975, Here Vol I, p 127.
7. Rammmanohar Lohia, "A Prophecy", *Mankind*, Vol III, Nos 1 and 2, January-February 1968, p 107.
8. Rammanohar Lohia, *Capitalism Misses the Bus*, *Congress Socialist* (Bombay), Vol-VI, No-2, March-April 1959, p 107.
9. Rammanohar Lohia, *Immediate Satyagraha,Harijan* Vol XXI, No 8, June-July 1946, pp 19-20.
10. Rammanohar Lohia, *The Mystery of Sir Stafford Cripps,* Padma Publication, Bombay, 1942, p 117.
11. Rammanohar Lohia, "Facts and Fallacies of Indian History", *Modern Review,* Vol X, No 4, March-April 1956, p 21.
12. Rammanohar Lohia, "Indian Foreign Policy", *National Herald* (Bombay), Vol VIII, No VI, July-August 1960, p 137.
13. Rammanohar Lohia, *Congress Conception of India's Freedom, National Herald* (Bombay), Vol XI, No VIII, March-April 1960, p 127.
14. Rammanohar Lohia, *Devaluation—A Note*, *Mankind*, Vol VII, No IV, October-November 1962, p 144.
15. Rammanohar Lohia, "International Balance Sheet", *Congress Socialist* (Bombay), Vol IX, Nos II and III, March-April 1965, p 127.
16. Rammanohar Lohia, "The Collapse of International Morality", *Congress Socialist* (Bombay), Vol XII, No VIII, January-February 1966, p 139.
17. Rammanohar Lohia, "India's Economy in Figures", *National Herald,* (Bombay), Vol XII, No VIII, September-October 1960, p 179.
18. A Appadorai, *Essays in Politics and International Relations*, Asia Publishing House, Bombay, 1969, p 140.
19. Barnett, *Communist China and Asia,* OUP, London, 1960, Introduction, p IV.
20. AR Desai, *Recent Trends in Nationalism,* Popular Book Depot, Bombay, 1960, p 171.
21. Rammanohar Lohia, *Two Years of P.S.P,* Praja Socialist Party Publications, Bombay, 1959, p 101.
22. Rammanohar Lohia, *We Build for Socialism,* Praja Socialist Party

Publications, Bombay, 1958, p 117.

23. Acharya Narendra Deva, *Socialism and National Revolution*, Padma Publication, Bombay, 1946, p 107.
24. Pran Chopra, *Uncertain India,* Asia Publishing House, Bombay, 1982, p 19.
25. Rammanohar Lohia, *Statement of the Policy of the Congress Socialist Party,* Padma Publications, Bombay, 1962, p 71.
26. Horst Hartman, *Political Parties in India,* Meenakshi Prakashan, Meerut, 1971, p 198,
27. DR Mankekar, *The Guilty Men of 1962,* Tulsi Shah Enterprises, Bombay, 1968, p 27.
28. HK Singh, *A History of the P.S.P. (1934-59)*, Laxmi Narayan Agarwal, Agra, 1970, p 91.
29. Rammanohar Lohia, *Socialist Self Criticism, Congress Socialist* (Bombay), Vol X, No VIII, March-April 1962, p 111.
30. Myron Weiner, *Party Politics in India*, Asia Publishing House, Bombay, 1963, p 27.
31. Woffrd, Jr, Harris, *Lohia and America Meet,* Snehlata Rana Reddy, Madras, 1961, p 117.
32. Jagdish Shah, *Socialist Paralysed*, Laxmi Narayan Agarwal, Agra,1970, p 129.
33. Asoka Mehta, *Politics of Planned Economy*, Sterling Publishers, Jullunder, 1975, p 184.
34. K Satchidananda, *Indian Foreign Policy*, Scientific Block Agency, Calcutta, 1999, p 194.
35. Sampurnanand, *Memoirs and Reflection*, Asia Publishing House, Bombay, 1960, p 115.
36. JP Narayan, *Towards Struggle*, People's Publishing House, Delhi, 1975, p 109.
37. Onkar Sarad, *Lohia,* Prakashan Kendra, Lucknow, 1972, p 105.
38. Madhu Limaye, *Evolution of the Socialist Party*, Chetan Publication, Hyderabad, 1952, Introduction, p 3.
39. GS Bhargava, *Leaders of the Left,* Meherally Book Club, Bombay, 1970, p 103.
40. Asoka Mehta, *The Political Mind of India*, Socialist Party Publications, Bombay, 1959, p 29.
41. MR Masani, *Socialism Reconsidered*, Padma Publications, Bombay, 1959, p 13.
42. PL Lakhanpal, *History of the C.S.P.*, National Publishers and Stationers, Lahore, 1971, pp 27-28.
43. OP Goyal, *Contemporary Indian Political Thought,* Kitab Mahal, Allahabad,

1990, p 37.

44. Sadiq Ali, *Towards Socialist Thinking in Congress*, AICC, New Delhi, 1961, Introduction, p IV.
45. PC Chakravarti, *India-Pakistan Relations*, Firma K.L. Mukopadhyay, Calcutta, 1994, p 23.
46. Ibid, p 23
47. Rammanohar Lohia, *Third Camp in World Affairs,* Socialist Party Publications, Bombay, 1967, p 119.
48. Ibid, p 119.

*Chapter 11*

# Sino-Pakistan Strategic Partnership: India's Countervailing Options

*Shubhodeep Chakrabarti*
Assistant Professor, Scottish Church College
University of Calcutta, Kolkata

## Introduction

The first decade of the 21st century is witnessing an unambiguous shift in global economic power differentials from the West to the Asia-Pacific region, where primarily China has emerged as the dominant economic power. Being the second largest economy of the world, a global manufacturing hub and the largest creditor to the US, holding the highest number of American treasury bonds, China which has notched up an astounding double digit GDP growth rate since the 1990s, has clearly emerged as a regional hegemon poised at the threshold of superpower status. Commensurate with their country's rising economic clout, the Chinese have embarked upon a massive military expansion and modernisation programme which has made the People's Liberation Army and its air and naval wings arguably the only military machine capable of posing a long term threat perception to American strategic interests in the Asia-Pacific region. While the US still remains the sole superpower and the preponderant military power capable of exercising and enforcing global hegemony in military parlance, the recession of 2008, the imbroglio of its Iraq and Afghanistan wars, and the consequent negative growth which the US economy and the Eurozone countries are grappling with since the last half a decade are all indicative of an unmistakable tilt in global power balance in favour of China. As per assessments by American experts China could very well be on its way to attain the military capability to dominate the Asia-Pacific region by 2020 on account of its overwhelming naval expansion and development of area denial capabilities.[1] The extraordinary growth of the Chinese economy is transforming the geopolitics of the Asia-Pacific region with China primarily focusing on establishing hegemony in Asia by preventing the rise of any rival power by concentrating on the accretion of its military might. India must take a holistic view of the security threats the Sino-Pakistan military alliance poses to its vitalnational interests and accordingly take steps for mitigating these threats.

In the immediate aftermath of the May 1998 Pokhran II nuclear tests conducted by India, noted strategic affairs expert, Henry Kissinger opined that India's decision to go for nuclear weaponisation was necessitated by the considerations of existing in a tough neighbourhood.[2] The unmistakable reference was to the two nuclear armed neighbours of India, namely China, a country with global power ambitions and possessing arguably one of the largest and most modernised militaries in the world. The second country being Pakistan, which went overtly nuclear immediately after India's Pokhran II by conducting six tests in response to India's five. However, it is significant to note that since the Sino-Indian border conflict of 1962, Pakistan and China have been engaged in one of the most intensive strategic partnerships, which transcended the vagaries of Cold War politics and extending to the 21st century, having significant ramifications as far as India's core security interests in South Asia are concerned.

The China-Pakistan strategic axis has been a determining factor in the evolution of India's strategic doctrines ever since the border conflict with China (1962) and the subsequent engagement of Pakistan by China. Since its inception in the 1960s, the Sino-Pakistan strategic alliance till date has followed the patterns of a 'patron-client' relationship, whereby China has been augmenting Pakistan's military capabilities, both in terms of conventional weaponry and also nuclear technology, primarily aiming at keeping India focused on a Pakistan-centric security orientation, and thereby confining it to South Asian region, thwarting its power ambitions of emerging as an Asian power. In order to neutralise Indian military capability, the Sino-Pakistan strategic cooperation has followed the realist paradigm of cementing a de-facto alliance against India.[3] During the Indo-Pakistan wars of 1965 and 1971, the Chinese adopted a hostile stance towards India, condemning it as the aggressor and also threatening military intervention in favour of Pakistan. The dismemberment of Pakistan in 1971 made India the preponderant power in South Asia along with upsetting Chinese security calculations in South Asia whereby it had envisaged making India beset with serious security constraints by assisting the Pakistani military on both India's western as well as eastern flanks. Following the violation of its territorial integrity with the birth of Bangladesh, and India's first nuclear test conducted on 18th May 1974, Pakistan signed an agreement with China in September 1974, through which the Chinese finally conceded to longstanding Pakistani requests for helping it acquire nuclear weapon capabilities and build the requisite delivery systems.[4]

The Sino-Pakistan strategic partnership was further accentuated after the Soviet invasion of Afghanistan in 1979. The US and China were equally alarmed at the prospects of Soviet military campaign in Afghanistan which they perceived as a Soviet expansionist move to get access to the warm waters of the Indian Ocean, thereby threatening the vital Sea Lines of Communication (SLOC) which facilitated the oil supplies coming from the Gulf. Pakistan, too was deeply alarmed at the prospect of Soviet presence in a country which it considered as a region of its 'strategic depth', and also the fact that the USSR was friendly to India, Pakistan viewed the Soviet occupation in Afghanistan as its existential threat. Pakistan thus became the 'frontline state' in the US-China-Saudi Arabia alliance which aimed at 'bleeding the Soviets white'. During the decade of the 1980s, the CIA channelized huge quantities of arms and money through the

Pakistani military and ISI for aiding the Mujahideen or the Afghan resistance against Soviet occupation. These arms were to be diverted by Pakistan for propping up militancy in Punjab from the early 1980s and after the withdrawal of Soviet forces from Afghanistan in February 1989, it started aiding and abetting militancy in Kashmir from May-June 1989, which till date continues unabated. It was during the 1980s that the US overlooked the acquiring of nuclear weapon capability by Pakistan, with active Chinese assistance in brazen violation of international arms control regimes. It was imperative for America to achieve its strategic objective of compelling the Soviet Union to withdraw from Afghanistan which was possible only by soliciting the support of the Pakistani army and the ISI whose role was vital in providing the logistics, training and arming of the Afghan resistance. India was confronted with grim security challenges of having to guard her sovereignty and territorial integrity against two nuclear armed neighbours, both having fought wars with her and having unresolved borders and territorial disputes. Chinese transfer of M-9 and M-11 series of ballistic missiles to Pakistan, coupled with their assorted transfer of technology and facilitation of production facilities is but another testimony of China's strategy of contributing towards the emboldening of Pakistani strategic capabilities for jeopardizing India's security.[5]

It is significant to note that from the mid-1960s China has actively instigated secessionism in India's north east by providing insurgent groups weapons, training and funding. Currently China is attempting to revive various secessionist groups in India's north eastern states by arms transfer, and funding in order for using these terrorist groups for espionage and subversive activities.[6] Pakistan too has adopted the same strategy of adopting terrorism as an instrument of state policy by waging a proxy war against India by aiding and abetting externally sponsored terrorism first in Punjab and then in Kashmir. It is significant to note that both, China and Pakistan have colluded to act in ways detrimental to India's interests, by following the policy of propping up internal instability in India through support to anti India secessionist and terrorist groups, in order to achieve their common objective of thwarting India's rise as a power of reckoning in the Asia-Pacific region. China has been using Pakistan as a bulwark to obstruct India's power ambitions, by transferring missile and nuclear technology to Pakistan, it aims at keeping India bogged down with its own security concerns in South Asia, so that it may never develop the requisite strategic capabilities to take on a more proactive role in furthering its national interests and emerge as a rival power to China. It therefore is a challenge to Indian policymakers to take a realistic assessment of the threat emanating from the Sino-Pakistan strategic alliance and revise India's options, both political as well as strategic to effectively deal with threat perceptions.

## A Brief Review of Sino-Pakistan Strategic Collaboration

The Sino-Pakistan strategic engagement was essentially based on a mutual convergence of their politico-security interests and objectives in the subcontinent, most importantly to thwart India's rise as a power of reckoning in South Asia.

Beginning the late 50s heightened border tensions between India and China on the boundary question, the flight of the Dalai Lama along with his followers from Tibet into India in 1959 and subsequent granting of political asylum by India and most importantly after the 1962 war, where India suffered a humiliating debacle, Pakistan seized the opportunity to forge close strategic ties with China. For the Pakistani establishment, the Chinese provided the ideal role model as a strategic counterweight to offset India's military superiority in the region. India's defeat in the 1962 war, also convinced Pakistan of the vulnerability of Indian war machine and thereby raised its hopes of coercing India into granting concessions on Kashmir. The Pakistani military in particular realised the importance of nurturing strategic ties with China in view of huge tracts of Indian territories lying under Chinese occupation (around 40,000 sq km of area in Aksai Chin area of Ladakh) and the hope of soliciting Chinese military intervention in any future conflict with India. Pakistan signed a boundary settlement agreement with China on 2nd March 1963, whereby it illegally transferred 5,180 sq km of territory to China from Pakistan occupied Kashmir (POK), without involving India into the negotiations.[7] In 1978, the two countries inaugurated the Karakoram Highway linking the Xinjiang province of China with Havelin, 90 km north of Islamabad, passing through Abottabad, Gilgit and the Hunza valley.[8] This highway acts as a major security threat to India, in terms of facilitating Chinese military intervention in Ladakh.

China has proved to be Pakistan's most reliable supplier of weapon systems, including nuclear technology and its requisite delivery systems (long range missiles). During the Indo-Pak conflict of 1965, China strongly deplored India as the aggressor and even threatened military intervention on side of Pakistan. In the preceding months of the 1971 war, China utilised the good offices of the Pakistani diplomatic establishment in order to fructify its détente with the then Nixon administration. Henry Kissinger made a secret visit to Beijing in July 1971 and this paved the way for the historic Sino-US engagement leading to the formal diplomatic recognition of the People's Republic of China by the US in 1972, during Richard Nixon's visit to Beijing.

## China-Pakistan Nuclear and Military Cooperation

The birth of Bangladesh in December 1971, followed by India's first nuclear test on 18th May 1974, significantly heightened Pakistan's security paranoia emanating from India's profile as the predominant power in South Asia. The quest for its own nuclear weapons further cemented the Pakistan-China partnership, with China providing clandestine technological help in Pakistan's nuclear programme, in complete contravention to international norms and its own commitments in containing nuclear proliferation as a member of the P-5 club. It is widely believed by international nuclear experts that Pakistan had by the early 1980s acquired de facto nuclear capability with active Chinese assistance in terms of technology related to uranium enrichment, supply of nuclear test data, supply of design information of nuclear bombs, advanced computer systems for command and control, supply of heavy water and also conducting nuclear test on Pakistan's behalf on Chinese soil. Chinese scientists and technicians helped Pakistan to produce highly enriched uranium at its Kahuta facility. The US intelligence agencies had knowledge about a nuclear test conducted by China in the Lop Nor desert of Xinjiang province, in 1983 which was actually the validation of technology for the bomb to be delivered to Pakistan.[9] In 1986, Pakistan concluded a comprehensive nuclear cooperation agreement with China and also received tritium, a key element to boost the production of fission weapons. China also agreed to extend various kinds of financial and technical assistance. In 1995-96, in blatant violation of its non proliferation commitments China supplied around 5,000 ring magnets to Pakistan for uranium enrichment and consequently increasing its nuclear warhead manufacturing capacity.[10] Given Pakistan's dubious proliferation track record, the increasing political instability, ethnic and sectarian violence, increasing radicalization of its society and armed forces by fundamentalist elements like the Taliban, and most importantly the collusion and linkages between global terrorist groups like the al-Qaeda and the ISI, rapid increases in Pakistan's nuclear weapons and their disposition in safe hands remains a matter of utmost concern for New Delhi. Recently China has announced that it was going to sell two new nuclear reactors to Pakistan. This action of Beijing is in gross contravention of its commitments under international law as a member of NSG (Nuclear Supplier's Group). Pakistan currently has three nuclear reactors functional and none of them is under international safeguards. The Chinese action proves that it is determined to augment the capabilities of Pakistani nuclear forces in their race to attain strategic superiority over India and thereby holding her hostage to Sino-Pakistan strategic coercion. Since the early 1990s, China in contravention to its commitments under the MTCR (Missile Technology Control Regime) has supplied Pakistan with ballistic missiles like the M-9, and M-11, with complete transfer of technology. China has also facilitated in setting up production facilities for these missiles at Pakistani factories at Sargodha and Taranwah.[11]

Unlike the standard operational procedures followed by most countries of testing missiles at test ranges located far away from inhabited areas, Pakistan often tests its missiles flying over heavily populated areas. The inference is strikingly clear, that the so called Hatf, Ghauri and Shaheen class of missiles are all actually Chinese M-9 and M-11 missiles. The Hatf 2 and 3 and Shaheen class of missiles are considered to be M-11 missiles, Shaheen-1 is believed to be M-9 and Shaheen-2 is supposed to be the M-18 missile of China.[12] Most of these missiles are in the intermediate range category which is well beyond the MTCR limit of 300 km. India's missile programme is being developed indigenously and the design, development and actual deployment of missiles in the inventory of armed forces takes a considerable period of time. Whereas on the other hand Pakistan is getting large number of tested and battle worthy missiles with advanced technology from China which can tilt the balance in its favour in case of war.

## Chinese Ambitions of Establishing Hegemony in Asia

China views India as its natural competitor of establishing hegemony in the Asia-Pacific region in general and South Asia in particular. India's rising economic profile, its demographic and natural resources coupled with its strategic power are a cause of concern. Keeping this is mind it has been one of the most coveted strategic goals of China to contain India economically as well as strategically and thereby keep its role marginalized as a South Asian power. For China its strategic ties with Pakistan acts as a bulwark for maintaining military pressure over its arch rival India. For Pakistan this alliance serves as the most reliable guarantee of maintaining strategic balance keeping in mind India's overwhelming superiority in economic, scientific technological as well as military realms over it. China's 'Grand Strategy' in South Asia has manifested itself at multiple levels, namely:

1. To exert military coercion on India's northern frontiers by keeping the contentious border issue unresolved and procrastinating the negotiations. It is significant to note that China with the exception of India has resolved its

border disputes with most of its neighbouring countries including settling its over 4,000 km long borders with Russia.The Chinese military routinely violate Indian sovereignty by crossing over the Line of Actual Control. China has also undertaken massive modernisation of its military infrastructure across Tibet by stationing thousands of troops, building up missile silos, and developing five fully functional air bases in Tibet besides opening the Lhasa railway line in 2006 which will aid in rapid mobilization of the Chinese army across the boder. China enjoys conventional superiority and has the ability to strike deep into the Indian territory. China will try to strike political and economic centres, major military bases and depots, command centres, communication and network systems and could also strike on major troop concentrations. Despite India's recognition of Tibet as an integral part of China, the Chinese have refused to relinquish their claim on the whole state of Arunachal Pradesh.

2. China is following a 'String of Pearls' strategy for the military encirclement and subsequent containment of India through its client states in India's neighbourhood. It has set up sophisticated reconnaissance posts on the Coco islands of Myanmar to gather intelligence on Indian missile launches across the Bay of Bengal. It is financing and providing the technical expertise for setting up the deep water port at Gwadar in Pakistan, which can at a point of time serve as a base for the Chinese Navy to get access to the Arabian sea and thereby posing a critical security threat to India. It is also setting up ports in Bangladesh, Myanmar and Sri Lanka (Hambantotta port). The Chinese are also selling weaponry to these countries and as a measure to negate Indian influence is offering huge economic assistance in developing strategic and economic infrastructure in countries like Myanmar and Bangladesh.

3. The Chinese assistance to Pakistan's nuclear and missile programmes has the primary objective of jeopardising India's security, and strategic stability and at the same time constraining her to remain confined within the South Asian region, in the process effectively neutralising India's chances to emerge as a strategic rival to China or emerge as a key power in the South and South East Asia. The Chinese ambitions of dominating the Indian Ocean region seriously impinges upon India's quest for energy security, and safeguarding her core interests in her strategic domain stretching from the Straits of Malacca to the straits of Hormuz. The Chinese have provided financial and technical assistance in building all three Pakistani nuclear plants at Chashma, Kahuta and Khushab. It is this Chinese gifted nuclear and missile capability that has emboldened Pakistan to pursue terrorism as an instrument of state policy with brazen impunity against India to further its goals of destabilising India and wresting Kashmir away.

## India's Options to Deal with the Sino-Pakistan Axis

Ever since the 1962 war with China, India has followed a policy of dissuasion with regard to China. It implies that India would try diplomatically to resolve all outstanding issues with China in a peaceful manner. India did not and still does not enjoy military or nuclear par militarily, this policy aimed at maintaining a defensive posture and following a non-provocative stance towards the Chinese. Regarding Pakistan, India has followed a policy of active deterrence, implying maintaining a qualitative and quantitative superiority to deter Pakistan from attempting any military misadventure. However, in the given Sino-Pakistan strategic collusion, and China's massive military modernisation, it is pertinent for India to view the long term Chinese threat with concern. India faces a greater threat from China than Pakistan because New Delhi knows little about Beijing's combat capabilities.[13] India needs to re-examine its no first use nuclear doctrine in the light of Pakistan's rapid increases in its nuclear inventory and China's massive military modernisation and its growing military asymmetry vis-a-vis India. Though India needs to keep China engaged in a dialogue to resolve the vexed border dispute, it is the need of the hour to strengthen the operational preparedness of the Indian armed forces so that they can achieve a capability of active deterrence against the Chinese from their current state of strategic dissuasion. The most vital aspect for developing the deterrent capability against China is the speedy operationalisation of India's second strike nuclear capability. India needs to develop submarine launched ballistic missiles having the requisite range to hit high value targets in China. Also it needs land based ICBMs (Inter-Continental Ballistic Missiles) in a range of more than 5,000 km with MIRVs (multiple independent re-entry vehicles) to cover the entire Chinese Landmass.

India also needs to expeditiously undertake modernisation of its defence forces. The government's apathy regarding defence modernisation despite India facing the risk of a simultaneous 'two-front war' from Pakistan and China can prove to be perilous for our security.[14] Critical areas like artillery modernisation, induction of long range firepower for the army, night vision capabilities, tackling the falling combat strength of air force and making efforts to develop a blue water navy, and the time bound development and deployment of a ballistic missile defence (BMD) system ought to be accorded top most priority by the government if India aspires to claim its rightful place in the 21st century global arena. The Army's 'Cold Start' doctrine which aims at rapid mobilisation at a short notice and undertake deep thrusts into enemy territory by integrated battle groups to achieve mission objectives in a short span of time needs to be operationalised at the tactical as well as strategic levels.

## Fostering Strategic Cooperation with the US, Japan and the ASEAN Bloc

India without compromising on the sovereign principles of its pursuit of an independent foreign policy, must strive to cultivate a deepening economic and strategic partnership with the US, Japan and the ASEAN bloc to counterbalance China's efforts of a strategic encirclement of India.

India and the US have a wide convergence of strategic interests and one of the most important one among them is to safeguard peace, security and stability of the Asia-Pacific region. India should exercise its diplomatic leverages to prevail upon the Americans to take note of Pakistan's complicity in acting as the main breeding ground of radical Islamic terrorism which poses an existential threat not only to India but also to the US coupled with its horrendous non-proliferation record, a crumbling civil administrative structure and its military and the ISI being in active collusion with the Taliban, Pakistan has emerged as the hotbed of global terrorism. India should make most of its diplomatic and economic prowess to pressurise America to compel Pakistan in dismantling its terrorist infrastructure targeting India. Another important aim of Indian diplomacy while engaging the US in a strategic partnership should be to highlight the serious violations against the international non-proliferation conventions and MTCR (Missile Technology Control Regime) committed by Pakistan while engaging in nuclear and missile collaboration with China which has contributed to a serious destabilisation of peace and security environment in South Asia.

The massive modernisation of the Chinese military which has heightened a sense of insecurity amongst all of China's neighbours including India and is also shared by American allies like Japan, South Korea, Philippines and the ASEAN bloc which makes it imperative upon America to reorient its strategic postures and security commitments in Asia. Japan too has its own security concerns from China's rising military might and has been advocating for a kind of a trilateral strategic alliance amongst India, Japan and the US. In 2007 the then visiting Japanese Prime Minister, Shinzo Abe, while addressing a joint session of the Indian Parliament mooted the idea of an 'Asian NATO',[14] covering the three arcs of democracy, viz, India, the US and Japan in a politico-strategic and economic alliance. Both India and the

US have a vital stake in maintaining peace and stability in the Asia-Pacific region and keeping the sea lanes of communication stretching from the Straits of Hormuz to the Straits of Malacca secure. In this regard cooperation between the navies of the countries becomes vitally important.

China's attempts to deter India from oil exploration in South China Sea demonstrate its hegemonic attitude and power projection goals.[16] India should attempt in forging a close economic engagement with these countries which would provide spinoffs in terms of convergence of strategic goals and interests. Chinese military modernisation, its hostile stance on the Spratly Islands dispute is a matter of concern for its neighbours in South East Asia. India should strive for closer strategic partnership with Vietnam which can include military sales to Vietnam like transfer of Brahmos supersonic cruise missiles, joint development of weapon systems, servicing and maintenance of Vietnamese naval submarines like the Kilo class ones MiG fighter jets both of which are of Russian origin, which India too has in its arsenal. The Indo-Vietnamese strategic ties can act as a counterbalance to the Sino-Pakistan alliance.

## Conclusion

China's ambitions of dominating the entire Asia-Pacific region makes it imperative on her part to prevent India's rise as a potential rival which can challenge its hegemony. Commensurate with its global power projection ambitions, China has prioritised the massive modernisation of the People's Liberation Army as well as developing aerospace capabilities. It is indeed a major challenge to Indian policy makers, strategic community, and the military top brass to undertake a comprehensive threat assessment to her core national security interests in the light of two nuclear armed neighbours which are importantly engaged in a very close politico-military partnership. India ought to undertake a comprehensive security review and implement the necessary policy formulations in the light of two critical challenges to her vital national security interests in South Asian region and beyond. First, Pakistan's policy of encouraging cross-border terrorism against India, its rapid increase in the number of its nuclear weapons and the misuse of the huge military aid it receives from the US in the name of fighting terror to bolster its offensive military capabilities against India. Secondly, the adoption of a recalcitrant approach by the Chinese on border negotiations, its aggressive territorial claims on Arunachal Pradesh, its massive military advantage vis-a-vis India both in conventional and nuclear arenas and its objective of keeping India tied down in South Asia, by aiding Pakistan militarily and economically to act as a strategic counterweight to India and above all its ambitions of establishing hegemony in Asia-Pacific.

India's engagement with China requires a cautious approach due to the delicate task of carrying out the negotiations on the vexed border issue while at the same time keeping a level of military preparedness to deter any Chinese adventurism. It is significant to note that irrespective of political irritants, China has emerged as India's largest trading partner and the economic engagement between the two countries has the potential to be Asia's growth engine in the 21st century. However given the high trade balance in favour of China, India ought to review its policies of economically engaging China for securing the commercial interests of her entrepreneurs. Given India's rising profile as an emerging economic power, her quest for securing reliable sources of energy, from the strategically important Gulf region, to Central Asia, Africa and Latin America, and her aspirations of acquiring a permanent seat at the UN Security Council, it is imperative for India to increase her military prowess which will play a key role in defending her core interests not only in South Asia, but also globally. India cannot afford to be in denial of the strategic challenges it faces. Ranging from defending her economic interests, tackling an increasingly volatile nuclear armed Pakistan which is getting increasingly radicalised, and witnessing the rise of a superpower on its northern borders, India needs to pursue a pragmatic security strategy and undertake military modernisation commensurate with her requirements of being the guardian of peace, stability and regional security in

South Asia and the Indian Ocean region. The pivotal role played by the Indian Navy in thwarting the activities of Somali pirates who threaten international shipping has pointed out the enhanced security role which India is expected to play in the Indian Ocean region in the near future. Above all, unlike China, India's economic growth is viewed as a precursor to the rise of a benign power in Asia by the ASEAN countries, Japan, Australia and importantly also the US. To fulfill its legitimate role in the future security architecture of Asia, it is imperative for India to first safeguard its own core national security interests against the Sino-Pakistan axis.

## References


1. Bhumitra Chakma, *Strategic Dynamics and Nuclear Weapons Proliferation in South Asia* (Bern: Peter Lang, 2004).
2. Swaran Singh, *China-South Asia:Issues, Equations, Policies* (New Delhi: Lancer's Books, 2003).
3. Swaran Singh (ed), *China-Pakistan Strategic Cooperation: Indian Perspectives* (New Delhi: Manohar, 2007).
4. PL Bhola, *Pakistan's Nuclear Policy* (New Delhi: Apt Books, 1993).
5. Rollie Lal, *Understanding China and India: Security Implications for the United States and the World* (Westport Connecticut: Praeger Security International, 2006).


## Notes

1. Matthew Pennington, "China may have largest Pacific fleet by 2020: US", *The Sydney Morning Herald*, November 21, 2013. Accessed on 27th November 2013. <http://www.smh.com.au/world/china-may-have-largest-pacific-fleet-by-2020-us-20131121-2xwib.html>
2. B Raman, "Pokhran II and Indo-US Relations", *South Asia Analysis Group*, October 10, 1998. Accessed on 1st December 2013. <http://www.southasiaanalysis.org/paper4>
3. Anindyo Majumdar, "The Changing Imperatives", in Swaran Singh (ed), *China-Pakistan Strategic Cooperation: Indian Perspectives* ( New Delhi: Manohar, 2007), pp 36-37.
4. PL Bhola, *Pakistan's Nuclear Policy* (New Delhi: Apt Books, 1993), p 52.
5. Bhumitra Chakma, *Strategic Dynamics and Nuclear Weapons Proliferation in South Asia* (Bern: Peter Lang, 2004), pp 170-172.
6. Sandeep Unnithan, "Gunrunners of North-East", *India Today*, June 6,

2011. Accessed on 10th December 2013. <http://indiatoday.intoday.in/story/chinese-agents-smuggle-arms-to-spread-militancy-in-north-east/1/139538.html>

7. Swaran Singh, *China-South Asia: Issues, Equations, Policies* (New Delhi: Lancer's Books, 2003), pp 72-73.
8. Virendra SahaiVerma, 'The Karakoram Highway' in Swaran Singh (ed), *China-Pakistan Strategic Coperation: Indian Perspectives* (New Delhi: Manohar, 2007), p 338.
9. Swaran Singh, *China-South Asia:Issues, Equations, Policies* (New Delhi: Lancer's Books,2003), p 195.
10. RollieLal, *Understanding China and India:Security Implications for the United States and the World* (Westport Connecticut: Praeger Security International, 2006), p 140.
11. Swaran Singh, *China-South Asia:Issues, Equations, Policies* (New Delhi: Lancer's Books,2003), p 198.
12. Rajiv Nayan, 'Ballistic Missile Technology Transfers', in Swaran Singh (ed), *China-Pakistan Strategic Coperation: Indian Perspectives*( New Delhi:Manohar, 2007), p 185.
13. Rahul Singh, 'China now a bigger threat than Pakistan, says IAF Chief', Hindustan Times, May 23rd, 2009. Accessed on 5th December 2013.<http://www.hindustantimes.com/india-news/china-now-bigger-threat-than-pakistan-says—iaf-chief/article1-413933.aspx>
14. RajatPandit, 'Army's modernization drive still to gather steam despite China, Pak threats', The Times of India, October 23rd, 2013.Accessed on 2nd December 2013.<http://timesofindia.indiatimes.com/india/Armys-modernization-drive-still-to-gather-steam-despite-China-Pak-threats/articleshow/24562691.cms?referral=PM>
15. Shekhar Iyer, "Japanese PM Abe moots 'Asian NATO' ", *Hindustan Times*, August 23rd, 2007. Accessed on 2nd December 2013. <http://www.hindustantimes.com/india-news/japanese-pm-abe-moots-asian-nato/article1-243902.aspx>
16. Dean Nelson, "China Warns India on Oil Exploration", *The Telegraph*, December 6th, 2012. Accessed on December 2nd 2013.<http://www.telegraph.co.uk/news/worldnews/asia/india/9726916/China-warns-India-on-oil-exploration.html>

*Chapter 12*

# India's Policy towards the Smaller Neighbours and South Asian Security in 21st Century

*Amartya Ray*
Research Scholar,
Department of International Relations
Jadavpur University, Kolkata

## Introduction

Indian foreign policy is a collection of complex strategies—both long term and short term aimed at achieving certain goals to best secure its national interest. Now national interest is something which varies from time to time, depending on the domestic needs and external environment. After gaining independence in 1947, for the next 40 years India followed a path in its foreign policy which was largely shaped by some values and principles, foundation of which was laid down by our first Prime Minister Pt. Jawaharlal Nehru. There were some exceptions, of course, when New Delhi had gone for a more hawkish attitude in the policy as well as in its execution; the ideal example being the liberation war of Bangladesh in 1971. But exceptions should never be confused as rules. If we study the period ranging from the end of World War II till the collapse of the USSR, it was values and principles (the idea of non-alignment for example) which worked as the main source, or at least the decisive force in thinking and making of Indian foreign policy.[1]

The collapse of the Soviet Union and the end of Cold War signalled a halt in this tradition and mode of operation. This happened for two reasons, one domestic and the other external. First, India embarked on a journey of economic liberalisation which drastically changed our domestic front and its needs, attitude towards life and worldview. As we have already mentioned, domestic need has always remained a major factor in making a country's foreign policy; thus this change inside India definitely called for some readjustment in its engagement towards the world. Secondly, the tendency or preoccupation of seeing the world through the Cold War prism was no longer remained necessary. States across the world were in a mood to rejuvenate and reshape their foreign policies as per their own choices and needs, rather as per the demands of the bipolar superpower system. India was no exception in this matter.[2] And so were its smaller neighbours.

This was the background of India's renewed engagement with its smaller neighbours in the present century, which was actually kicked off in 1990s.

## The Impact of Globalisation

Economic liberalisation or structural readjustment—these were the key words dominating Indian politics after Narsimha Rao-led Congress took over in New Delhi in 1991. This was probably a historical coincidence, the fall of the 'Socialist Fortress' in Russia and the emergence of a forward-looking cabinet in New Delhi. It marked the end of an era symbolised by license-raj and went for opening up of the Indian market for foreign capital, the process of which is still on and even after 20 years which raises heated debates in the country. Some people like to call this change as LPG which denotes three components of the opening up process, Liberalisation-Privatisation-Globalisation. This LPG phenomenon had brought about three gradual developments, viz: *First,* foreign investment entered India and generated jobs which helped a large population to earn and save a few bucks and then eventually changed the consumption pattern of Indian population, especially the middle class. *Second,* Indian industries got a major boost in the form of foreign capital investment in their firms. Production had risen significantly and new markets were needed. The newly emerged middle class population, which had propped up after 1991, was not sufficient to feed the hunger for new markets of Indian trades and industries. For that they needed to look beyond the national boundaries. A lot of foreign companies also opened their production units/plants in India to reach out to the corners of the newly opened South and South East Asian markets. *Thirdly,* to meet the needs of the trades and industries, the first thing Indian government could do was to reach out to the markets of our immediate neighbours. And that was precisely what New Delhi did when globalisation knocked the doors of South Asian region. And that marks a departure from the long drawn strategy of engaging our neighbours more politically (and socially) and keeping economic objectives as the second priority.

This stress on economic engagement rather than on the traditional socio-political ones had created a new set of challenges for the Indian diplomatic community. Here we need to remember that our neighbouring states, as well, were going through different kinds of changes/ transitions in the backdrop of the post-Cold War developments. Thus this period presented a complete new scenario where India had found itself trying to readjust its modes of engagement with neighbours when they themselves were in flux.

Thus the domestic as well as the external environment for India's foreign policy had changed after 1991. Again these changes had factored in reshaping of its conventional idea of 'national interest' in the backdrop of a sweeping process called globalisation.[3]

## India's Failure in the Neighbourhood

In the context discussed so far, during the initial times, in its neighbourhood Indian foreign policy had failed in two ways. First, politically it failed to assert its authority in the region. We have seen there was a major shift in India's national interest in its neighborhood in the changed circumstances of globalisation and industrial growth. This development called for new markets where competition for Indian goods and services would be less or nominal. The best way to get this was to open up the neighboring states which were further lagging behind India and had a very little presence of European/American or Asian MNCs. So it was clear to New Delhi that economic diplomacy was the call of the day. But in a hurry to meet this new challenge it ignored the traditional job of keeping its presence deep in social and political spheres of these states. That is why the royal massacre in Kathmandu and the decade-long civil war in Nepal caught India ill-prepared. It was obviously a major intelligence failure for India. And that intelligence failure led to a situation where India did not have any 'natural ally' in Nepal other than the traditional friend, the Nepali Congress which was bleeding badly during those times of law and order chaos and political uncertainty.

The situation in Nepal had put India in trouble in two ways. The Maoists of Nepal helped the Communist Party of India (Maoist) with arms and ammunition, let alone moral boost and a safe haven to take refuge in the face of encounters with the Indian security forces. It also helped China enter South Asian politics more directly and decisively.[4] It was a long standing custom that any new Nepali head of the state/government (be it the king/president or the prime minister) would come to New Delhi in his/her first state tour abroad. When Prachanda (the general secretary of the Communist Party of Nepal, Mr Puspa Kumar Dahal) occupied the chair of the president, though for a brief stint, he went to Beijing on his first official state visit...a major break in tradition and a clear threat to India's interests in Nepal.

Nepal was not the only case where India had failed during this period. It had substantially failed in the Maldives and lost almost all traditional friends. The way the Maldives' interim government scrapped the deal with India based GMR-led consortium for upgradation and maintenance of the Male International Airport was a blatant expression of distrust and lack of commitment. It had failed to respond to the humanitarian crisis in Sri Lanka as well. In both the cases the vacuum left by Indian failure was immediately filled up by China. In Bangladesh, there remains a big question mark on India's motive and credibility. Dhaka alleges that New Delhi has always remained slow and late in delivering on its promises. Whatever it does, does too late...to reap any mutual benefit. The latest example of India's lacklustre attitude is regarding the implementation of the Teesta water sharing.

Thus we can say India has lost much of its goodwill and positive image in its immediate neighbourhood of Nepal, Bhutan, Bangladesh, Sri Lanka and the Maldives, in the post-Cold War era. Only exception, perhaps, has been Myanmar with whom India has maintained a stable relation, if not extremely cordial. The western neighbours, Pakistan and Afghanistan do not come under the considerations of this article as they always call for special attention and India's shared history with them is quite different from the countries that we have taken into account.

Now let us move on to the second failure which had come up in the economic front, for which analysts argued India had neglected its traditional socio-political ties with the neighbours. It is now beyond any doubt that India has reaped the benefits of globalisation quite successfully. It saw a telecom and information revolution. It has become self-sufficient in food and electricity. Per capita income and purchasing power of common people have increased significantly. Jobs have been created and poverty has decreased quite rapidly. India has also become polio-free. Health infrastructure has developed after the introduction of the National Rural Health Mission. In short, in the domestic front, though there are certain dissenting voices, India has developed significantly with regard to almost all the parameters of economy/ society/ health/education, etc. And here lies the second problem. India could not or rather did not try to take its smaller neighbors along in the path of this development. The neighbours allege that India has always dealt with them separately and bilaterally. But it had never tried to draw a plan for overall development of the

South Asian region. They further say because of its preeminence in the region, it is India alone which can take leadership role for an all round development of not only itself but for its smaller neighbors as well. These neighbors insist that when India had gained handsomely in its trade and commerce with the smaller neighbours, these countries suffered trade deficits. This is a serious allegation that India needs to take care of and such hostile attitude in the neighbouring capitals is not a very good sign for an aspiring superpower.[5]

## India's Goals in the Neighborhood

India has precisely three inter-connected goals in its neighbourhood, viz:

*First,* to attain a superpower status, India needs to have a peaceful neighbourhood so that it can engage itself in matters of global importance in a more comfortable and confident manner. Western borders do not promise anything good. Relations with Pakistan would dramatically improve overnight—no one expects that. But at the best it could pacify and secure its northern, eastern and southern borders with smaller neighbours. A peaceful border on three sides and warm, friendly relations with the neighbouring capitals would definitely give New Delhi an edge not only in international politics, but also in its relationship with Islamabad.

*Secondly,* a friendly neighbourhood would ensure China's limited access and influence in the South Asian region. Chinese 'string of pearls' strategy can be countered with a much benign and cost-effective measure of sincere and committed engagement with the neighbours.[6]

*Thirdly,* this region has already proved to be a good market for Indian goods and services. If India shows even more sincerity and commitment, these smaller neighbours can also become suppliers to Indian industries. Ancillary industries can be set up in these countries which will give

Indian industries cheap components and jobs to their citizens. This will further lessen Chinese influence and the prevailing resentment against New Delhi in some constituencies.

## Recent Improvements

As we have mentioned earlier, most of the failures came up during the initial years when India was trying to adjust itself with the new realities in its 'all-known' extended courtyard. Deterioration of relations with the Maldives or Sri Lanka are relatively new issues though. But in the last couple of years, it seems New Delhi has realised what went wrong in the 10-15 years that followed the decisive, benchmark year of 1991. The way it has responded to the political crisis in Bangladesh over the general elections or the way it has sidelined the Maoists from the Constitution making exercise in Nepal, shows some credible and pragmatic approach to the problems brewing up next door. The newly elected Maldivian president had come to New Delhi in his first state tour and assured that he would look into the GMR contract issue; a good sign for Indo-Maldivian engagement. Relations with Sri Lanka have become much smoother than what it was 5-6 years back. Transition in Myanmar is being closely followed and New Delhi is quite active in regard to the developments of that country, especially having a natural ally in Aung San Suu Kyi. Thus, during the end of the last decade and in the current one, few things have been achieved in the neighbourhood and few damages have been successfully repaired. New orientations and doctrines like the *Look East Policy* have worked effectively in regard to the eastern neighbours and can be replicated in dealing with the north and south as well.[7]

## Long Way to Go ...

Though India has achieved a few goals of immediate importance and has been in a better position during last 4-5 years as far as the smaller neighbours are concerned, it is yet to travel distant roads to attain the long term goals, the objectives which are imperative for it to climb up the ladder to get the superpower status. Some of these long term goals are being discussed here and some ideas have been forwarded. These are:

*First,* India should clearly separate the set of strategies meant for Af-Pak region from the set meant for the smaller neighbours of northern, eastern and southern sides. This clear cut distinction would enable the foreign policy makers and diplomats think and function more precisely and effectively. In fact New Delhi may consider the western border as a different region altogether; and may deal with the smaller states of remaining three sides by clubbing them together, with special focus on an individual state as and when necessary.

*Secondly*, New Delhi should try and integrate these states in its development trajectory in a mutually beneficial way.

*Thirdly*, India needs to deliver on its promises in a time-bound manner. The way it is dealing with Bangladesh over the Teesta water sharing is not a good example of diplomacy.

*Fourthly,* New Delhi needs to understand that it is necessary to develop more than one constituency or natural ally inside the neighbouring states so that repetition of Nepal could be avoided.

*Fifthly,* cultural and educational linkages with the elite of the neighbouring states are very much important as these people would be the decision makers in near future in the neighbouring capitals. But while doing so India needs to remember the elites who do not belong to the political sphere; i e business class, military, social activists, etc, are to be equally taken care of.

*Sixthly,* India needs to handle media in a proper way. In the changed circumstances post 1991, its image has been damaged in many ways. An image makeover is possible if it remains committed to the growth of these nations and at the same time publicize its contributions using the popular media of those states.

And finally, as our neighbours call for, India needs to take a multilateral approach to issues concerning all of the countries in the region; like introduction of free trade zone or environmental issues, etc.

## Conclusion

Security is something which can be ensured in various ways, depending on the objectives and the players involved. South Asian security is attainable only when India functions well in the region as well as globally. If we exclude Pakistan and Afghanistan from our discussion, South Asia means India along with some satellites revolving around it, if not dependent on it. Thus if India can sanitize its western borders and remains friendly to the neighbours sitting on other sides, larger South Asia can be peaceful. But in reality, it is easier said than done.

Unequal friendship hardly yields any result. Now in the given context, India cannot shrink in its size or presence in this region. And this sheer preeminence creates misperceptions and distrust in the neighbouring capitals. So it remains India's both duty and obligation to win their trust and confidence by delivering on its promises. We have started this article with the presumption that the end of Cold War had brought about some serious changes in global politics and South Asian region could not remain insulated from those changes. India, during its over enthusiastic journey en route to globalisation, somewhat ignored the traditional ties with its smaller neighbours and that ignorance backfired pretty soon. New Delhi has been in a damage control exercise since then. But very recently, as we have seen, there seems to be some improvements in bilateral relations with almost all of our neighbours. So this is high time India stresses on its commitment to these countries. This will also help in isolating Pakistan in its own region and curbing the Chinese influence.

Economic development and engagement is undoubtedly the necessity of the time. But New Delhi should never ignore again the traditional political ties with these countries. It took 40 years to build up that trust and mutual dependence and only 10-15 years to disrupt all those ties. Time and situation have given New Delhi a precious second chance which it should nurture with great care. If India really disconnects its western borders from the rest of the three sides, and treat the northern, eastern and southern neighbours with respect and on the basis of equality, we can expect to revert to the situation of 1950s or 60s. And South Asian security will be a reality at that point of time. Mutually beneficial economic engagement while maintaining the deep rooted political ties is the only way to move forward...together!

## Notes

1. Ganguly, Sumit; *India's Foreign Policy: Retrospect and Prospect; www.ufmg.br/cei/wp-content/uploads/*indianforeignpolicy*_ganguly.doc* (electronically accessed on 26.01.2014)
2. India Writes Network (IWN); "A Free and Prosperous India: Five Principles of Foreign Policy"; Official website of the MEA, Government of India; *http://www.mea.gov.in/articles-in-indianmedia.htm?dtl/22430/A+Free+and+Prosperous+India+Five+Principles+*
   of+Foreign+Policy (electronically accessed on 26.01.2014)
3. Gujral, IK, "The Post Cold War Era: An Indian Perspective"; *World Affairs*; Vol 1, No 1, Jan-Mar 1997, pp 44-55
4. The UCPN-Maoist supremo's clear tilt towards China is reflected in the interaction with the Chinese state news agency, Xinhua on 28th May 2013. *http://news.xinhuanet.com/english/china/2013-05/28/c_132415023.htm* (electronically accessed on 23.01.2013)
5. Behuria, Ashok K et al; *'Does India Have a Neighborhood Policy'*; Strategic Analysis, Vol 36, No 2, March 2012, pp 231-233.
6. Haidar, Suhasini; "In the Neighbourhood, it's India Fading"; *The Hindu*, p 7, 3 Jan 2013.
7. "India's Look East Policy: Critical Assessment"; An interview with Ambassador Rajiv Sikri; South East Asia Research Programme, Institute for Peace and Conflict Studies, October 2009, pp 5-8.

*Chapter 13*

# Rethinking the Indo-Pak Ties in the Context of Democratic Peace Thesis

*Somali Mukherjee*
Assistant Professor, Gurudas College
University of Calcutta, Kolkata

## Scope and Theoretical Basis

India-Pakistan relations are one of the most widely researched areas of International Relations and South Asian studies. The justification of this proposed paper therefore faces a stiff task. The proposed paper is a theoretical study that seeks to apply the democratic peace proposition (DPP) or thesis to study the role played by different regime types in constructing relations with India. As the literature survey would readily establish, while there is an enormous body of literature on geo-political, historical, and realist readings of India-Pakistan relations, and there exists a considerable body of work on Pakistan's domestic politics, there is no systematic work yet on the subject that applies the DPP to study the orientations, practices, institutional basis, power struggles, and related aspects of Pakistan's myriad regimes in their relations with India. The research gap is therefore self-evident. There is no published work in the public domain which has applied DPP to India-Pakistan relations and this proposed paper is an attempt to fill in this gap.

There is a growing conviction among the scholars that widespread democratisation will lead to a more peaceful world. One thought-provoking question is whether the democracies are in general peaceful, that is the monadic version holds true or whether the democracies are peaceful only towards other democracies and does behave aggressively towards other non-democracies, that is the dyadic version is more plausible. This paper would like to investigate some of the contemporary debates regarding the democratic peace thesis and would try to assess whether the democratic peace holds in the case of India-Pakistan relations, and if so which version is more plausible. This is because while India has remained a democratic polity since independence, Pakistan has been often ruled by military regimes.

Several criticisms can be labelled against this thesis. One, that the literature has been unconcerned about the possible lag effect between a country's regime change and its foreign conduct and between its regime change and the other's recognition and confidence in this change.[1] Further it has been alleged that DPP fails to distinguish between the initiators and defenders of international hostilities. Also as pointed out by Joanne Gowa it fails to distinguish between the norm based and interest based attributions of the foreign policy conducts. These issues are vital parameters of this study.

It is well acknowledged that often the Indo-Pak foreign policy behaviour exhibits strong short term orientations and are helpless prisoners of their past memories which often adversely shape their future expectancies. Hence, it can be argued that these ties are not affected by the change in regime type. However, the second image matters in foreign policy and domestic variables need to be investigated systematically to ascertain what kind of impact these generate over time. Even if the finding turns out to be negative, the exercise would carry significant heuristic value in itself. The second major problem in applying the democratic peace thesis in case of Pakistan consists of the popular allegation that the military is the real power centre in Pakistan's political system, no matter what kind of regime actually rules the state. While this is a powerful argument, yet two considerations stand paramount. *First, it does not necessary follow that civilian governments in Pakistan carry no foreign policy autonomy and, secondly, the degree of autonomy or control cannot be pronounced without empirical investigation.*[1]

The Democratic Peace Proposition is primarily based on two empirical claims that democracies are unlikely to conflict with one another, secondly democracies are more prone to conflict with non-democracies as non-democracies are with one another. The Democratic Peace Proposition (DPP) can be subdivided into two parts: (a) Source of peace, and (b) Patterns of interactions.[2] The sources of peace can be divided into Political norms (it includes the socialization of leaders within the domestic environment, treated amply in the works of Maoz, Russet, Raymond. It basically emphasizes non-violent conflict resolution. It further opines that non-democratic leaders are socialised in an environment in which coercion and violence are widely accepted as legitimate means for resolving political disputes. It further presumes that norms of conflict resolution practices employed by the political leaders when involved in domestic disputes are also used when the leaders seek to resolve international disputes and crises. The second premise on which the sources of peace build upon is the role of institutional structures. It has four propositions: (1) A central goal of state leaders is to retain their positions in the domestic political arena. (2) In all political systems, the domestic political opponents of a regime will attempt to mobilise political opposition when the domestic and foreign policies pursued by the regime have failed to achieve the stated policy goals. (3) In domestic political system counter elites are better able to mobilize opposition in order to challenge the incumbents for their policy failures. (4) In all political systems, state leaders believe that a foreign policy set back for their country stemming from a diplomatic retreat or military defeat could pose a threat to their domestic political position.

Another contested area is whether democracies are more pacific in their actions towards all other states, ie the Monadic version or is the Dyadic version which states that democracies are more pacific in their actions only towards other democracies is more valid. We shall come back to this debate shortly. *If one has to trace the origin and the trajectory of the development of DPP one has to definitely start with Immanuel Kant and his immortal work "In Perpetual Peace"* (1795), *where he states that a republican form of government is exemplified by the Rule of Law, provides a feasible basis for the states to overcome structural anarchy and to secure peaceful relations among themselves. DPP can be further traced to the work of Dean Babst in the Industrial Research (journal).* Here he reported that "no wars have been fought between independent nation with elective governments between 1789 and 1941." Melvin, Small, David Singer (1976) found that democracies participate in fewer wars than non democracies from 1815 to 1964. At present the debate can be summed up as revolving around three competing interpretations. Democracies are generally more peaceful than non-democracies. Democracies are more peaceful towards each other. Democracies are no more peaceful than non-democracies.

*The survey of some of the major texts in the arena of Indo-Pak relations shows that there has virtually been no work on the applicability of theoretical models as the Democratic Peace Thesis in this field.* Various aspects of India-Pakistan ties like the psychological dimensions of leaders and the masses, the historical legacy, the nuclear question and the role played by the outside foreign powers have been exhaustively delved into. However, there is a dearth of theoretical explanation of the relationship. And the little theoretical work done is essentially realist in inspiration. *The proposed paper is therefore expected to provide valuable insights into the domestic-external relations and the general dynamics of the Indo-Pak relations.*

## The Presumptions

*The first hypothesis is to test whether the 'pact of non-aggression' among democracies necessarily holds or not.* Is true as Doyle has posited that the very constitutional restraint, shared commercial interests, international respect for individual rights that promote peace among the liberal societies can exacerbate conflicts between the liberal and non liberal societies. Some eminent scholars have argued that what is important is how constrained the leaders are. For example Morgan and Sally Campbell writes "...our hypothesis is that governments facing the most decisional constraints... should be least war prone." It implies leaders who are not elected could be as constrained or even more constrained than their elected counter parts. John Mearsheimer has alerted us that the possibility always exists that a democracy can revert back to being an authoritarian state. Although a large number of countries have recently adopted the democratic structure of governance (ie universal suffrage, multiparty competition, contested elections, and legislative oversight), it is still not evident that leaders and people have internalized such democratic norms. *Hence, further research in this arena should seek to find out how far Pakistan's civilian regimes internalized democratic norms and sought peace with successive democratic Indian regimes or not.*

Status quo and revisionist states often have divergent foreign policy orientations regardless of their regime types. Thus young and revisionist democracies may not act like mature and status states. Sorensen et al have maintained that the democratic progress made in the "Third Wave" (as proposed by Samuel Huntington) has been fragile, tentative and reversible. Rousseau and his colleagues have argued that democracies are less likely to be involved in crisis initiation because they are satisfied with status quo. *Therefore the second hypothesis which can be tested is whether revisionist democracies are more likely to initiate crisis than mature and satiated democratic powers.* The tortuous trajectory of India-Pakistan relations affords an excellent case to test this proposition.

Kant had proposed three factors that could promote peace among the democracies; public opinion—it constitutes a powerful force against belligerence. Spirit of commerce that contributes to peace and the creation of pacific union among democracies which restrains war among them.[3] Russet counters that public opinion can be quite permissive and often reacts only to policies. Walter Lippman has remarked that in their foreign policies democracies are likely to be "to be too late with too little, or too long with too much, too pacific in peace and too bellicose in war, too neutralist or appeasing or too transparent." This characterisation is especially apt in describing democracies relations with non democracies. It is pointed out that established democracies have less confidence in the stability and dependability of their more immature and fragile counterparts (Russet, 1993). Further Maoz and Russet have noted that when a democratic state confronts a non democratic one it may be forced to adopt the norms of the international conduct of the latter lest it be exploited or eliminated by the non-democratic state that takes advantage of the inherent moderation of the democracies.[4] All these are open ended research questions, which can be taken up for further investigation. According to Bueno de Mesquita and Lalman, minor democracies are more likely to be challenged by the non democracies. The general tendency on being attacked is that major democracies seem to be more restrained while minor democracies seem more war prone, corroborating the claim that "democratic lions squeak and democratic mice roar."

Another point which deserves attention is the fact that that transparency boosts reciprocal confidence whereas its absence complicates communication and coordination between democracies and non democracies.[5] The condition of trust does not apply to mixed dyads therefore accounting for their tumultuous relations. Indeed, non democracies lack of trust worthiness and transparency accentuates democracies felt need to demonstrate resolve when facing them in crisis. *Accordingly, further studies may investigate the nature and quality of trust consecrated by the different democratic regimes in their relations with India.* This would necessitate a close study of India's responses to peace overtures of such civilian regimes in Pakistan, to find what responses were elicited in New Delhi and reasons put forward in support of the same.

## The Applicability of the Proposed Model

I propose to apply the DPP in the context of Indo-Pak relations. Ever since its inception, Pakistan has been living under long periods of military dictatorship with short intervals in the form of civilian rule. India cannot remain totally unconcerned because militarism in Pakistan has been in the past a source of pressure and tension for India. The military rulers of Pakistan have invariably always indulged in strengthening their legitimacy by creating a fear of Indian aggression against Pakistan by justifying the need to strengthen the military power of Pakistan. I shall explore the rules of Pakistan's military dictators, starting from Ayub Khan, whose stated objective was the security and preservation of Pakistan and its ideology, as articulated in his autobiography *Friends not Masters*. Apart from the ideology and Kashmir, the main source of friction between India and Pakistan at that point of time was the Indus Water System. After independence India had constructed several multipurpose projects on the eastern boundaries of Indus. Pakistan feared that India might repeat a 1948 incident that curtailed the water supply.

On the other hand an entente between Pakistan and China evolved in inverse ratio to the Sino-Indian hostility, which ultimately climaxed in the border dispute in 1962. The 1965 war began as a series of border flare ups along the undemarcated territory at the Rann of Kutch. The Runn of Kutch conflict was resolved by mutual consent and through British sponsorship and arbitration but the Kashmir conflict proved to be more dangerous. There was a sharp spurt in infiltrations towards India. Pakistan it seems, hoped to support an uprising by the Kashmiris against India. Finally on September 23, a ceasefire was arranged by the United Nations Security Council. In January 1966, Ayub Khan and PM Lal Bahadur Shastri signed the Tashkent Agreement. The Tashkent Agreement proved to be the turning point in Ayub Khan's administration.

In February 1966, a national conference was held in Lahore, where most politicians criticised Ayub Khan's unnecessary capitulation towards India. Meanwhile, Mujibur Rehman presented his six-point economic and political programme for East Pakistan's provincial autonomy. Ayub Khan also lost the services of his very able foreign minister Bhutto who later became a vocal opposition leader and the founder of the famous Pakistan's People

Party. In January 1969, several opposition parties formed the Democratic Action Committee with the declared the aim of restoring democracy through mass movement. Ayub Khan reacted by alternating conciliation with repression Ultimately Ayub Khan invited Democratic Action Committee to meet him in Rawalpindi, promised a new constitution and said he would not stand for re-election in 1970. On March 25, 1969, martial law was proclaimed. Agha Mohammad Yahya Khan the army commander in chief was designated the Chief Marshall Administrator. Ultimately Ayub Khan announced his resignation and Yahya assumed presidency.

Relations reached a new low when in 1971; India intervened in support of the secessionist forces in East Pakistan, playing an instrumental role in the creation of Bangladesh. General Yahya launched a new wave of repression in East Pakistan. These events led to the third Indo-Pak war in 1971. On 25th March Mujib was arrested and transported to West Pakistan and the West Pakistan forces started executing a planned genocide of the Bengalese. There was an exodus of about 100 million Bangladeshis to India. Yahya Khan gave a call to the people of Pakistan to be prepared for a war with Hindu India. In October 1971, the uprising in East Bengal gained further strength and momentum due to the organisation of the Bengalese into a guerilla force called Mukti Bahini. Ultimately the Simla Agreement was signed in 1972. Mr Bhutto declared that his country wanted to make a break with the past strife and that he would work for securing good relations with India.

The Simla Agreement can legitimately be described as an important land mark in the bilateral relations of India and Pakistan because its provisions successfully provided a sound and a practical basis for Indo-Pak normalisation in the post-1972 period. It ushered in a new era of good-will, cooperation and friendship. It can in fact be described as the new charter of the Indo-Pak détente. Interestingly one needs to note the fact, that, weeks after the Indo-Pak 1971 winter war, it was Bhutto who authorised, orchestrated and administered scientific research on nuclear weapons and it is he who is known as the father of Pakistan's nuclear deterrent programme.[6] In his book on the Pakistan Army, South Asia expert Stephen Cohen quotes a senior Lieutenant General as warning the late Zulfikar Ali Bhutto against using the military to control political opposition too often saying "If you use the stick too often, the stick will take over."

Regime of Zia is further regarded as not a healthy factor in the growth of Indo-Pak relations. In August 1977, General Zia announced the release of nearly 200 prisoners who were languishing in the Pakistani jails. India reciprocated the gesture by announcing the release of 200 Pakistani prisoners from the Indian jails. In February 1978, Mr Vajpayee paid an official visit to Pakistan and tried to create a more helpful and congenial environment. He declared that India fully respected the sovereignty and territorial integrity of Pakistan. He emphasised that though India is a big and a large country it would never play the role of a big brother in South Asia. Talks in New Delhi produced on 12th April 1978, an agreement over the Salal Dam Project. It marked the ending of a thirty-year dispute.

In 1978, Desai-Zia meet at Nairobi further improved the environment of Indo-Pak relations. In at Mumbai and Karachi respectively. In November 1978, Indian cricket team visited Pakistan and the cultural and sports relation between the two countries started to make a good head way. The premature end of the Janata era and in June 1980, the development of India-Pakistan differences over the crisis in Afghanistan gave a new twist to the Indo-Pak relations. In 1982, the Indo-Pak Joint Commission was institutionalised, which included the sub-commissions for trade, economy and travel. Indira Gandhi received Zia on November 1, 1982, in New Delhi and during their meeting they authorised the Foreign ministers and Foreign Secretary level talks to proceed with the talks leading ultimately to the formation of SAARC. In the late 1980s Indo-Pak settled relations settled into a pattern of ups and downs. Despite significant economic and trade agreements little progress was made concluding a comprehensive long term agreement to have non-discriminatory bilateral trade. Siachin conflict occurred in 1984, New Delhi charged Pakistan for arming and training Sikh terrorists in Punjab. In December 1985, the visit of Zia to India, culminated in both the sides agreeing not to attack each other's nuclear facilities, ushered in a brief phase of cordiality.

The cordiality evaporated in early 1986, with India's unhappiness over Pakistan's alleged interference in Punjab and the bungled Pakistani handling of pan-American airliner in which many Indians died. For its part Pakistan was disturbed by anti-Muslim riots in India and Zia accused India of assisting political campaign for Benazir Bhutto. Between November 1986 and February 1987, India and Pakistan conducted provocative missile maneuvers along their border that raised tension considerably. India's Operation Brass Tacks took place in Rajasthan across Pakistan's troubled Sindh province and Pakistan's manoeuvres were located close to India's state of Punjab. The crisis heightened when Pakistan's premier nuclear scientist AQ Khan revealed that Pakistan had manufactured a nuclear bomb. The tensions created were diffused at the foreign secretary level talks in New Delhi (January 31st to February 9) during which the two sides agreed to a phased troop withdrawal. Sudden death of Zia in an air crash in August 1988 and the assumption of the Prime Ministership by Mrs. Bhutto after 1988 elections provided the two countries with unexpected opportunity to improve relations.

Rajiv Gandhi's attendance at the SAARC summit in December 1988, permitted the two Prime Ministers to establish a personal rapport and sign three agreements, including one proscribing attack on each other's nuclear facilities. However, domestic political pressures in Sindh, Punjab and Kashmir destroyed the chances for improved relations in 1989 and 1990. For her part, Benazir Bhutto backed away from her comments on Simla Accords and continued to press the Kashmir issue internationally and public opinion forced Rajiv Gandhi and V P Singh to take hard line on events relating to Kashmir. In fact during her second tenure, the cordiality with P V Narsimha Rao almost disappeared.

Again in June 1991, Pakistan PM Nawaz Sharif proposed talks with India, Pakistan, the USA, the USSR and China to consider making *South Asia a Nuclear free zone* but the minority governments of Chandra Shekhar and Narasimha Rao declined to participate. Nevertheless, negotiations concerning Siachin Glacier resumed in November1992 after a hiatus of three years. By the mid-1990s little occurred to improve the bilateral relations as unrest in Jammu and Kashmir accentuated and the domestic politics in both the nations were unsettled. Sharif ordered Pakistan's nuclear tests code-named Chagai 1 and 2, in response to the Indian nuclear tests. However, it also needs to be stressed in 1999, it was under Sharif's stewardship that the Lahore Declaration was signed with Vajpayee. Vajpayee inaugurated a bus service that connected New Delhi with Lahore, It dawned on the two powers that the possession of nuclear weapons brought in added responsibility to avoid conflicts and promoted the idea of CBMs.

Eight years of Musharraf era has seen a sea change in the Indo-Pak bilateral relationship. General Musharraf, when he staged his coup against Sharif was the most unpopular in India than perhaps any Pakistani leader since Jinnah. He was the architect of the Kargil misadventure. Musharraf started his India file by virtually rejecting the Lahore Declaration made by Vajpayee and Nawaz Sharif and even refused to recognise the 1972 Simla Agreement signed by Mrs Gandhi and Zulfikar Ali Bhutto. He maintained this position during the Agra summit in July 2001 when he refused to accept any reference to the cross border terrorism in Kashmir. The seminal event that changed the course of the India-Pakistan relationship was the attack on the Indian Parliament in December 2001. The relationship between the two countries remained frigid, so much so that the SAARC meeting was cancelled because of the Indian Leader's refusal to sit at the same summit table with Musharraf. Thereafter the momentum was built slowly resulting in Vajpayee's visit to Islamabad in January 2004, when the Islamabad Agreement between the two countries were signed, resuming the bilateral composite dialogues suspended during Musharraf's coup d'etat. Musharraf ordered all cross-border Jihadi activities to stop. Vajpayee conducted the first free elections in Indian Kashmir which resulted in the ouster of the unpopular government of Mufti Mehmood. The bilateral talks led to the opening of bus travel between the two Kashmirs for the first time in nearly sixty years. Thereafter one can safely conclude that the Indo-Pak peace process had made some good strides while the General was in command.

India is convinced that Pakistan was involved in the attacks against the Indian parliament in 2001 and those perpetrated in Mumbai in 2008. Pakistan on its part is persuaded that India is fanning the flames of Balouch Separatism and manipulating the Afghan government to catch it off guard. At the beginning of 2012, South Asia was still held hostage to the India-Pakistan confrontation. India wanted bilateral negotiations on Kashmir while Pakistan favoured international mediation. During his recent visit to the US, the Indian PM Manmohan Singh rejected Pakistan's demands that Kashmir dispute should be settled in accordance with the UN resolutions. Manmohan Singh said "I have publicly stated that there can be no redrawing of borders (in Jammu and Kashmir)...but our two countries can work together to ensure, that these are borders of peace...."

Myra MacDonald, the author of *Heights of Madness* a book about the Siachin War between India and Pakistan noted that for the first time in the history of Pakistan, a civilian government was pushing a comprehensive constitutional reform package through the parliament to curtail the undue provisions introduced by the dictators to tighten their grip on power. Zardari had urged the parliament to pass amendments that would turn him into a titular head and remove his rights to sack the PMs which has been used by previous military dictators. General Kayani had repeatedly said that he wanted to keep the military out of politics. However the environment at Pakistan was volatile, with Zardari imposing Governor's rule in Punjab to replace an administration run by the Sharif brothers. The Taliban insurgency also fast spreading from the tribal areas to The North West Frontier Province. The situation was already on the edge with the government agreeing on a ceasefire with the Taliban militants in the Swat Valley in exchange for introducing Sharia laws. Further corruption allegations had tainted the Zardari government, and despite successive orders from the Supreme Court proceedings were not initiated against Zardari by Geelani, who had through such acts earned Contempt of Court proceedings against him. An editorial in *The Hindu*, offered a very interesting analysis suggesting that rather than being investigated and being branded as a corruption infested regime, the Zardari-led government would prefer a coup by the military so that they go down in the annuls of history as a Shaheed.

The beginning of 2013 had been marked by a number of skirmishes along the Line of Control. Mid-January onwards the region had witnessed perhaps the worst bout of fighting in the last ten years. Despite talks between Lieutenant Vinod Bhatia and Major General Ashfaq Nadeem, where an attempt was made to ease the situation, the skirmishes continued unabated resulting in eight Indian casualtics and nine Pakistani casualties. The incident incited even the usually calm Indian Prime Minister Dr Manmohan Singh to say that "after this dastardly act, there cannot be business as usual with Pakistan." As a sign of protest the Indian Government decided to send back Pakistani Hockey players, who were in India to participate in the Hockey India League. The death of the Indian soldier Sarabjeet Singh in the Pakistani custody further worsened the situation.

2013 was the year of transformation in Pakistan. Many analysts hoped that the transfer of power to a new civilian government would perhaps bring a thaw in the tension; however the Pakistani Jihadi forces or Army do not seem to be in the mood to allow it. It was amply manifested when on the eve of high profile talks between Sharif and Dr Singh; militants crossed the Pakistani border and killed eight Indian military personnel. The deliberately timed attack resembles earlier attempts by the terrorists to frustrate the bilateral process.

The new Pakistani Prime Minister Sharif must indeed overcome the obstacles in his own country before trying to negotiate peace with India. Both the Jihadi elements and the Army have vested interest in exacerbating tensions with India, lest they might face a curtailment in their powers or worse, deep cut in the defense budget. Matters worsened when the Mumbai terror mastermind Hafiz Saeed was seen to lead the Eid prayers before a massive gathering at the Gaddafi Stadium in Lahore on August 9. He was also seen to lead a parade of several thousands on August 14, to mark the Pakistani Independence day. The final nail in the coffin was the announcement by the Pakistani Finance Minister, that a plan to grant India Most Favoured Nation, was at present offs the table.

Shelling already marked the heaviest exchange since the 2003 ceasefire. Indian analysts remain convinced that Pakistan uses shelling as a cover for Jihadi elements crossing the border to attack the Indian installations. Rough estimates show, there have been 42 ceasefire violations in 2013 as compared to 17 in 2012. Elections scheduled in India in April-May 2014, may further compel the present UPA government to take a hard line and this fact has been corroborated with the coming to power of Congress backed Presidential candidate, Pranab Mukherjee and his deft handling and dismissing of the pending mercy petitions, which ultimately led to the hanging of Kasav, the lone survivor of the Mumbai attackers. Of late the Indian Army has become a major irritant in the Indo-Pak relations. Aggressive statements against Pakistan, army's veto against Siachin reflect the increasing role of army in political affairs. At present, settlement regarding Kashmir, Siachin and Sir Creek seem unlikely. The heralding of 2014, could witness the 'game' to grow more perilous. The US withdrawal from Afghanistan, would leave both the countries to jostle for power in the region. Further it shall again rivet the attention of the Pakistani terror groups back on India, as its prime enemy. The internal dynamics of both the countries, like the secessionist and Jihadi elements along with the Pakistani military establishment and the newly elected Indian government are going to play crucial role in shaping the foreign policy dynamics in the days to come.

The quest for security has been at the heart of Pakistan's foreign policy since independence, and it is perhaps not unnatural as it was the prodigal child of partition and its accompanying bloodshed. The cessation of Bangladesh delivered a major blow to the ideology which justified its existence, therefore the Indo-Pak conflict is both asymmetric and enduring but the power asymmetry is truncated and mitigated by many factors in particular the weaker state Pakistan has been able to reduce the asymmetry through strategy, tactics and alliances with outside powers and acquisition of qualitatively superior weapons.[7] The Indo-Pak conflict is simultaneously over territory, national identity and power position in the region. The political status of Kashmir from Pakistan's perspective is unfinished business of partition along religious lines in 1947. TV Paul says some of India's domestic constraints arise from the tendency of democratic states not to make territorial concessions, especially to non-democratic states.

## Conclusion

Since Pakistan has gone through several democratic regimes punctuated by spells of military rule, it is a fit case to investigate if the nature of Pakistani foreign policy towards India has varied by the nature of regimes or not. The proposed research questions which can later be delved into are the following ones: The chief research question is "has democratic Pakistan been more peaceful towards India compared to the dictatorial regimes?" Does the Indo-Pakistan case corroborate the claim that mixed dyads are more war prone than dyads with similar regime types? What should count as evidence of peace? Is covert violence and aid to terrorism war like situation? To what extend are democratic factors responsible for hostile image building? Is there any evidence that people and civil society movements reduce the prospects of war? Does the dyadic democratic theory hold in this critical bilateral tie?

It is perhaps time to take a fresh look at the Indo-Pak situation, realism still holds but the answer to bombs by delivering more bombs shall only wreak in more destruction and havoc and increase human suffering. It is about time that the Pakistani military comes out of its insecurity and realise that though low intensity conflicts may continue a major war is unlikely due to the presence of nuclear deterrents. More and more CBMs (Confidence Building Measures) should be encouraged between the two countries. The successive Indian governments too need to abandon hawkish stands and take a more humane approach. We need to comprehend the internal multiple cancers that are bleeding Pakistan, that it is a country ravaged by hunger, illiteracy, diseases, with only a small 'selectorate', to borrow from Bueno de Mesquita controlling the reins of power. Does common man want war? Following Amartya Sen one can say that peoples capabilities need to be improved and only fruitful engagement can reduce the flame of mutual mistrust burning the two countries. More people to people contacts, and track two diplomacy needs to be encouraged, forums like SAARC should be reformed.We need to take advantage of the germinating seed of democracy in Pakistan, we can perhaps rethink our foreign policy orientation and attain a delicate balance between realism and constructivism, which with time and effort might hail in an era of at least 'peaceful co-existence'.

## Notes

1. Sebastian Rosato, "Explaining the Democratic Peace", *The American Political Sciense Review*, Vol 99, No 3, August 2005, pp 468.
2. Steven Chan, "In Search of Democratic Peace: Problems and Promise", Mershon International Studies Review, Vol 41, No 1, May 1997, pp 63.
3. John Macmillan, "Liberalism and Democatic Peace", *Review of International Studies*, Vol 33, No 2, April 2004, pp 179.
4. Barbara Farnham, "The Theory of Democratic Peace and Threat Perception", *International Studies Quaterly*, Vol 47, September 2003, pp 180.
5. David L Rousseau, Christopher Gelpi, Dan Reiter, Paul K Huth, "Assessing the Dyadic Nature of the Democratic Peace", *The American Political Science Review*, Vol 90, No 3, September 1996, pp 520.

6. Shankar Bajpai, "Untangling India and Pakistan", *Foreign Affairs*, Vol 82, No 3, May-June 2003, pp 125.
7. TV Paul (ed), *The India-Pakistan Conflict: An Enduring Rivalry*, Cambridge University Press, UK, 2005.

## Bibliography

1. Dennis Kux, *India-Pakistan Negotiations: Is Past Still Prologue?*, United Institute of Peace, Washington, 2006.
2. William R Thompson and Richard Tucker, "A Tale of Two Democratic Peace Critiques", *The Journal of Conflict Resolution,* Vol 41, No 3, June 1997, pp 428-454.
3. David L Rousseau, Christopher Gelpi, Dan Reiter, Paul K Huth, "Assessing the Dyadic Nature of the Democratic Peace", *The American Political Science Review,*Vol 90, No 3, September 1996, pp 512-533.
4. James Mahoney, "Qualitative Methodology and Comparative Politics", *Comparative Political Studies,* Vol 40, No 2, February 2007, pp 122-144.
5. James Mahoney, Erin Kimball, Kendra L Koivu, "The Logic of Historical Explanation in Social Sciences", *Comparative Political Studies*, Vol 42, No 1, January 2009, pp 114-146.
6. John Gerring and Rose McDermott, "An Experimental Template for Case Study Research", *American Journal of Political Science*, Vol 51, No 3, July 2007, pp 688-701.
7. John Gerring, "What is a Case Study and What is it Good for?", *The American Political Science Review*,Vol 98, No 2, May 2004, pp 341-354.
8. Shaul R Shenhav, "Political Narratives and Political Reality", *International Political Science Review*, Vol 27, No 3, July 2006, pp 245-262.
9. Sumit Ganguly, *The Conflict Unending. India Pakistan Tensions Since 1947,* Oxford University Press, UK, 2002.
10. Kuldip Nayyar, *Wall at Wagah India Pakistan Relations,* Gyan Publishing House, New Delhi, 2003.
11. Sumantra Bose, *Kashmir: Roots of Conflict Paths to Peace,* Harvard University Press, Massachusetts, 2003.
12. TV Paul (ed), *The India-Pakistan Conflict: An Enduring Rivalry,* Cambridge University Press, UK, 2005.
13. Major General (Retd) Mahmud Ali Durrani, *India and Pakistan: The Costs of Conflict and the Benefits of Peace,* Oxford University Press, Pakistan, 2001.
14. Major General Ashok Krishna, PR Chari (eds), *Kargil: The Tables Turned,* Manohar Publishers and Distributors, New Delhi, 2001.
15. Rafiq Dossani and Henry S Rowen (eds), *Prospects for Peace in South Asia,* Stanford University Press, CA, USA, 2005.

16. Amitabh Mattoo, Kapil Kak, Happymon Jacob (eds), *India and Pakistan: Pathways Ahead,* KW Publishers Pvt Ltd, New Delhi, 2007.
17. J N Dixit, *India-Pakistan in War and Peace,* Routledge, London, 2002.
18. Summit Ganguly (ed), *India's Foreign Policy: Retrospect and Prospect,* Oxford University Press, New Delhi, 2010.
19. Sebastian Rosato, "Explaining the Democratic Peace", *The American Political Science Review*, Vol 99, No 3, August 2005, pp 467-472.
20. Steve Chan, "In Search of Democratic Peace: Problems and Promise", *Mershon International Studies Review*, Vol 41, No 1, May 1997, pp 59-91.
21. John Macmillan, "Liberalism and Democratic Peace", *Review of International Studies*, Vol 30, No 2, April 2004, pp 179-200.

# Section II

# Non-Traditional Security

- Security Challenges in South Asia: A Commoner's Observation.
- The Idea of 'Security' in the 21st Century South Asia
- How to Meet the Security Challenges of South Asia by Democratization and Secularism
- Kashmir Dispute in South Asian Security
- Beating the Security/Development Trap: Using Geography to NE's Advantage
- Livelihood Concerns, Migration and Trafficking: Gender and Security in South Asia
- Environmental Security and India: Global, Regional and National Dimensions
- Security Perspectives of Pakistan and Afghanistan: Looking through the Lens
- Non-Traditional Security Issues and the Challenges of Globalisation in South Asia
- The India-Bangladesh Border: A Rising Threat to Human Security
- Food Security and Human Development in South Asia
- The Maldives—Fighting for Life
- Water Conflict Between India and Bangladesh: A Threat to Human Security
- A Journey from Present to Future Perfect through the Prism of Health Security.

# Section II

# Non-Traditional Security

- Security Challenges in South Asia: A Commoner's Observation
- The Idea of Security in the 21st Century South Asia
- How to Meet the Security Challenges of South Asia by Democratic Norms and Secularism
- Kashmir Dispute in South Asian Security
- Bridging the Security/Development Gap: Using Geography to Its Advantage
- Livelihood Concerns, Migration and Trafficking: Gender and Security in South Asia
- Environmental Security and India: Global, Regional and National Imperatives
- Security Perspectives of Pakistan and Afghanistan: Looking through the Lens
- Non-Traditional Security Issues and the Challenges of Globalisation in South Asia
- The India-Bangladesh [illegible] Emerging Threat to Human Security
- Food Security and Human Development in South Asia
- The Maldives—Fighting for Life
- Water Conflict between India and Bangladesh: A Threat to Human Security
- A Journey from Present to Future: [illegible] through the [illegible] of Health Security

*Chapter 14*

# Security Challenges in South Asia: A Commoner's Observation

*Sanghamitra Sarker*
Associate Professor
Department of Political Science
Surendranath College for Women, Kolkata

South Asia comprises of the sub-Himalayan countries and topographically, it is dominated by the Indian Plate; it comprises of the countries of Afghanistan, Bangladesh, Bhutan, India, Maldives, Nepal, Pakistan and Sri Lanka. South Asia is home to well over one fifth of the world's population, making it both the most densely inhabited and the most densely populated geographical region in the world. Hence, security becomes a quintessential factor in this region. By definition, security means absence of threat or a state of being free from danger or threat. South Asia is a dynamic and complex region that presents the world with significant opportunities and challenges to global security, stability and human well-being. According to *Oxford Dictionary*, commoner is an ordinary person without any rank or title. Generally this term is used to refer those people who are not privileged or do not have any connection with privileged section of the society. National security is the prerequisite to maintain and to preserve the survival of the state through the exercise of economic power, diplomacy, and power projection and political power. This paper attempts to come to a critical understanding of the links between commoners' perception and state's traditional perception of security by examining the constraints on commoner in the backdrop of South Asia in the 21st century. By examining the constrains on commoners' daily livelihood contesting general insecurity in this region, this paper argues that commoners' daily security is constrained by seven main factors. Poverty which is the deprivation of basic requirement of life; higher rate of illiteracy which make them insecure in every walk of lives; poor health condition which ultimately endanger their lives and negatively portrays human resources of the region; the construction of gender-bias, personal and customary laws which prevents women i e half of the population from their equal opportunity and benefit sharing in the developmental process of this region; the poor management of state-owned distribution system for which budgetary allocation remains unreached to the commoner. Security threats to states of this area which include cross-border armed conflicts, external and internal threats which certainly jeopardizes the safety of the inhabitants of the region and final constraints to security, is the power of corruption which endangers the commoners' daily existence as well as top national armed security in this region.

The issues examined in this paper are the causes of insecurity experienced by commoners' of South Asian region and insecurities derived from the absence of human security. Human security shifts the focus of security away from the state and armed conflict to focus on other threat parameters affecting human life and to treat these as security threats, placing the security of individuals, not states, at the center stage of security study.[1]

In the post-Cold War period particularly in this century, the dynamics of security became stronger. Its urge to distinguish between 'hard' and 'soft' security threats had increased manifold. Asia is confronting serious and unprecedented security challenges in the 21st century. Many of these challenges are traditional in nature—including geopolitical readjustments among the major powers, weapons proliferation, and shifting alliances—but many others are non-traditional, such as energy security, transnational terrorism, and natural disasters. There is an emergent argument on the need to expand the traditional notions of security to address the non-traditional threats and so develop a more comprehensive approach to security. This is mainly because the traditional security paradigm does not address the rapidly growing non-traditional threats to security like, "the struggle for resources embedded in the pursuit of energy, security, environmental degradation, forced migration, international terrorism, insurgency ascendancy of non-state actors in drugs, arms, money-laundering and financial crime organization."[2] The main questions that are being asked today are security from what, when, where and how?

In the 21st century, globalization has led to softening of borders, it has also, inappropriately, aided many security problems to attain dangerous dimensions. Post 9/11, terrorism has moved centre stage in the security discourse. The shadowy non-state actor—a terrorist who was in the fringes of security discourse—is now the new threat. The South Asian region has faced a series of terrorist activities which are sometimes sponsored by their neighbouring states.For example, Indians have suffered cross-border terrorism for decades. In Jammu and Kashmir, the Pakistan-sponsored terrorism has paralyzed normal life since the 1980s. According to Indian estimates, terrorism has claimed 34,000 lives since 1990 including over 12,000 civilians and 18,000 terrorists. Pakistan has also been involved in the supply of arms and financial assistance to Naxalites and separatist groups active in India.[3] Apart from Pakistan, Liberation Tigers of Tamil Eelam (LTTE) is known to have trained the United Liberation Front of Assam (ULFA) and Maoists from India and Nepal, respectively. Similarly, it has been reported that Maoists in Nepal also work closely with the People's War Group (PWG) of Andhra Pradesh. On the other hand, Bangladesh, Pakistan, Sri Lanka, Nepal and Bhutan have their own analysis of terrorist attacks apprehending foreign hands behind the terrorist attacks in their homelands. In most of the cases, state or common people indicate India as a foreign player in these cases.

We should keep in mind that in this region, India and Pakistan both are nuclear powered states and both are heavily militarily equipped and safeguarded. As per the 2013 budgetary allocation, after Sharif came to power there has been 10 per cent increase in allocation. In case of India, according to the 2014 interim budget, there has been an approximate 10 per cent rise in budgetary allocation for defence. The death toll in India, Pakistan and Sri Lanka has been one of glaring instance. India accounted to 843 deaths in 2013 due to Naxal attacks, Kashmir conflict, Muzaffarnagar riots and North-east insurgency. In Sri Lanka, according to official reports, the death toll has reached to 70,000 (till 20th Sept, 2013). Pakistan records to a death toll of 5,682 people in 2013.Apart from this, however, there are intermittent terror strikes and bomb blasts that occur every other day in different cities of the country, thereby increasing the death toll to a mammoth level.[4] Why two militarily well-equipped states of South Asia have failed to address the physical security of their own citizens? Is it enough to blame each other for the insecurity of their own people?

In spite of this blame game, large sections of common people of this region mostly remain insecure in terms of fooding, lodging and clothing. The concern of food is catered to by a number of factors—land, irrigation, crops, labour and many other things, without which food cannot reach to the population of any country. Different factors like low quality crops, insufficient irrigation facilities, adulteration hampers the development of food security and hence, the common man perceives a threat from that region. Likewise, sometimes border issues and forced displacement for varied reasons including developmental issues, change of river-bed and cross-border conflicts often snatch away shelters from innumerable people, thus, creating a potential security threat. Therefore, for a common man the absence of availability of the basic requirements of life indicates serious security intimidation. Apart from these, rising terror strikes and killing of innocent lives by both state and non-state actors add fuel to the fire of perceived security threat.

On the other hand, curbing the voices and the rights of the civil society and the intellectual section of any country is not only a gross violation of basic rights but also threatening the security build-up of the population. In fact, violation of the rights of any citizen of the country threatens security. In case of the female population, security remains a key area of concern in South Asia. Combatting female feticide, child abuse, trafficking, crime against women which includes rape, honour killing and sexual harassment is the need of the hour for the South Asian states. In the last century the genocides or riots or conflicts—in whatever way it is expressed, the killing of innocent women and children have been rampant in South Asia. However, statistics show that no genocide has occurred in the 21st century in South Asia. But intolerance among different groups is increasing in this region. The buffer state of Cold War era, Afghanistan is still continuing as a breeding ground of various ethno-religious group perpetrating terror. In this century Bangladesh witnessed intolerance between political and religious groups. India is the witness of many forms of intolerance between politico-ethno-linguistic groups, religious groups and comparatively less in case of class-caste groups. Pakistan is the worst recipient of immense politico-ethno-religious (inter-religious) conflicts in this century. Even Maldives was not spared from any security threat. However, Nepal has been struggling its battle to combat internal and external threats to their democratic tradition. On the other hand, Sri Lanka has witnessed worst form of ethnic conflicts which from various international platforms has been termed as genocide.

This paper begins by discussing the related position of security of common people vis-à-vis security as perceived by traditional state power. Traditional security has always been a concern for the South Asian states. The Indo-Pak and Sino-Indian border conflict and the ripples surrounding it have suffered the entire region. These tensions have led to wars, indefinite period of crisis and in procuring nuclear expansion. Intermittent interventions across the border have complicated the security scenario of the region. Water disputes in various degrees and with more than one country has kept the region disturbed and under scrutiny. Apart from these, there have been numerous issues that have fractured the unity and stability of the zone. Cross-border terrorism and terror activities have aggravated the conflict of the region.

Fundamentalism, radicalism, insurgency, violation of maritime laws, cyber-crimes add to the galore of South Asian security threat in the 21st century. The internal insurgencies in Bangladesh, India, Sri Lanka, Pakistan and Nepal have been rampant and the rising fundamentalist activities in these countries have been serious threats to the stability and peace in South Asia.

South Asia has experienced express economic and social development in this century. The region underwent extensive liberalization in trade, which has been one of the important components of structural reform efforts among the South Asian countries in this century with Sri Lanka leading the way.[5] However, in spite of all this progress and an optimistic road ahead, the subcontinent faces certain significant stresses which can be categorized into external and internal threats. Terrorism turned into a serious armed intra-conflict phenomenon in the post-Cold War era. However, counter-terrorism came on to the global itinerary after 9/11. In this 21st century, South Asia portrays an image of an area which has been disturbed by violent religious and radical fundamentalism and fanaticism where groups like al-Qaeda, Taliban, Indian Mujahideen, Laskar-e-Toiba, LTTE and Left extremists are active.[6] Groups like Jamaat in Bangladesh and Maoists in Nepal also posed serious security challenges to the respective states. In this sphere, challenges were well taken by the state powers, though success rate is not always very high. Nepal can be cited as the best example of contrasted image of security. On one hand, they failed to provide security to their royal family and on the other hand, they were successful in handling challenges from ultra-groups. In case of Sri Lanka, it can be called as the most negative portrayal where UN passed resolution against them for human rights violation. In the recent past, the major incident took place in Abottabad, Pakistan, where

Osama Bin Laden was killed by US troops. When incidents not only significant in world security studies but also raise some crucial questions regarding the concept of sovereignty in the 21st century.

However, apart from these spheres of terror activities, security threats also emanate from other intrinsic social issues like human security, ethnicity and identity issues, racism, food security and poverty. In the contemporary world, poverty seems to be the biggest setback for South Asia's overall development. Therefore, poverty has now emerged as one of the major threats that have adversely affected the South Asian region.

## Human Security and Scarcity

South Asia represents one of the most vulnerable regions in terms of human development and gender disparity. It fares poorly in several human development indicators and faces colossal challenges to improve the quality of life for all its 1.4 billion citizens, almost one-fourth of the world population. The quality of growth and poverty is being weakened by rising inequality and insecurity in many Asian countries. South Asian countries (Bangladesh, India, Pakistan, and to a lesser degree Sri Lanka) have large proportions of the rural population living in poverty with high levels of illiteracy. The region remains one of the most disadvantaged in the world: more than 40 per cent of its 1.4 billion people live on less than one dollar a day, making South Asia home to nearly half of the world's poor.[7] Poverty is a permanent infliction in most of the countries of this region. According to UNDP's 2012 Human Development Report, Afghanistan ranked among the lowest countries, ranking 175th. Bhutan has been ranked 140th, while Bangladesh (160th), India (136th), Pakistan (147th), Maldives (104th) and Sri Lanka (92nd) out of 187 countries in the 2012 UNDP Human Development Index (UNDP Human Development Index 2012).

Moreover, share of distribution of GDP among the South Asian countries indicate that there is a lack of balanced

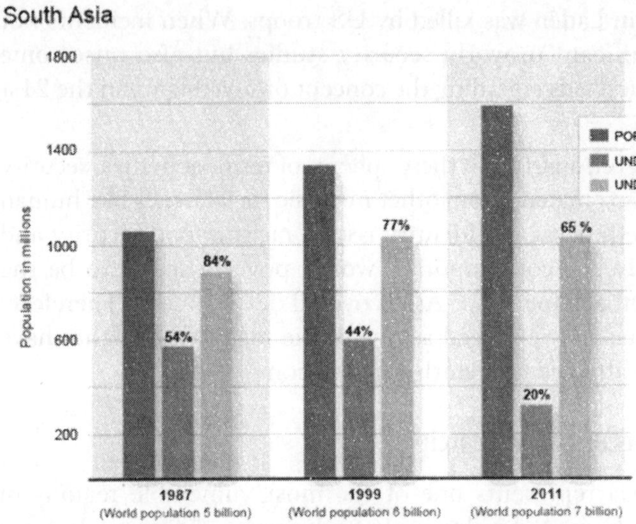


Population: Poverty ratio (*Source:* Reuters, 2011)

distribution. The Human Development Report of 2013 confirms that in most South Asian countries, the score in terms of the HDI is very low. Although Sri Lanka and the Maldives are comparatively better, as per the HDI parameters, this region is still in an appalling condition in terms of access to income, health and education which is necessary for a decent living as per the international standards.

South Asia also accounts for one-third of the world's maternal deaths. Child malnutrition, however, despite some drop, continues to remain among the highest in the world with almost 50 per cent of children are below the standards for weight by age (UNICEF). Environmental degradation, insufficient infrastructure, and social exclusion are among other abundant obstacles to growth and poverty reduction.[8] The majority of the South Asian population is suffering from destitution, deprivation and misery.

## Health

Issues of health and poverty are conjoint as one depends on the other in an immense way. In South Asia, according to the World

Bank Report 2012, there have been a marginal improvement (though there is an upward growth) in the access of sanitation facilities since 2010—29 per cent in Afghanistan, Bangladesh accounts 57 per cent, Bhutan accounts 47 per cent, India records 36 per cent, Maldives records 99 per cent, Nepal traces 37 per cent, while Pakistan and Sri Lanka traces 48 per cent and 92 per cent respectively.

In case of drinking water facilities, the Southern Asian regional average regarding the access to improved water sources is 30.9 per cent (UNICEF and World Health Organization 2012). Thus, this array of data substantiates the argument that security in the south Asian region in health and sanitation sector is thoroughly challenged.

India's one billion plus population, together with young and large populations in Bangladesh and Pakistan, means that the region has the world's second largest population of children. Of the three countries, only Bangladesh, with a lower rate of child mortality than either India or Pakistan, is on track to meet United Nations MDG 4. It reduced under-five deaths to almost half of its 1990 level by 2002, at an average of annual rate of reduction of 5.2 per cent. In contrast, the slowdown in child mortality reduction seen in India and Pakistan in the 1990s has left them lagging behind. India must accelerate its annual rate of reduction to over 6 per cent to meet MDG 4, and for Pakistan, the required rate is 7 per cent.[9]

Gender and poverty issues are highly intertwined and are of major importance in the region of South Asia. While nearly two-thirds of the world's poor are in South Asia, more than one-third of the region's poor are women. And poverty is particularly acute for women living in rural areas. In poor families, the gender division of labour, and responsibilities for household welfare, mean that the burden of poverty falls most heavily on women. Given gender disparities in education, health care, economic participation, and incomes, women are the most vulnerable category. Hence, the above mentioned scenario is enough to conclude that "poverty is violence", as Elaben Bhatt, the Indian activist mentioned. However, we can perceive that in addition to poverty, if you are a female then your gender identity can be a cause of another round of terror.

## Gender-Bias Legal Structure

In addition to these above constraints to secured and peaceful lives of common people, the role of personal law, customary laws, even social practices prevailing in this region create a serious challenge to dignity and equal status of women and backward sections of society. This ultimately deters the legal security of the majority population of South Asia. In case of women security of Pakistan, the Women Protection Bill 2006 can be considered a positive attempt to minimise the gender gap of Pakistan, but that does not mean that women in Pakistan are equally secured by their legal structure. In Afghanistan, security in all perspectives is under threat, and hence it is remarked, "President Hamid Karzai's government has let down Afghan women," according to the new EU ambassador to Kabul, who singled out the failure to end prosecution of rape victims and other abused women for 'moral crimes' as a particular 'disgrace'.[10] In Bangladesh and India, in the name of personal and customary law, the legal protection to several minority and tribal women in the case of marriage, divorce, alimony and property inheritance is denied.

In this paper, my argument is that high expenditure on armed security cannot be treated as enough safeguard measurement for ensuring security of the human race. It should be linked up with the developmental issues with human face. With this view, in this century most of the South Asian states have increased their budgetary allocations in the social service sectors. However, defeating poverty will not be possible without challenging the prevailing model of development in South Asia. In 2005, the Parliament introduced National Rural Employment Guarantee Act (NREGA), which till date can be considered the most available approach to rural India for poverty alleviation through employment generation. In fact, in 2013, the World Bank had indicated an assured annual funding of $3-5 billion for the next four years to push development projects and poverty eradication programmes.[11] In the case of Bangladesh, Bangladesh Garment Manufacturers and Exporters Association (BGMEA) came up with a massive employment scope for the people and most importantly for the deprived sections and women in the country. Experts say that while the garment industry has benefited from the cheap labour offered by women—who tend to work for less than men—the industry has reduced the marginalisation of women who were excluded from formal sector jobs, hence bridging the gender disparity.[12] In spite of several criticisms against micro-finance it is undeniable fact that the concept of micro-finance in Bangladesh has been a guide for development in the region.

Assessing and studying the above mentioned threats—traditional or non-traditional, I have observed that the biggest challenge in implementing all security tools is corruption, which affects a range of services from military to social security like Janani Suraksha Yojana of the Indian government which guarantees only 500 INR to 800 INR for reduction of maternal and neonatal mortality among poor pregnant women. This mechanism of corruption has spread its tentacles to the extent of not sparing even the minimum allocation for the health security of underprivileged sections and also not sparing large amounts of contributions for the military security of the country.

In the year 2000, United Nations declared the Millennium Development Goals, for which the whole world came together to make a solemn pledge for 2015. (The Millennium Development Goals, UNDP) The goals are:

- The promise of primary education for every child
- The promise of an end to avoidable infant and maternal deaths and
- The promise of a halving of poverty

The Millennium Development Goals (MDG) included a whole range of other promises—to help improve water supply, to recover sanitation, to shrink child deaths and maternal deaths—to do a whole range of good things. Till date, the pledges required to meet the Millennium Declaration efforts in South Asia to tackle poverty, inequality, injustice and bring sustainable development have been grossly insufficient. The region will continue to remain vulnerable as long as threats are coming from poverty, inequality and injustice which will hamper the sustainable development of this region.

"South Asia emerged as a political actor in the global politics only after the Partition of India in the year 1947. In this region the partition left many places as 'killing fields', made million peoples refugees. But the main victims were women. They were killed, maimed, violated and abandoned."[13] All of these transformed the socio-political culture of this region. The year 1971 carried the legacy of 1947 once again. In the backdrop of this tragic past one should address the security paradigm of South Asia. The challenging security and initiatives of conditioning security, there is a frequent oxymoron that for some unknown reasons the efforts to maintain security and status quo is often hampered by the state machineries of the region. Thus, to conclude, it may be said, "points to be raised and points to be deferred." (Gramsci: Selections from *Prison Notebooks*).

## References

1. A Comparative Study on Women's Right in Bangladesh under Hindu and Muslin Personal Laws,
2. Women's Rights in Family Law in Pakistan—Publications—Heinrich Boll Foundation.
3. http://www.seea.org.in/special_issue/vol1/33.pdf (accessed on 27th February 2014).
4. http://www.thehindu.com/news/national/world-bank-promises-big-push-to-poverty-alleviation-schemes-in-india/article4506331.ece (accessed on 24th February 2014).
5. http://www.brecorder.com/money-a-banking/198/1187220/ (accessed on 26th February 2014).
6. http://www.worldbank.org/en/country/srilanka/overview (accessed on 25th February 2014).
7. http://med.gov.lk/english/?page_id=21 (accessed on 25th February 2014).
8. "Nari Andoloneer Panch Dashak", Maleka Begum, Anyaprokash Publication, Dhaka, 2002.

9. http://www.ids.ac.uk/files/socprotSA.pdf (accessed on 24th February 2014).
10. http://www.idsa.in/system/files/Book_TerrorChallengesSouthAsia.pdf (accessed on 25th February 2014).
11. Bangladesh Mahila Parishad, Uniform Family Code, Edition II (Dhaka): Legal Aid Sub-Committee of Bangladesh Mohila Parishad, 2006.
12. Anupoma Ray, Gendered Citizenship, Edition I (Delhi): Orient Longman Pvt Ltd, 2005.
13. http://www.unicef.org/progressforchildren/2004v1/southAsia.php (accessed on 28th February 2014).
14. Rioting over Women's Right in Bangladesh—12 April 2008: Al Jazeera's Hannah Belcher Reports, 12th April 2008. http://www.youtube.com/
15. http://www.theguardian.com/world/2014/mar/07/hamid-karzai-afghanistan-women-eu-mellbin (accessed on 1st March 2014).
16. http://www.thehindu.com/news/national/world-bank-promises-big-push-to-poverty-alleviation-schemes-in-india/article4506331.ece (accessed on 24th February 2014).
17. "Women Garment Workers in Bangladesh", Syeda Sharmin Absar, *Economic & Political Weekly*, Vol 37, No 29 (Jul 20-26, 2002), pp 3012-3013+3015-3016.
18. *India after Gandhi*, Ramchandra Guha, p 94, Pan Books, 2008.
19. Agnes Flavia (2009), Recent Development in the Uniform Civil Code in India.

## Notes

1. http://www.brookings.edu/research/topics/south-asia (accessed on 24th February 2014).
2. Dipankar Banerjee, Security Studies in South Asia: change and challenge (New Delhi: Manohar, 2000) p 50.
3. http://cps.org.za/cps%20pdf/pia20_2.pdf (accessed on 29th March 2014).
4. http://www.globalsecurity.org/military/world/war/index.html (accessed on 1st March 2014).
5. http://www.ids.ac.uk/files/socprotSA.pdf (accessed on 24th February 2014).
6. http://www.idsa.in/system/files/Book_TerrorChallengesSouthAsia.pdf (accessed on 25th February 2014).
7. http://www.ids.ac.uk/files/socprotSA.pdf (accessed on 25th February 2014).
8. http://www.saape.org/index.php/news-room/news/31-saape-s-south-asia-poverty-report-2013-launched-in-karachi-pakistan (accessed on 25th February 2014).
9. http://www.unicef.org/progressforchildren/2004v1/southAsia.php (accessed on 28th February 2014).
10. http://www.theguardian.com/world/2014/mar/07/hamid-karzai-

afghanistan-women-eu-mellbin (accessed on 1st March 2014).

11. http://www.thehindu.com/news/national/world-bank-promises-big-push-to-poverty-alleviation-schemes-in-india/article4506331.ece (accessed on 24th February 2014).
12. "Women Garment Workers in Bangladesh", Syeda Sharmin Absar, *Economic & Political Weekly*, Vol 37, No 29. (Jul 20-26, 2002), pp 3012-3013+3015-3016.
13. *India after Gandhi*, Ramchandra Guha, pp 94, Pan Books, 2008.

*Chapter 15*

# The Idea of 'Security' in the 21st Century South Asia

*Suranjan Das*
Vice-Chancellor
University of Calcutta, Kolkata

We perhaps need to complement the security based on military power, balance of power and strategic issues of security with the understanding of security based on human issues and socio-economic development, human rights, gender equity and environmental degradation. It is security of the territories from external aggression or as protection of national influence in foreign policy or as global security from the threat of nuclear holocaust forgotten by the legitimate concern of the ordinary people to sub-security in daily lives of many of them.

Security symbolises protection from the threat of diseases, hunger, unemployment, crime, social conflict, political depression and environmental hazards. It is being stressed by many scholars that the security based on political independence, national defence and territorial integrity, cannot have an enduring appeal for the masses unless it is supplemented with concerns of freedom from threat to one's survival. In this context socio-economic progress of a nation-state based on equity, access, sustainability and good governance are also-pre-equated for achieving national security for South Asian states and once this real national security is guaranteed, co-operative bilateralism and regional co-operation should follow. Civil societies and governments across the states of the region need to realise that they share a common colonial past; they shared common experiences of nation building and they shared common issues generated by the process of globalisation. We need to realise that the resolution of identity politics in Sri Lanka is not only required for national peace in the island but also its implications for the identity politics in South Asia, especially in Pakistan, Bangladesh and Nepal. We also need to appreciate the fact that strengthening of democracy and containment of fundamentalism and terrorism in Pakistan and Bangladesh are not only required for good governance in those countries but are also necessary for sustenance of democracy and multiculturalism in India.

Again bringing the Maoist groups within mainstream politics is not only crucial for the Nepalese democracy but also a positive implication for the Indian state which is also involved with meeting the Maoist challenge. To develop a discourse, to generate popular consciousness across regional-national boundaries in South Asia, to make the people and government of Asia realise that for insuritical security it will be beneficial for the individual states to learn from the experience of its neighbours. For instance the process in which India has been able to sustain its democratic, secular and federal polity in the face of domestic and external challenges, should bear lessons for the other states of South Asia or Bhutan's model of Gross National Happiness (GNH) and their method of preserving ecological balance could have lessons for other South Asian states as they prepare their future developmental blue prints.

In other words, the notion of South Asian security has no 'right' dimension, it has multiple dimension. At one level there is certain importance in military security and balance of power but at the same time there has to be realisation that national security cannot be sustained without effective realisation of the demands of development which should promote constructive regional ingredients. When the conversion of the two levels should be attained, only then South Asian Free Trade Area (SAFTA) will be a reality and enable us to rectify a situation valued only about

4 per cent of import and export trade of South Asian countries at a time to their region. At a time more than 64 per cent of the West European commerce represented Intra-European Economic Community.

It is, however, believed that India being the strongest economy of the region and the rising global power has to play a leadership role in creating a healthy regional order in South Asia. Of course, this could not be done by making India a soft state or by converting national boundaries to soft boundaries but New Delhi has to project and protect South Asian interests in global forums. India has to emerge as a model of good governance for the region and India's recent moves in South Asian politics have been in consonance with this requirement. For instance, despite degrading security environment inside Pakistan and continuous cross-border terrorism, New Delhi had resumed Indo-Pak bilateral dialogue in July 2011 which raised the creation of possibility in trade, movement of people and liberalisation of research.

In fact, the recently organised Indian show in Lahore where 200 Indian exhibitors participated and Pakistani traders are shortly to organise show. The 15th meeting of the special representatives of India and China held in Delhi on 16th and 17th January 2013, resulted in the adoption of what has been called a New Yearly Verdict Mechanism for consultation and co-ordination of India-China Border affairs. And one would argue that this had largely been possible because of India's constructive approach to the Chinese question. Again on 11th February 2013, our Prime Minister Dr Manmohan Singh rightly asked the Maldivians to resolve the crisis themselves. It is again an example of Indians constructive response to domestic crises in the neighbouring state. India's role in the first ever Ministerial Conference of 49 least-developed countries may also be seen as an example of India taking a lead to project South Asian interest in world affair.

In conclusion it would be asserted that South Asian unity today is very important if the region has to take advantage of the current trade of decline of the traditional great powers. All analysts are now talking of the rise of Asia or even of Asian century. In South East Asian scenario South Asia falls to be of strategic importance. Leading American commentator Robert Kaplan had recently remarked on the importance of the Indo-Pacific and the Western Pacific and India and mainland South East Asia. The security of the nation states in this holistic context will be strengthened by constructive relationship. South Asia has the possibility of emerging as a new powerhouse. Pundit Jawaharlal Nehru's remarks in 1955 Bandung Conference is of great relevance for its future implication—"*We should not increase the feeling of dislike and hatred*." Let this seminar be conducted in the spirit which Nehru wanted Bandung Conference to be conducted in.

*Chapter 16*

# How to Meet the Security Challenges of South Asia by Democratisation and Secularism

*Pradip Bhattacharjee*
Member of Parliament, India

South Asia is a region characterised by complexity—geographically, ethnically, politically and militarily. It is constituted by a continental landmass, located between southern China and India, and one part by an archipelago dividing the Pacific Ocean and the Indian Ocean. This position acts as a bridge between two world seas and also between the continents of Asia and Oceania, which has situated the region as a point of convergence. The diversity in religion, beliefs, cultures and ethnic groups, not only portrays the characteristics of a junction but it also demonstrates the differences in regional conditions and common similarities of South Asian countries. The governments of the states of South Asia range from totalitarian, democratic, royal as well as communist regimes, which strongly add to the regional diversity.

Debates about the appropriateness of democracy for developing nations were common during the Cold War years. Now, the majority of the world's independent nations have opted for democratic forms of governance. But now the leaders in these new democracies face a serious problem. That is, how to create strong, sustainable democratic institutions that will fulfills the high hopes of their people for political freedom and opportunity.

Here the question arises, what is the relative importance of international and domestic causes in explaining the survival of domestic regimes and the more recent transitions from authoritarian regimes to democratic ones? And how the leaders of democratic states, multilateral development organisations, and non-governmental organisations support democratic transitions most effectively? In this context there will be an attempt to cover five South Asian countries—Nepal, Bangladesh, Sri Lanka, Pakistan and India to understand critical change in the region. In Nepal, an enthusiastic social movement has reigned in an autocratic monarchy and reclaimed the people's democracy. As Bangladesh moves towards elections, the trust and credibility of its institutions and democratic processes are yet to be proved. Sri Lanka has yet to resolve the role and status for its minorities and for decades has experienced violent conflict. In Pakistan, the army continues to influence national politics, which lives little room for political development and democracy. The scenario is a bit different in the case of India. India is an emerging global economic force. So, there is a daunting need to secure social and economic equity. For this reason India has successfully expanded its democratic institutions.

Democracy faces three main challenges in South Asia. It faces a foundational challenge which is the demand of establishing a democratic government that will not be undermined by authoritarian challenges. But democratic institutions sometimes fail to secure democratic environment within a state. For example, the 2013 Bangladesh election could not protect democratic trends as one of the major political party Bangladesh Nationalist Party (BNP) boycotted general election which resulted in the outbreak of violence throughout the nation. In this particular case, the leader of BNP Khaleda Zia's unrealistic approach was criticised by many political analysts, experts and scholars. Zia understood that, the political atmosphere of Bangladesh was not favourable for her party. So, may be it was her planned strategy to avoid election. But this gravely hampered the picture of democratic Bangladesh to the world.

Secondly, several countries of this region had shown their weakness to the army and non-democratic forms of government. This is one of the serious problems to establish functioning democratic institutions ensuring a functioning state in the whole territory. In many countries of the region, the laws of the state do not run to remote areas. Electoral processes are often undermined which ultimately reduces faith in democracy among masses. The third challenge is to strengthen democracy and to take it beyond institutional routines. In South Asia it is a celebration of diversity within the different societies. On the other hand, the demographic realities of South Asian region are compelling—an increasingly young population in old societies is controlled by an ageing leadership with old and traditional mindset; large scale population shifts from rural to urban areas of the country and the declining importance of land-based occupations as an importance of the global economy increases rapidly. But one should understand that, the social change must go hand in hand with political transformation. The political practice of South Asia has given rise to a new language of democracy although it has generated home grown challenges like terrorism and anarchist trends. South Asia needs to develop an alternative approach to think about democratic reforms that will respond to the promise of democracy. If it is possible to introduce the bi-party system in the states of the region, situation can be improved. The United State of America and European countries like the United Kingdom follow bi-party system and a better administration and governance is seen there. Multi-party system usually is an obstacle in the path of prompt decision making. In South Asian context, the states mostly have multi party system. Therefore, usually no party gains absolute majority after general elections. It makes formation of the government a crucial job in this region. Multi-party system opens the paths of coalition government which is one of the most remarkable features of the South Asian politics and it should be remembered that, coalition government is not capable of strong and fast decision making as tremendous political pressure lies on the government. As a result, often addressing sensitive issues becomes problem-some in these states.

For South Asia's security, democratisation in this region is very important. Only through this, political stability of this region can be assured. In contemporary world politics, democratisation is accepted and welcomed by most of the nations. In South Asia, if democratisation can reach every state, the security concern can be reduced in a more meaningful way. India and Bangladesh share their border with Myanmar, which chose the path of democratisation in the recent times. The release of the hugely popular political leader Aung San Suu Kyi is a positive sign that Myanmar is embracing the idea of democratisation more and more.

The lack of religious tolerance is another serious problem in this region. The meaning and interpretation of secularism varies within South Asian states. The countries with Muslim majorities (Pakistan and Bangladesh) give a different colour to it than the others. In the former, there is a desperate intention to equate secularism with atheism and agnosticism. It is a strategy that automatically puts those who disagree on the defense and ultimately removes the topic from the realm of reasoned debate. In South Asia, democracy based on universal-suffrage preceded the secularisation of societies that in any case lacked an indigenous push for secularism. Nowadays, secularism has become an instrumental ideal of the state. The ideals of secularism have always been important, though precarious, in South Asia. Because of its diverse population, the region has long been a sphere of conflict between several religious communities. In such circumstances it is secularism that has been eroded. But despite the weaknesses of actual practice, the understanding of secularism has been an essential part of the accepted political values of South Asia.

*Chapter 17*

# Kashmir Dispute in South Asian Security

*Aswini K Ray*
Retired Professor
Jawaharlal Nehru University
New Delhi

The Indo-Pakistan dispute on Kashmir much predates the emergence of South Asia as a distinct geopolitical concept in international relations, and consequently of SAARC as a regional entity in global diplomacy. In fact, the concept is still in search of a distinctive identity in the popular imagination within the region, which could partly explain its progeny, SAARC's lack-lustre progress so far. One problem haunting all the countries is their historical roots in the wombs of British colonial India, and with their territorial borders tied with the umbilical cord. This remains a political liability for purposes of nation-building of the sovereign states in the region, and consequently, for economic cooperation among them. Since the post-colonial territorial demarcations could not have clinically separated the diverse ethnic clusters of colonial India within their new sovereign jurisdictions, cross-border cultural vibes are predictable in this diverse multi-cultural region; and they are often perceived to be threats to national security by the regimes in these inadequately evolved nations as states, and fuels inter-state tensions. Attempts at insensitive and ham-handed repression of such manifestations by the regimes, saddled with their varying levels of democratic and governance deficits, have stoked greater regional tensions further undermining their nation-building agenda that was anyhow aborted by the global Cold War coinciding with their emergence as sovereign states. Thus, almost all the states in the region are faced with inter-state disputes of varying dimensions, affecting regional co-operation within the SAARC that could have reinforced South Asia's distinctive geopolitical identity. Not surprisingly, both South Asia as a concept and SAARC as an institution of regional cooperation within the global system have remained 'poor cousins' of most of their comparable counterparts.

Among all the inter-state disputes in the region, incubated by comparable macro-level factors mentioned above, the Indo-Pakistan dispute on Kashmir has remained the major threat to regional security, being the source of three full-scale wars, two near-wars, a prolonged proxy-war with cross-border terrorism, and now two nuclear neighbours with long-range delivery capacities as adversaries threatening global security, and possible mutual destruction. Paradoxically, the adversaries, between themselves, are also inhabited by the world's largest number of absolute poor; and one of them often described as a 'failing state' and the other as an 'emerging super power', but both afflicted by weak structure of governance, replete with corruption, violence, and un-administered areas affected by insurgency. This paradox lends greater poignancy to the dispute, and some urgency to explore possible options towards confidence-building among the two historical adversaries, and dominant powers in SAARC, to promote regional cooperation. Towards this end, history could be a useful guide.

Historically, a legacy of colonial rule, the Indo-Pakistan dispute on Kashmir began with Pakistan's unsuccessful attempts to militarily annex this Muslim-majority multi-religious 'Princely State'; followed by India's reference of the aggression to the UN Security Council after partially thwarting the Pakistani attempts, and thus creating the 'Line of Control' (LOC) that now divides the region between the Indian state of Jammu and Kashmir (including the Buddhist-majority Ladakh) and the Pakistan-occupied Kashmir. Since then, the experience of Pakistan's three unsuccessful attempts of full-scale wars, continuous proxy-wars through cross-border aid to insurgency, and terrorism, has eliminated the possibility of any military solution to the dispute, which, despite Pakistan's military alliance, the US has not endorsed either in 1965 or during the Kargil war; even during Pakistan's most opportune moment of India's war with China in 1962. President Kennedy 'persuaded' the Pakistani President to assure the Indian Prime minister of the status quo in Kashmir. At any rate the US, now faced across the world with Islamic militancy, including in the Af-Pak region, and in the present stage of its strained relations with Pakistan, is unlikely to view the militant Islamisation of the politics of Jammu and Kashmir across the 'Line of Control' with Pakistani collusion with any sympathy, as during the Cold War. The G-8 countries, including Russia and China, both faced with Islamic militancy at home, are also unlikely to view the present trend in the Islamic politics of the region with any sympathy. Even the Islamic world, now in political turmoil triggered by the 'Arab Spring' and the 'Orange Revolution' is too busy at home to be of help to Pakistan. Hence, the possibility of any resolution through the UN or third party mediation is also ruled out.

That leaves the only option for resolution through bilateral negotiations for which the situation is now conducive, globally, regionally, as also in the domestic political economy of the two countries, with both tied to the economic 'conditionality' of their globalisation agenda and faced with many comparable problems in varying degrees to learn from each other. In fact, with comparable historical inheritance of the colonial era, both now globalised, and with strategic alliance with the US, Pakistan, in its new political incarnation with an elected civilian regime, a pro-active judiciary and media appears to present a more evolved version of some of the incipient problems in India for both the neighbours to learn from each other and promote mutual cooperation; also as a potential role-model for regional cooperation. The case for some steps, howsoever small, for resolution of the dispute is quite compelling and the time is propitious.

At the political plane, despite the scars of 26/11, and the compulsions of coalition politics, the Indian Prime Minister has publicly acclaimed the Pakistani Prime Minister as 'a man of peace' and, the Pakistani Prime Minister recently in Davos lauded the Indian Prime Minister as a 'genuine person' who is keen to resolve all issues with Pakistan, including the 'core issue' of Kashmir; his party colleague, President Zardari through his 'memogate' has sought the US help to try the guilty of 26/11 and hand them over to India for punishment. Even the flamboyant Imran Khan as a leader of the emerging *Tehrik-e-Insaf*, accused of support from the Army-ISI clique, has publicly demanded the continuity of civilian rule in the country, democratic governance with judicial and media freedom, along with peaceful relations with India, complete ban on cross-border terrorism to be replaced by free flow of people and goods across the 'Line of Control' and also bilateral negotiations in a de-militarised Kashmir in both parts of the dividing line, with the Intelligence agencies of both out of bounds to help confidence-building. Interestingly, he has also demanded Pakistan's relations with the US to be modified to become less 'demeaning and survile' for Pakistan, and be 'more like India's' relations. Such public pronouncements by Pakistani leaders, including a potential political winner on the eve of elections reflect the mood of the Pakistani civil society vis-à-vis India, as distinct from the powerful military-ISI clique underwriting its many Jehadi outfits. Quite clearly, the present 'democratic' Pakistan, despite its many democratic deficits, is conducive for relative peace in Indo-Pakistan relations for possible steps towards resolving the Kashmir dispute through peaceful bilateral negotiations as mutually agreed in the Shimla Conference in 1972, but repeatedly violated by the Pakistani regimes marionetted by the Army-ISI clique by involving either third parties or exporting cross-border terrorism and Islamic jehadi insurgencies in the region.

Even within the Kashmir valley, there is some lull in jehadi terrorist violence with Omar Abdullah's National Conference leadership in firm political control of the valley articulating local grievances with the national government with a stridence reminiscent of his iconic grandfather than his populist father. He has also sent many olive branches to the departed Pandits to return to the valley with promises of security. Tourism in the valley has picked up, and the local traders are able to market their goods. These policies have partially helped in assuaging the wounded pride of a section of the valley's youth and motivate them away from the Pakistani-inspired insurgencies, and some also to the democratic mainstream, as the last peaceful local elections testified. In this context, some conclusions of a recent (2011) Government of India commissioned survey by an NGO (Institute for Research on India and International Studies) are quite revealing of the prevalent mood of the valley's youth. It rates the general political awareness of the youth as 'very high' and 'inward-looking', rooted in Kashmir and not exposed to either India or Pakistan; 67 per cent of the youth want the Kashmiri Pandits to return to the valley, despite their perceptible inclinations towards Islamic religious sermons; 67 per cent also feel corruption, misgovernance, and Human Rights violations as the main problems in the valley; 56 per cent respondents felt *'Azadi'* and a separate Kashmir as their birthright; and most significantly, 75 per cent supported peaceful political protest as the most effective form of demand articulation, and 72 per cent rejected the 'gun option' which was supported by only 24 per cent of the youth. But for the demand for Azadi is stoked by the turbulent politics of the valley in recent times, and supported by 56 per cent of its youth.

The results of the survey are unlikely to be strikingly different from the most other states of India and, arguably, Pakistan and the rest of South Asia. But the more striking part of the optimistic reality is the 75 per cent of the youth who still support 'peaceful protest' and reject the 'gun option' despite the turbulence. This opens the possibility of peaceful bilateral negotiations, including civil society interactions and 'soft power' diplomacy of cultural exchanges and trade across the border as a substitute for 'cross border terrorism' to slowly and informally transform the 'Line of Control' as the 'Line of Interaction', and the border porous enough to be inconsequential for human interactions of culturally kindred communities.

Beyond this humanisation of the border, and continuous second-track diplomacy to reduce points of tension and widen areas of cooperation—a continuing process initiated by India's Lahore Bus journey, that was aborted by Pakistan's misadventure in Kargil—any expectation of a dramatic resolution of the dispute, or reversal of long entrenched positions by either side is unrealistic. Pakistan's position based exclusively on the Muslim majority in the valley, and involving a second partition based on religion, is totally unacceptable to India's secular democratic state with a Muslim population more numerous than in Pakistan; and India's case, of the valley being an integral part of the Indian state of Jammu and Kashmir is totally unacceptable to Pakistan which still views it as the unresolved problem of the partition of the colonial era; and, a possible case of quid-pro-quo to settle score with India for its support to the secession of East Pakistan. For the Pakistani regime, Kashmir is the 'core issue' with India which views it as non-negotiable. These entrenched positions are unlikely to change in a hurry.

Thus, that the realistic option is to maintain the status-quo created by the 'Line of Control', and devise ways of transforming it as a 'Line of Interaction' to promote mutual cooperation as a role-model for regional cooperation by the two dominant members of the SAARC.

*Chapter 18*

# Beating the Security/Development Trap: Using Geography to NE's Advantage

*Aloke Sen*
Indian Foreign Service (Retired)

The close connection between security and development is explained in a paper at the Centre for Research on Inequality, Human Security and Ethnicity (CRISE) of Oxford University in the following terms:

(a) human security forms an important part of people's well-being and is, therefore, an objective of development;

(b) lack of human security has adverse consequences for growth and development; and

(c) unbalanced development is an important cause of conflict and insecurity.

In other words, lack of security hampers development, and lack of development fosters insecurity, a classic vicious cycle, of which the North East of India can be a prime example.

Let us look at the current state of play in this important region. Economic activities are very basic, with the agriculture sector stagnating, and performance of industries and services sectors grossly inadequate. There are raging insurgency problems over land distribution, immigration, ethnic identity issues, religion, political autonomy, etc. And there are three principal actors—the central government, the state governments, and the separatist groups.

Development deficiencies include connectivity and infrastructure, the lack of a proper industrial base, and all-pervasive corruption which means continual leakage of funds earmarked for specific developmental goals. Security issues include insurgency, external threats, economic crimes such as extortion and smuggling, etc.

One feeds off on the other. This is the *'trap'* I am referring to in this presentation. To understand how the environment of insecurity is impacting on development, one only has to recall the recent Manipur *'blockade'*. Lack of a proper business climate is sapping entrepreneurial confidence and leading to flight of capital, making sure that the economic base that the NE seeks remains ever elusive. Poor border point facilities translate to an inability to penetrate external markets that could have helped these states to optimise their prospects and opportunities outside the country.

In the given circumstances, the two questions are:

(i) What should be NE's first priority—security or development?

(ii) Can economic development alone solve the complex problems of the NE?

My own answers would be: (i) both, equally; and (ii) maybe not, but development can surely shrink the field of conflicts.

Security establishment and development economists are often found to hold contrary views on these questions. Faced with them, the government alternates between political pacification and jerky development initiatives, and recourse to stringent law and order measures. The Armed Forces Special Powers Act (AFSPA) is a case in point.

When it comes to assign priority to security or development, I would take a chance and vote for the latter, taking all due precaution, of course, and trusting that the benefits of development would over time douse the fire of insurgency and separatism. To trigger development activities an array of strategies can be brought into play, but in this presentation I would confine myself to only one—namely cross-border linkages. NE has to effectively connect with the outside world.

Here is a paradox. Geography, widely considered to be the villain of the piece, is actually NE's asset. The region has Bangladesh, Myanmar and China for development partners; the first two offering all-important access to the sea, and the third an economic superpower which can both help and hinder NE. The Kaladan multi-modal project through Myanmar offers two kinds of transit: one looping back to the Indian mainland and the other running outwards to South East Asian markets.

Consider a list of maladies: backwardness and poverty, weak industrial base, unresolved social problems, environmental challenges, drug trafficking and other crimes. The problems obviously are of India's NE, but were they transposed to China some years ago, they would have also described that country's Yunnan province.

In a comparable situation of under-development, China decided to lift Yunnan's fortunes by working out a poverty alleviation plan that focused on large projects to improve infrastructural facilities such as roads and power; using Yunnan's geographic location as an advantage in regional and border trade with South East Asian countries like Myanmar, Laos and Vietnam; trying to strengthen the local economic base through use of locally found natural resources; at the same time paying attention to socio-economic issues like poverty, environment, migration and drug trafficking.

China can today claim much success for its strategy for Yunnan which stands elevated to a higher plane of prosperity and purpose. Yunnan is China's deliberate instrument to penetrate South East Asian markets and boasts key infrastructural links that bring steady dividends to the local people.

I feel for NE, China's Yunnan strategy would be appropriate and worth trying. These states can deliver for India's Look East policy what Yunnan has achieved for China's South East Asia policy. But due attention would need to be first paid to the following:

(a) NE has to behave like a composite and cohesive economic whole. An analyst has aptly described the NE states, thriving on their social and cultural 'differences', as 'politically correct but economically unviable'. The pride of being 'unique' that an outsider often senses in these states would need to be surrendered when it comes to developmental matters. A regional approach rather than one focused on the well-being of individual states should work better;

(b) Synchronisation would need to be achieved between efforts being made outside and within the region. For example, for cross-border projects that may be built by India in Myanmar or Bangladesh, there would need to be matching investments and progress on India's side of the borders. Only then the domestic dividends of India's external investment/trade policy would be available to the people of NE;

(c) NE has to actively attract talent from the rest of the country—out-of-region business has to be convinced of the advantage of creating and using an operational base in the NE to reach desired external markets. Use of local resources by them would be greatly beneficial to the local economy; and

(d) An element of protectionism for a while would not be amiss, as premature throwing open of the gates to aggressive economic actors like China would only swamp and kill fledgling domestic business ventures in the region.

*Chapter 19*

# Livelihood Concerns, Migration and Trafficking: Gender and Security in South-Asia

*Saswati Ghosh*
Associate Professor, City College (North)
University of Calcutta, Kolkata

> "Trafficking of women and children must be seen in a broader context of labour migration, movement of people from conflict zones, refugees and Internally Displaced People."
> —Noeleen Heyzer
> (Executive Director, UNIFEM)

The movement of population is a topic of serious discussion among social scientists and has gained much attention of policymakers as well in recent times. Migrating in search of a better life—within a country or across national borders as an outcome of political or economic reasons—has always been undertaken by people around the world and was confined particularly to male population. Emerging research, however, indicates that a change has come around, and now women are also migrating as individuals, for paid work.

This paper would look into existing gender inequality leading to migration decisions, greater feminisation of migration, migration associated with human poverty issues and social exclusion, gender-based as well as human rights' violation in the process of migration, violation of international law in the process of migration, and the poverty-migration-trafficking nexus. The fact that rights of women migrant workers and trafficked persons are serious security concerns for both origin and destination regions or countries has been looked in to, and emphasises ensuring safe migration and fair work places at the core of all labour recruitment and deployment policies and practices initiated by any authority and hails all anti-trafficking efforts.

This paper strongly dissociates itself to any measure that takes away the right to migrate and propagate the preservation and nurturing of the right to migrate to ensure women's mobility.

## Greater Feminisation of Migration

Traditionally, the idea of migration was closely linked to male workers, as they provide major share of both work and labour force and provide for family's livelihood. But by the 1980s, women in South Asia were found to constitute, on an average, about 35 per cent of the labour force in the region, though the distribution across countries differed and a growing part were migrant workers (UNDP HDR, 1995). Up to the 1990s, female migration in South Asia was a family decision, mostly for marriage and not necessarily linked to employment, as was the case for men. Data from India's 1991 census show that the reason cited for migration by 77 per cent of female migrants was marriage, while 60 per cent of men cited employment as their reason, though no single 'South Asian' pattern of labour migration has emerged. (Srivastava and Sasikumar (2003), Srivastava and Hussain (2008))

Migration experience indicates that factors that had prompted some people to migrate while others stayed home—so identifying such factors has become important to both social scientists and policy makers. Traditional economic theories focus on opportunities, on the push and pull factors which force or entice people to migrate. Labour migration came up as an integral part of the process of economic development (Lewis, 1954; Todaro, 1976), the mainstay of Neoclassical Economics at the macro level. Correspondingly, the neo-classical economics theory at micro level (Todaro, 1989) puts the onus on the individual actors, presumed to be rational agents, to migrate as the inherent cost-benefit calculation leads agents to expect a positive net return, usually in monetary terms, from such movement. People choose to move to where they can be the most productive, given their skills. The 'New economics of migration theory', which was developed as challenge to many assumptions and conclusions of the neoclassical theory (Stark and Bloom, 1985) asserts, migration decisions are not made by isolated individual agents but by larger units of related people—typically families or households—only to maximise expected income and also to minimise risks. Gradually, came up the 'dual labour market' theory which goes beyond individuals or households, but emphasises the intrinsic influence and control of markets. (M Piore, 1972; P Doeringer and M Piore, 1972)

**Who are the mobile populations?**

- Construction workers, factory workers, miners
  - Domestic workers
  - Agricultural labourers
- Military, para-military, uniformed personnel
  - Transport sector workers
  - Sex workers/Prostitutes
  - Students, tourists
  - Refugees, etc.

Though economic factors are always important, they are not the only determining factors in the decision to migrate. These economic theories have conspicuously failed to consider psychological, social and political motivations, religious persecution, natural calamities and conflict as source of migration. That migration may not be a conscious choice, but an outcome of misinformation is also absent in these theories, which have made them questioned in real life. Migrant networks are also very important determinant, as these networks provide sets of interpersonal ties that connect migrants, former migrants and non-migrants in the regions or countries of origin through kinship, friendship and shared community origin. So there are many economic, social and physical reasons why people emigrate, and they can usually be classified into push and pull factors. Push factors are those associated with the area of origin, while pull factors are those that are associated with the area of destination. The dominant motive for migration is economic, and pull factors tend to be higher wages and greater demand for labour perhaps found in centres of industry and commerce. Economic push factors can include overpopulation and the absence of economic opportunity. Social and physical reasons tend to involve forced migration, and an example of a social push factor would be intolerance towards a certain religious or cultural group. An example of a physical push factor would be a natural disaster.

## Livelihood-Poverty-Migration

The 1997 Human Development Report offered us a broader understanding of poverty from just income poverty:

> "Poverty can mean more than a lack of what is necessary for material well-being. It can also mean the denial of opportunities and choices most basic to human development—to lead a long, healthy, creative life and to enjoy a decent standard of living, freedom, dignity, self-esteem and the respect of others.... Poverty must be addressed in all its dimensions, not income alone."

As already discussed, there may be a host of push and pull factors in migration decision, poverty being the most important one in a developing country like India. Failure of rain in rainfed agriculture, low agricultural productivity, rural indebtedness, landlessness, death of the earning member, sudden illness in the family—any single factor or a combination of them can onset a process of displacement from native places. Large scale urbanisation and emerging trend of industrial-based employment has created economic incentives for migration and resulted in an approximately three-fold increase in population mobility in the last half century. With increasing pressure on land, resulting from over-population, large number of the rural unemployed people move to cities or other rural areas in search of seasonal or permanent employment. While there is a rising middle class, figures indicate that 30 per cent of all urban residents still live below the poverty line, the majority of whom are migrants who live in urban slums.

Increased demand for migrant labour and economic opportunities that have traditionally led men to migrate within their national borders in search of work has grown stronger over time and expanded to include women. The same incentive, fueled by globalisation and liberalisation of trade, has increased the external migration of low skilled labourers across most of the region over the past 15 years. On the one hand, it is leading to transformation of rural-based livelihoods like farming, fishing and all other agriculture-based livelihood activities in such a way that has taken away many jobs, on the other hand, it has flooded the market with consumer goods and marketing strategies which increase demands on individuals and societies.

Livelihoods in the rural areas of the South Asian countries continue to depend largely on agriculture, which is primarily rain-fed in most places. A study by WOREC (Asia Foundation et al, 2001) for prevention of trafficking in Nepal found that, for the majority of families studied, migration was clearly linked to landlessness or near landlessness. That study has shown that among the families from the Terai region with at least one migrating member, 61 per cent had only up to 1 bigha of land (a marginal holding, incapable of providing year-long food) and 17 per cent were landless, where majority claimed their primary livelihood being rainfed agriculture. Natural calamity adds to that shock. In Bangladesh, 80 per cent of the total population of 140 million live in rural areas, the poverty situation is aggravated by frequent floods, cyclones and droughts. Agricultural production is often below subsistence which leads to seasonal and long term borrowing for consumption and production (Vidya Shah et al 2002).

Agriculture is so far the biggest employer for women. An estimated 68.5 per cent of women work in farming, or around

77 million women. The majority of them are involved in crop farming, while the rest rear livestock. While male farmers may outnumber female, a far higher percentage of women work in farming than men. Only 46.6 per cent of Indian male workers are employed in farming.
(http://censusindia.gov.in/Census_And_You/economic_activity.aspx)

The intersections between trafficking and labour can be linked with an increased demand for migrant labour—cheap, exploitable workers; enhanced by a lack of regulation around informal labour sites and lack of monitoring sites of bonded labour; lack of monitoring of child labour; lack of regulating labour recruitment practices; lack of mechanism for enforcing labour standards and recruitment practices and an absence of anti-trafficking partnerships with unions, employers and those lobbying for labour rights—all contribute to worker vulnerability. States often were trying to control migration of young women but there is very little work to actually control the regulation of agencies which are operating. In India, restrictive migration policies force people to travel through irregular means. Girls under the age of 18 are not allowed to travel to other countries for work.

This impact is felt most by the women. For example, mechanisation of agriculture, fisheries and many other farming activities has reduced the demand for certain types of labour performed by women, particularly those who were traditionally engaged in harvesting and processing works. Simultaneously, the entrance of large corporate interests into industry and structural shifts away from production for local markets to production for international export has led to growing rural poverty and unemployment, which in turn put increased pressure on rural communities to move beyond their immediate locations in search of income. Many such factors lead to such aggravated conditions of poverty that women are pushed from their lives of subsistence into outright destitution, which prompts them to migrate in search of survival. The UN Special Rapporteur on Violence

Against Women, Radhika Coomaraswamy has observed that the state failed to protect and promote women's human, economic and social rights and this absence has created a situation in which trafficking flourishes, trafficking further subjects women to numerous additional human rights violations. (Position Paper on the Draft SAARC Convention on Preventing and Combatting Trafficking in Women and Children for Prostitution: UN Special Rapporteur on Violence Against Women, cited in Shah 2002.)

## Women: Discrimination Leads to Trafficking

Women in South Asia constitute the poorest of the poor as a result of gender insensitivity, discrimination, lack of social status and of basic rights, together with grueling domestic roles and responsibilities. These factors reduce their access to resources, education, training and labour markets. The Gender Empowerment Measure (GEM) for South Asian women is 0.23—the lowest value amongst all regions in the world. (UNDP, HDR 2012) Preferential treatment for boys in this region is reflected in selective education enrolment and school dropout patterns. A study from Nepal shows that nearly 30 per cent of illiterate girls felt that they were powerless and could do little to change this situation. (UNICEF, 2001) In this context of discrimination, lack of choice and vulnerability, increasing numbers of young women and girls, many of whom are between the ages of 10 and 20, are being trafficked in the region, mainly for the sex industry.

The significant increase in the phenomenon of human trafficking over the past decade, both globally and in the South Asian countries is an admitted fact but it is exceedingly difficult to establish accurate figures about the number or figures about the women trafficked because of its illegal and clandestine nature. Globalization, the professionalization of traffickers, syndicates and the extension of modern transportation, as well as sex tourism, the feminisation of poverty and the changing nature of prostitution, have all worked towards increased demand for, and supply of, bonded or unfree labour especially that of young women. (Shah, 2002)

Prostitution is not the only reason for trafficking in women. Many are trafficked into domestic labour, agricultural and factory work, begging, and other circumstances where they are also vulnerable to sexual and physical exploitation and abuse. The majority of trafficked women, however, find themselves in brothels where they have little or no control over their bodies and lives. Many are physically locked into the brothels in poor living conditions, facing daily violence, with little or no access to health care. Coercion, an alien environment, fear of deportation and other psychological factors keep them away from seeking any kind of help.

## Trafficking in Women and Girls

Existing studies and information provide only a partial stature of the extent and magnitude of trafficking in the region. While governments and civil society organisations are increasingly making efforts to collect data, there are often discrepancies in the numbers resulting from the hidden nature of trafficking itself. As the 'Position Paper on SAARC Trafficking' (www.twnside.org.sg/title2/women/1999/e.equity/TWR110-111p62.doc) suggests that information is becoming gradually available about the geographic patterns of trafficking in the region, with points of origin, transit and destination of internal and trans-border trafficking.

Migrant workers have also been referred to as irregular, undocumented, illegal, trafficked workers or population. The terms migration, trafficking and smuggling often overlap, so they should be made clear in the outset:

- *Migration* is a movement from one place to another (legal or illegal);
- *Smuggling* is when one is moved illegally by a third party across borders for profit;
- *Trafficking* is when one is *moved* and *exploited* by a third party. In the case of adults, via deceptive or coercive means. Trafficking can be legal or illegal movement, within or across borders.

International Labour Organisation (ILO) has provided a clear definition of trafficking lest it be confused with regular migration and people smuggling. Once there is coercion, force or exploitation, migration turns into trafficking. The following description from an ILO publication will contrast the nuances of people smuggling and trafficking:

> "In practice, it is not always easy to differentiate between people smuggling and trafficking, because 'voluntary' agreement may be a result of deception, or may involve an individual or family entering into debt to pay for the travel, debt that puts them at the mercy of the lender. It may result in physical confinement when the human cargo is locked into a vehicle or into a sending or reception centre." (International Labour Organisation, 2003)

There are various forms of trafficking, though country to country variation becomes important. It may be forced or bonded labour; which can be male adults or female adults; or it can be for domestic work and/or Commercial Sex Worker with kids or a cross-over between labour and Commercial Sex Worker. Labour may also include conscription like child soldiers, as girl children were claimed to constitute even up to 40 per cent in Sri Lanka with the LTTE and they may, again, also be exploited sexually

A 'Good Practice' and serious effort on the part of the government can be cited from Indonesia with its 'National Action Plan for Abolishing Women and Child Trafficking' which was endorsed through Presidential Decree no 88/2002, on December 30, 2002. It put succinctly:

- Trafficking will include: by using threats, verbal and physical abuse, abduction, fraud, deception, misuse of vulnerability (eg if someone has no alternative, is isolated, is addicted to drugs, trapped in debt),
- giving or receiving payments or profits in cases in which a person is used for prostitution and sexual exploitation (including paedophilia),
- legal or illegal migrant workers, child adoptions, fishing

platform work, mail order brides, domestic helpers, begging, pornography,

- drug dealing, selling of body organs as well as other forms of exploitation.

Any such document and subsequent action taken reports are yet to emerge from any other country.

## Numbers? Not Known!

As already mentioned, due to its illegal and clandestine nature, it's difficult to calculate the exact number of migrants as well as those who have been trafficked. Here is a glimpse of the claimed numbers from various sources. (STOP-India 2001, Maiti Nepal-Nepal, NNGAT-Nepal cited in SARIQ, Shah 2002)

- **Migration:**
  - India: 6.3 million people migrate for employment. UP and Bihar alone account for 41.5 per cent of total migration.
  - Bangladesh: 2,00,000 foreign employment second source of foreign earnings, after garment.
  - Pakistan: 3 million remittances equivalent to 44 per cent of total merchandise exports (1993).
  - Sri Lanka: 7,80,000 remittances highest foreign exchange earning source.
- **Trafficking:**
  - 2,00,000 persons trafficked annually are from South Asia.
  - 15,000 women and children are trafficked from Bangladesh annually.
  - 5,000-7,000 Nepali girls are trafficked to India annually.

  4,50,000 trafficked annually from Asia-Pacific: about half from South Asia (STOP, 2001 cited in SARIQ)

Despite the variations in data there is an overriding composite picture of an increase in trafficking, indications that trafficking from new areas and from population groups not previously involved in prostitution. Figures also suggest a growth in demand for increasingly younger girls.

The figures below give an indication of the level of trafficking in the region:

- Between 5,000 and 10,000 girls and women are trafficked to India every year from Nepal (STOP-India, Maiti Nepal-Nepal, NNGAT-Nepal, cited in Hageboeck et al, undated), ie at least 50,000 over the last ten years.
- During the last ten years, it is estimated that over 30,000 women and girls have been trafficked from Bangladesh to India; and this is continuing at a rate of 200-400 women monthly. (STOP, 2001, cited in Hageboeck undated)

Studies from Odisha and Bangladesh have indicated a sharp increase in trafficking after natural calamities. For example, the trafficking of girls from Nayagarh, Odisha increased after the cyclone of 1999 and subsequent floods in coastal Odisha, with 15-20 girls being trafficked from the cyclone-hit areas to Jhansi, Madhya Pradesh on the pretext of marriage. Same experience has been recorded after cyclone Aila and trafficking from South 24 Parganas in West Bengal (cited in Hageboeck, undated).

## Trafficking and Sex Trade

Those who get trafficked for sexual purposes constitute the largest share and they rarely come out of choice. Again, the data is limited and difficult to ascertain. Research, though based on sample survey have shown that of the sample of 495 trafficked women from Bombay brothels who have come from both India and Nepal (N=495), 51 per cent were under the age of 18 and 15 per cent under age 15. About half of them (56 per cent) have been recruited via economic lures; 17 per cent kidnapped via drugs; 9 per cent abducted via force; 46 per cent trafficked by strangers; 29-40 per cent by acquaintances; 9-16 per cent by family members and those who have come voluntarily, 49 per cent provided family disruption as proximal context (38 per cent family violence). (Silverman et al, 2007)

Those who are forced to join the sex trade are usually forced to go through mostly 'unnatural and painful' sex that their clients cannot get from their partners. Further research show that the Recent Risk/Violence faced by the Commercial Sex Workers entering as Adolescents in Mumbai brothels in 2010 (Silverman, 2011):

Unprotected sex in the past 90 days—36 per cent (if adolescent) vs. 22 per cent (among entering at 18 years or older)

Anal sex in past 7 days—8 per cent vs. 3 per cent

Sex after client condom refusal in past 7 days—10 per cent vs. 5 per cent

Violence in past 7 days—52 per cent vs. 34 per cent

It's a long-standing debate whether prostitution is exclusively a form of exploitation or there is a question of choice involved in it. The present contributor holds it to be exploitation as no real choice exists in an patriarchal unequal power relation. However, the question of choice has been promoted by none other than the ILO, through a highly debated report named "The Sex Sector: The Economic and Social Bases of Prostitution in Southeast Asia". The report, released in 1998, based on research of the 'sex' industries in Malaysia, Indonesia, Thailand, and the Philippines, the ILO gave an overall favourable review of the business of sex: It called for prostitution and sex industries to be officially recognised as a legitimate economic sector because they are already "integrated into the economic, social and political life" of countries and "contribute in no small measure to employment, national income, and economic growth."

But the expansion of the so-called 'sex industry', 'sex tourism' has forced others to raise the question of trafficking and migrant workers' rights. This leads to the security concerns for the migrant woman labour, who may unwittingly become trafficked.

## Why Trafficking is a Security Concern

Receiver countries usually adopt a legalistic immigration approach, and this gives little consideration to the fact that the woman trafficked is a victim. The rights of the trafficked woman or child simply gets lost in this process, and it does not matter whether the person has been trafficked for prostitution or forced labour; there is not much sympathy for the victim and it is generally left to NGOs to try to sort out the resulting disaster for the women concerned. (Denis Wright, 2008)

Trafficking of women and children raises a security concern from three sides:

- They migrate due to inadequate livelihood options in their country of origin.
- The women and children are not safe while migrating.
- They, due to their mobility, can be perceived as potential security risks for the host country, so the denial of rights at per with the citizens is perceived legitimate.

Mobility and entry into the work force have brought benefits to many of these women and their families, narrowing the gender gap in many spheres including social prestige, control over income and decision making. At the same time, socialisation and the education of women and girls, especially in traditional societies, do not prepare them adequately for the experience of migration. In comparison with men of the region, women have even less access to information, are hardly exposed to the outside world, and often lack the confidence and independence required to negotiate and make decisions. These factors heighten their vulnerability, as do the uncertainties and irregularities they encounter when trying to find work (Shah et al, 2002). This violation of human rights needs urgent intervention to make the migration safe.

## Safe Migration: Law, Good Practices

Population movement and migration must be looked into from a

Human Rights perspective which asserts:

> "Violations of human rights are both a cause and a consequence of trafficking in persons. Accordingly, it is essential to place the protection of all human rights at the centre of any measures taken to prevent and end trafficking." (OHCHR, Recommended Principles and Guidelines on Human Rights and Human Trafficking, 2002)

Migration is a complex continuum having various domestic and external dimensions along which voluntary migration may become involuntary and legal migration may become illegal. The following box shows the continuum, where the left portion show how the migration can become and remain a free one, while as we move to the right, it gradually become perilous and unfree.

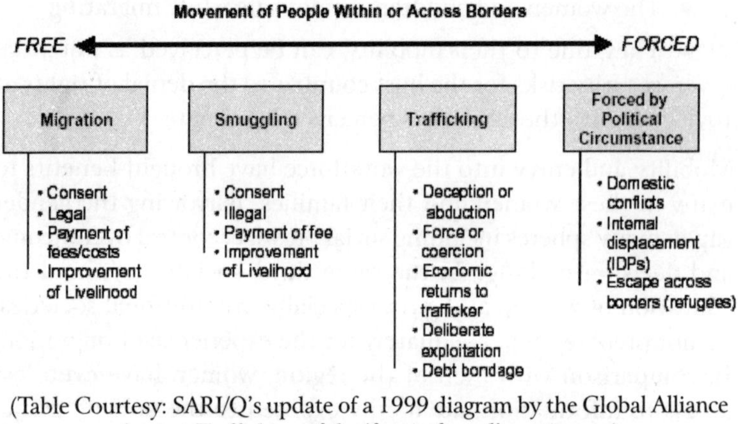


(Table Courtesy: SARI/Q's update of a 1999 diagram by the Global Alliance Against Trafficking of the 'free to forced' continuum)

The risks associated with migration are high, particularly for low skilled individuals, both male and female. The vulnerabilities can be divided into three stages:

(Diagram Courtesy: SARI/Q)

At the preparatory stage, the risks include deceptions by unauthorised agents that transform would-be legal migrants into illegal migrants or trafficked victims at the point of destination. Equally important are the problems that could make a legal migrant's experience in the destination country a nightmare. The range of unacceptable outcomes at a migrant's destination, whether she or he is legal or illegal, include the confiscation of passport and restricted movement; long hours and poor working conditions; verbal, physical and sexual abuse; contracting HIV/AIDS and, at the extreme, death at the hands of traffickers in human organs. The critical issue is to ensure safe mobility, particularly for women, so that their rights and security can be protected at points of origin, transition and destination. While laws and policies can provide a framework for empowerment and protection of rights, their implementation can be limited without the acceptance and active involvement of the people themselves. Activities are now being directed towards facilitating safe movement. Migration information centres have been set up to provide information on safe passage, in order to prevent migrating women and girls from falling prey to abusive and exploitative practices.

Safe-migration model developed by Jabala Action Research Organisation included by UNODOC as a good practice.

Jabala's Safe Migration Project gets panchayats in West Bengal to keep track of women who migrate into urban areas, providing a safety net for women who get trapped into sex work or slave labour.

Jabala Action Research Organisation, a Kolkata-based civil society organisation (CSO) has embarked on a Safe Migration Project with the help of gram panchayats, to prevent the exploitation of young girls and women who migrate from rural areas to metropolitan cities and major towns in search of work.

Formally launched a year ago, the Safe Migration Project operates in 13 blocks (including Jalangi, Hariharpada and Beldanga) in Murshidabad district, Joynagar and Kakdwip blocks and Bhutiarisharif panchayat in South 24 Parganas, Bashirhat I, Gaighata and Swarupnagar blocks in North 24 Parganas and Kaliganj block in Nadia district of West Bengal.

A natural corollary to a UNICEF-sponsored module developed by Jabala in 1998, which sought to rope in local self-governing bodies in rural areas to stem the flow of women into red-light areas, the Safe Migration Project uses tracking booths in the blocks to keep track of women who migrate into urban areas across the country, or across the Indo-Bangladesh international border in search of employment as domestic or factory workers.

The project, in its pilot stage, restored 47 girls to their families. Of these, 15 were rescued from Delhi, two from Mumbai, and 30 from in and around Kolkata and West Bengal.

Some of these women had found their way into brothels, while many had been sexually abused as domestics in the homes they were employed in. Once the girls got in touch with the local police and lodged their complaints, minor girls were taken charge of by the respective child welfare committee in the areas they were in. From thereon, the cards they were carrying helped Jabala and its partner CSO restore them, through the local panchayat, to their families. Where majors were concerned, the police worked through their counterparts in West Bengal and Jabala to restore the women to their families.

Plans are afoot to extend Jabala's operations to Lucknow, Pune and other cities.

(Rina Mukherji, Info Change News & Features, December 2006)

Safe migration is both a question of programmes, and of policy. We need to raise the question how have anti-trafficking laws impacted migration? Remittances through migrant workers turn out to be an important source of foreign exchange for the host countries but these are only tracked and published by Sri Lanka and Bangladesh. However, these figures do not seem to impact on the migration-related policies of these governments. Whereas Sri Lanka has a pro-migration policy with extra emphasis and safeguards for the safe migration of domestic workers, both Bangladesh and Nepal ban the migration of women as domestic workers. (Molly Hageboeck/SARIQ) In India, trafficking is associated with sex work so when women travel or migrate, people assume that women are migrating for sex work. Women are then placed under India's ITPA or anti-trafficking prevention act. India's policy is neutral, but on a case-by-case basis it retains control through the issuance of certificates for external travel. (Molly Hageboeck/SARIQ)

As the SARIQ programme experience sums it up: migrant women workers' rights can be ensured with a three-prong approach:

- Safe Migration—the perils migrants face today and solution strategies;
- Laws and their effective implementation—as deterrents to both trafficking and the kinds of domestic violence against women that can drive them into the hands of traffickers, and
- Caring for victims—ensures that they receive appropriate protection, whether as survivors of violence, witnesses in criminal cases, or both, and helping them rebuild their lives.

Victims'/Survivors' Rights have been clearly identified in the UN Convention on Justice and Support for Victims of Crime and Abuse of Power and International Convention on the Protection of all migrant workers and members of their families (2003). Though very few countries have ratified it, these are a truly rights based Convention; it covers the entire migration process; it gives the right to live and enter the country of origin; the right to be free from torture, inhuman and degrading treatment; the right not to be held in slave-like conditions; and is applicable to all migrant workers without any discrimination.

Important migrant rights in any country must include but would not stop at accepting the dignity of labour, right to employment, right to safe employment/working conditions; migrants' rights protection in the destination country and from the recruitment agency; right to collective bargaining, freedom to join a trade union; making labour contractors/recruitment agencies more accountable and enforce penalties; enhancing transparency of migration policy; free flow of information about migration (structure of placement fee, visa application) should be granted to all people, and in language that everybody can understand; MoU between sending country and receiving country like the one between Cambodia and Thailand mentioned below; reproductive rights for migrants in destination countries and right to job mobility and direct hiring, without requiring intermediaries such as recruitment agencies. These are the basic minimums for protecting the rights of the migrant worker and ensuring basic human rights.

Cambodia-Thai MoU on Trafficking can be placed a 'good practice', replicable in clearly identifiable other areas (www.no-trafficking.org/content/pdf/thai_cambodia_bilateral_mou.doc):

- Trafficked children and women shall be considered victims, and not violators and offenders of the Immigration Law.
- Trafficked children and women shall not be prosecuted for illegal entry to the country.
- Trafficked children and women shall not be detained in immigration detention centers during the time awaiting the official repatriation process…shelter and protection shall be provided to the victims according to the policy of each state.
- The relevant authorities shall ensure the security of trafficked children and women, victims shall be treated humanely throughout the process of protection, repatriation, and the judicial proceedings.

Can we have a similar MoU between India-Nepal-Bangladesh to reduce the vulnerability of women and girls, and ensure their basic human rights?

[Grateful to Baitali Ganguly, Secretary Jabala Action Research Organisation for allowing me to work with Jabala as a close associate, however, the inferences and conclusions are mine.]

## References

Hageboeck Molly, Manish Subharwal and Deepika Naruka Review of Issues and South Asian Initiatives on Safe Migration, Rule of Law (Trafficking and Violence Against Women) and the Care of Victims; South Asia Regional Initiative / Equity Support Programme (SARIQ) (Undated). http://www.academia.edu/1646841/Review_of_Issues_and_South_Asian_Initiatives_on_Safe_Migration_Rule_of_Law_Trafficking_and_Violence_Against_Women_and_the_Care_of_Victims

Indonesia: The National Plan of Action (2002): http://www.solidaritycenter.org/files/IndoTraffickingPlan%20of%20Action.pdf

International Labour Organisation (2003): Trafficking in Human Beings: New Approaches to Combating the Problem, Special Action Programme to Combat Forced Labour, May

Lewis, W Arthur (1954): Economic Development with Unlimited Supplies of Labour, Manchester School, Volume 22, Issue 2, pages 139-191, May 1954

M Piore, "Notes for Theory of Labor Market Stratification," Working Paper No 95, Dept of Econ, Mass Institute of Technology, Oct 1972.

Office of the High Commissioner for Human Rights (2002): Recommended Principles and Guidelines on Human Rights and Human Trafficking http:/ /www.ohchr.org/Documents/Publications/Traffickingen.pdf

P Doeringer and M Piore, Internal Labor Markets and Manpower Analysis, Lexington, Mass. 1972

Sarkar, Jyoti Parimal ( 2010): Bangladeshi Migration To West Bengal: A Cause of Concern http://www.scribd.com/doc/93086910/BANGLADESHI-MIGRATION-TO-WEST-BENGAL

Sasikumar, SK and Zakir Hussain (2008): Managing international labour migration from India: Policies and perspectives. October http://www.ilo.org/wcmsp5/groups/public/—asia/—ro-bangkok/—sro-new_delhi/documents/publication/wcms_123412.pdf

Shah, Vidya Beverly Brar and Sonam Yangchen Rana (2002) Layers of Silence: Links between women's vulnerability, trafficking and HIV/AIDS in Bangladesh, India and Nepal Draft paper prepared for the UNRISD project HIV/AIDS and Development March http://www.maitinepal.org/admin/uploaded/1383371891.pdf

Silverman JG, Decker MR, Gupta J, Maheshwari A, Patel V, Willis BM, Raj A (2007): Experiences of sex trafficking victims in Mumbai, India; International Journal of Gynaecology and Obstetrics, June; 97(3):221-6. E pub 2007 Feb 22

Silverman JG, Raj A, Cheng DM, Decker MR, Coleman S, Bridden C, Pardeshi M, Saggurti N, Samet JH (2011): Sex trafficking and initiation-related violence, alcohol use, and HIV risk among HIV-infected female sex workers in Mumbai, India: Journal of Infective Diseases, Dec 1;204 Suppl 5:S1229-34.

South Asia Regional Initiative/Equity Support Programme (SARIQ) (Undated) Prevention of Trafficking and Protection of Victims of Violence: Replicable Approaches—A Guide

Srivastava, Ravi and SK Sasikumar (2003): An Overview Of Migration In India, Its Impacts And Key Issues 22-24 June http://www.eldis.org/vfile/upload/1/document/0903/Dhaka_CP_2.pdf

Stark, O, and D Bloom (1985): "The new economics of labor migration", American Economic Review, 75: 173-178

The Asia Foundation and Horizons Project Population Council (2001): Prevention of Trafficking and the Care and Support of Trafficked Persons In the Context of an Emerging HIV/AIDS Epidemic in Nepal http://www.popcouncil.org/uploads/pdfs/horizons/trafficking1.pdf

Todaro, Michael P 1976, Urban Job Expansion, Induced Migration and Rising Unemployment: A formulation and Simplified Empirical Test for LDCs, Journal of Development Economics, 3: 211-225.

Todaro, Michael P, *Economic Development in the Third World*, Longman (New York), 1989.

Towards a SAARC Convention against trafficking in women and children (1999): Third World Resurgence No 110/111, October/November

United Nations Development Programme (1997): Human Development to Eradicate Poverty Technical Report. UNDP, New York.

Wright, Denis (2008): Forced Labour, Trafficking and Migration of Women in South Asia; UNEAC Asia Papers No 24.

*Chapter 20*

# Environmental Security and India: Global, Regional and National Dimensions

*Satabdi Das*
Assistant Professor
South Calcutta Girls' College
University of Calcutta, Kolkata

Traditionally the notion of security implies minimising the military and political threats directed towards national sovereignty. But in the post-Cold War period the notion of non-traditional security issues comes into prominence. Climate change is one of such issues which leads to redefine the concept of national security. The increased use of natural resources and their degradation, excessive industrial activities and increased use of fossil fuels have resulted in the accumulation of Greenhouse gases in the atmosphere which ultimately leads to climate change. Such effects are transboundary in nature; therefore, they have the potential to spur conflict among nations. When climates change significantly for which necessary resources like crop-lands, forests and water supply are not properly available to many, societies may become stressed, sometimes to the point of collapse. To quote Thomas Homer Dixon: "Unlike non-renewable resources such as oil and iron ore, renewables are replenished over time by natural processes.... Unfortunately in the majority of regions where people are highly dependent on renewable resources, they are being depleted or degraded faster than they are being renewed. From Gaza to the Philippines to Honduras, the evidence is stark: aquifers are being overdrawn and salinised, coastal fisheries are disappearing, and steep uplands have been stripped of their forests leaving their thin soils to erode into the sea."[1] Thus some major areas can be identified where environmental degradation and climate change have the potential to cause critical negative developments like the reduction of arable lands, impairment of food production, scarcity of water resources and the increase in extreme weather events. As an indirect result to these developments climate change induced migration may increase in some of the vulnerable regions of the world. Against such a backdrop it is essential to analyse these events as to whether these can trigger or amplify violence and social unrest.

Since the Stockholm Conference, the concern for environmental security has grown rapidly and its growing significance was evident in other major environmental conferences and symposia. As a result, various conventions and landmark protocols related to environmental protection came into prominence, like the Convention on Biological Diversity, the Framework Convention on Climate Change and the Kyoto Protocol. The Brundtland Report (1987) which is named Our Common Future' also asserts the responsibility of environmental degradation and climate change behind the conflictual relationship between and among nation-states: "Environmental stress is both a cause and effect of political tension and military conflict...nations have fought to assist or resist control over raw materials, energy supplies, land, river basin, sea passages and other key environmental resources. According to the report such conflicts are likely to increase as these resources became scarcer and competetion for them will increase."[2]

Against this backdrop in India the green dimension of politics has also emerged as a significant policy concern both at national and international level. In India the burgeoning population has created a pressure on the natural resource base, as a vast majority of them depends on climate-sensitive sectors like agriculture, forestry, and fishery for their livelihood. As a result climate change may intensify interstate and intrastate competition over natural resources, making resource conflicts more likely.

The adverse impact of climate change in the form of declining rainfall and rising temperatures, and thus, increased severity of drought and flood, is bound to threaten food security and livelihoods in the economy. Moreover, diversification of land into non-agricultural purposes and non-food crops may also exacerbate the situation thereby leading to large scale displacement, and cross-border migration with profound debilitating impacts on the economy and society. Food production is also directly threatened by water scarcity as rainfed production and irrigated farming consider water as the key factor for food security. As a result groundwater depletion has emerged as a major concern in India. Moreover the awefully limited adaptation measures and poor water management system may harbour potential for conflicts over water as well as destabilisation among communities. When water resources are widely shared between two or more nation-states or between two states of the same country the problem becomes more accute with political implications. Water sharing problems between India and Pakistan, India and bangladesh and between China and India are potential sources of discords. The problem has further been augmented by higher frequency of extreme weather events and a rise in ocean levels which are likely to result in greater interstate and intrastate migration—especially of the poor and the vulnerable—from the delta and coastal regions to the hinterlands.Thus India could face refugee influx from Bangladesh that may threat internal and regional security. Even within India, climate refugee influxes take place due to cyclones, floods and other calamitious situations which are potential enough to undermine social stability and internal cohesion.

The impact of climate change could also hinder India's development and delay progress in economic growth. If India has to reduce its carbon emissions, it would mean a major reorientation of her energy strategy. With the threat of climate change India is called upon to change her energy strategy based on coal and to use other energy sources instead, which may turn out to be expensive. As a result the question of energy security comes to the scene. So India's concern in any international treaty on climate change should take into account her economic development route also. Because, economic vulnerability and resource dependency of the developing South over developed North may lead to inequity in the sphere of burden sharing. Climate change impacts may fuel the politics of resentment between those having historical responsibilities for climate change and those most affected by it. Against this background, to consider the security implications of climate change India needs to frame the concept of security more broadly and redefine its defense planning and preparedness accordingly. Our systems for environmental management are basically national. But the consequences of climate change do not respect border. As a result border controls are not possible options for managing transboundary pollution or impact of carbon emissions. Furthermore, as national security is no longer about fighting forces and weaponry alone and it relates increasingly to watersheds, forests, soil cover, croplands, genetic resources, climate and other factors, military experts and political leaders of our country should consider them as equally crucial to the country's security as military prowess. In various Conferences of Parties cooperation among nations is proved vitally important. India in these conferences, specially ranging from Copenhagen to Durban, while emphasising the need to combat climate change, tried hard to protect her national interest vis-a-vis global concerns as well. Against this background, to deal with the national security implications of adverse climatic conditions, India needs to establish greater state capacity at all levels—federal, provincial and local for mitigation or adaptation or to devise strategies to reap benefits from the both. The National Action Plan on Climate Change in India is an initiative in the right direction as it provides a blueprint for changes at the national level in policy, planning, and public-private partnerships, and lays out a global vision for modifying longer time trends for sustainable development. So to address environmental challenge to national security calculas, India's climate policies can be more effective if consistently embeded within broader strategies designed to make national and regional development paths more sustainable. Action on climate change must not sharpen the division of the world between Northern countries and an impoverished South. Indian diplomatic stand should be shaped in a manner which ensures that the country is not saddled with unfair obligations that compound its challenges. However the trans-boundary nature of global environmental problems suggests that cooperation and not competition, between states, represents the best strategy for addressing these concerns effectively. Therefore, responding to environmental problems through prompt collective action could be an important means to generate trust and goodwill among disputing states. South Asian region is not an exception in this regard as mitigation and adaptation co-benefits can be achieved through regional cooperation. For example, here the nations have different energy resource endowments like coal in India, gas in Bangladesh, hydro potential in the himalayan nations of Bhutan and Nepal as well as strategic location of Pakistan for the transit routes linking South Asia with the vast gas and oil resources of Central Asia and the Middle East[3] which may help in taking care of diverse contingencies of climate change induced security paradigm. However, what we require is a collaborative spirit which acknowledges the pervasive threat of climate change to humanity and seeks to find answers that enhance, and not diminish the prospects of development particularly of developing countries.

## References

1. Thomas F Homer Dixon, "Environmental Scarcity and Mass Violence", *Current History*, Vol 95, No 604, November 1996, p 360.
2. World commission on Enviroment and Development, "Our Common Future", Brundtland Report, Oxford University Press, London, Newyork, 1987, p 290.
3. PR Shukla, "India's GHG Emission Scenarios: Aligning Development and Stabilization Paths", *Current Science*, Vol 90, No 30, 10 February 2006, p 392.

*Chapter 21*

# Security Perspectives of Pakistan and Afghanistan: Looking Through the Lens

*Shankhamala Ray*
Research Scholar
Department of International Relations
Jadavpur University, Kolkata
Journalist, ABP Group, Kolkata

In her book *I Am Malala: The Girl Who Stood Up for Education and was Shot by the Taliban* (Little Brown and Company, 2013), Malala Yusafzai wrote: "When we decorated our hands with henna for holidays and weddings, we drew calculus and chemical formulae instead of flowers and butterflies."

In one of her paintings, Malina Suliman depicted a country encircled by brown mountains and pile of books wrapped with brown papers. Some of the books are flying like birds. They have spread their brown wings to fly beyond the shackles of the mountains. (http://uk.reuters.com/article)

Malala and Malina, these two individuals from Pakistan and Afghanistan respectively, gained a good amount of international media attention last year. Pakistani school student and education activist Malala was shot in the head and neck in an assassination attempt by Taliban gunmen. She remained in critical condition for some days but later she was sent to a hospital in the United Kingdom for intensive rehabilitation. On the other hand, 23 years old painter and installation artist Malina's art has to take place away from public view. She waits until after dusk, working with a dim flashlight. In her first exhibition in Kandahar, she trembled as she made her way towards the gallery in fear of it being bombed.

Their freedom of expression, their zeal to spread education, above all, and security of their lives are in serious jeopardy. The increasing threat to the human security, especially child security and gender related security in Afghanistan and Pakistan, emanating from the religio-ethnic and socio-political sources have been minutely sketched in a number of recent films made by internationally acclaimed filmmakers. This paper's focus will be on the non-traditional security, to be very specific, the depiction of child security and gender related security concerns in two critically acclaimed Islamic films by renowned Iranian director Mohsen Makhmalbaf and Pakistani film-maker Shoaib Mansoor. Makhmalbaf's 'Afghan Alphabet' (2002), a documentary, shows the life of the children of the Afghan villages bordering Iran, and how their life and culture were affected by the Taliban regime. On the other hand Mansoor's Bol (2011) highlights the regressive outlook of a male-dominated society that offers no liberty to women. These two films have opened up new dimensions for academic inquiry regarding child security and gender related security.

In the documentary film 'Alefbay-e afghan' or 'Afghan Alphabet' (2002) Makhmalbaf tracks the children who do not attend school in the border villages between Iran and Afghanistan and questions why they are not being educated. He finds girls studying in UNICEF classes in one region. One of the girls is not willing to come out of her *burqa* despite the fact that she has run away from the shadow of the Taliban. She just can't escape the excruciating terror of god that the Talibans have created. Basically, a projection of Makhmalbaf's 'Afghan Children Education Movement' the discernible theme here is the rampant illiteracy among Afghan émigrés to Iran and the various bureaucratic matters that stand in the way of those who want to learn. (http://variety.com/2002/film/reviews) But Makhmalbaf's real interest lies in the way the religious rhetoric has already affected the minds of so many Afghan youths.

Makhmalbaf first ingratiates himself with his camera-shy

subjects and then asks them zesty questions. To a class of young boys chanting passages from the *Quran,* he shoots the question: Who and where is God? To a class of *burqa*-clad girls, his query is: Why do you have to cover your face? He seizes upon one girl who refuses to uncover her face even to perform her classroom exercises. Her potential unveiling becomes the kernel of the movie.

In 2002, about three million Afghan refugees were living in Iran. From those about 7,00,000 were Afghan children who were not allowed to go to Iranian schools because of their illegal status in Iran. After this movie was made, this subject became controversial and finally the Iranian *Majlis* (Parliament) passed a bill in which the Afghani children were allowed to go to school and it resulted in 5,00,000 Afghan kids getting education. (http://www.iraniantorrents.com/index)

During conflicts education can create a precinct of security for children. Through education children can enjoy the company of their friends while benefitting from regular contact with teachers. It can help the children to cope with the trauma of the conflict (Machel, 2001). In this context, I will refer to a sequence, which has been used a number of times by Makhmalbaf in this single documentary. A class full of children are reciting with the teacher—'a be ab (آب âb)'. In Pashto language âb is water. Water is another name for life or life is another name for water. The symbolic sequence connotes a simple truth—education is a life affirming activity and the children are demanding with a militant zeal their right to lead a life of dignity.

After tackling the issues of terrorism in his masterpiece 'Khuda Kay Liye', director Shoaib Mansoor from Pakistan swings focus to discuss domestic concerns of Pakistan, in 'Bol'.

The story unveils in the flashback mode as Zainab (Humaima Malick) narrates her life history to the media, minutes before being sentenced to death. Born in a conservative Muslim family, Zainab is the eldest amongst half a dozen daughters of Hakim Saab (Manzar Zehbai). The father's pursuit for a male successor in his family is thwarted when a son is born with effeminate traits. As the son Saifee (Amr Kashmiri) grows up amidst sisters, the father almost disregards his presence in the family (http://timesofindia.indiatimes.com)

Director Shoaib Mansoor uses this family as an archetype to address various concerns associated with the community. The film primarily objects to the idea of procreating human beings without taking complete responsibility of their existence. Concurrently it also highlights the regressive stance of a male-dominated society that offers no liberty to woman in choosing life-partner, refusing reproduction, gaining education or working independently. However, the concerns are very much contemporary with the film set in modern-day Lahore. This very context reminds me of a painting called 'Today's Life' by Afghan artist Malina Suliman. It depicts a tree with wombs and female embryos. The embryos are reluctant to come out of their mothers' wombs as they know an unfriendly world awaits them outside. (http://uk.reuters.com/article)

Almost all the issues are brought to light by the conformist characterization of the father figure in the film. The director attributes his fanaticism to his orthodox upbringing and bigoted beliefs. At several instances, the narrative underscores the irony of life. While we have often witnessed woman getting into the flesh trade for survival, here the male species falls prey to the situation. The fact that all his children were only girls, which had always been his biggest weakness, turns Hakim's strength when he gets money to impregnate a courtesan (Iman Ali) with a girl child. Later the Hakim wanted to kill this girl child. The Hakim killed his own child Saifee, after the boy got sexually abused. If we replace the Muslim Hakim with a staunch Hindu man, and set the film in India, and it would be true to each frame. It is often worse with literally hundreds of thousands of women being killed before birth or during it annually in India. Humaima Malik is brilliant as the defiant daughter. She dares to question his father and takes drastic measures to ensure that justice triumphs. 'Bol' is a strikingly bold movie that strongly depicts the blemishes but not without showing a ray of hope at the end.

The development of fascist tendencies combined with staunch

religious support portends an ominous future for women in Pakistan. Interestingly, in Peshwar University of Khyber Pakhtunkhwa Province the launch of Malala's book *I Am Malala* had been stopped. The Pakistani Taliban had warned the local shop owners not to keep Malala's book. The provincial police had informed the organizers that they would not be able to provide adequate protection! (http://www.dawn.com)

The feminist movement in Pakistan is the victim of the double tyranny of class and gender. Women have to struggle to win concessions from society and face difficulties maintaining themselves and their families. Militaristic culture enhances machismo and reinforces the concept of men's superiority. The historic importance of women's movement is that it has established that violence begins at home and continues into the society and state. (Samiuddin and Khanam, 2002)

During the last two decades women of Pakistan have shown that they will not submit themselves to attempts to remove them from the public sphere and diminish their legal rights. Strangely, bitter opposition to women activists came also from *Daughters of Islam* who espouses religion-centric propositions. The agency of South Asian women in creating, inflicting, perpetuating and pulling off insecurity on the one hand and in creating, sustaining and extending a sense of security on the other, can be investigated during peace and war time. The exploration of the agency extends into the realm of intellectual discourse and policy making. (Faizal and Rajagopalan, 2005) These intricate issues had been very rarely taken up by the indigenous filmmakers. The majority of filmmakers in Pakistan have most of the time tried to play safe, opting for risk-free topics, sprinkled with songs, dances, comedy, sentiments and brawls. (Vasudev, Padgaonkar, Doraiswami, 2002) However, there were courageous directors, like Khalil Qaiser and Riaz Shahid. Perhaps they have strong influence over Shoaib Mansoor.

There are a number of other startling movies on non-traditional security aspects of Afghanistan and Pakistan which have been released in the last decade by filmmakers like Mohsen

Makhmalbaf, Samira Makhmalbaf, Siddiq Barmak, Michael Winterbottom, etc. The films are 'Kandahar' (2001), 'At Five in the Afternoon' (2003), 'Osama' (2003) and 'In this World' (2002). However, 'Bol' and 'Afghan Alphabet' are two of the finest movies pivoting around child and women security.

Poet Faiz Ahmed Faiz, in one of his poems, had written, 'Bol ke lab azad hain tere...' (Speak that thy lips are free). In this, and in the film 'Bol', lies a message to speak out against oppression, be it in the political sphere or the personal.

In the Film 'Afghan Alphabet' we also find the narrator moaning:

> *If only Afghan girls were born in another land*
> *If only the sky was a bit kinder with the earth*
> *And if rain poured instead of fire.*

## References

1. Alvi, H and Rause, S, "Pakistani Feminism and Feminist Movement" in Abida Samiuddin, R Khanam (eds), *Muslim Feminism and Feminist Movement* (*South Asia*), Vol 2, Global Vision Publishing House, 2002, pp 1-5.
2. Rajagopalan, Swarna, "Women and Security: In Search of a New Paradigm" in Farah Faizal and Swarna Rajagopalan (eds), *Women, Security, South Asia: A Clearing in the Thicket*, Sage Publications, New Delhi, 2005, pp 20-21.
3. Gul, Aijaz, "A Diffused Light" in Aruna Vasudev, Latika Padgaonkar, Rashmi Doraiswami (eds), *Being and Becoming the Cinemas of Asia*, Macmillan India Limited. 2002, p 337.
4. Machel, Graca, "Education for Survival and Development" in *The Impact of War on Children*, Orient Longman, 2001, p 92.
5. http://www.dawn.com/news/1083168/kp-govt-stops-malala-book-launch (last accessed on 26.01.2014)
6. http://uk.reuters.com/article/2013/01/29/uk-afghanistan-kandahar-art-idUKBRE90S05C20130129 (last accessed on 28.01.2014)
7. http://timesofindia.indiatimes.com/entertainmant/movie-reviews/hindi/Bol/movie-review/9797368.cms (last accessed on 27.01.14)
8. http://variety.com/2002/film/reviews/the-afghan-alphabet-1200550194/ (last accessed on 26.01.14)
9. http://www.iraniantorrents.com/index.php? page=torrent-details&id=d1c16f19f18d11f15173c4d53abc10671ad275af (last accessed on 27.01.2014)

*Chapter 22*

# Non-Traditional Security Issues and the Challenges of Globalisation in South Asia

*Moutusi Paul Choudhury (Naskar)*
Research Scholar
Department of International Relations
Jadavpur University, Kolkata

**Abstract**

Security in the context of the Third World does not simply refer to the military dimension, as is often assumed by the western discussion of the concept. With the end of the Cold War, the idea of security assumed an integrated approach encompassing socio-economic, environmental and human factors which clearly establishes the primacy of non-traditional security in the whole gamut of global security structure. This very idea of Third World security is further complicated by the phenomenon called Globalisation, which often leads to homogenisation of testes and preferences of the people across the world, resulting in the need to assert various indigenous beliefs and cultures.

Against this backdrop, this paper tries to analyse some unconventional non-traditional security threats facing the South Asian countries, in the light of the challenges posed by the process of globalisation.

## Introduction

'Security', traditionally has been conceptualised in terms of protection of state's territorial integrity and political sovereignty.

But in the post-Cold War scenario, it is evident that the traditional concept of security has failed to address various security issues that surfaced owing to the dominant trend of the time—globalisation, and its impact on the socio-economic structure of the developing and undeveloped countries of South Asia.

Thus, with the speeding up of the process of globalisation, new perceptions of security with far reaching implications for international politics have come up. The world today is increasingly challenged by new security threats. Both academic and policy institutions have begun to focus on 'new' challenges that nation-states face. Such threats are labelled as Non-Traditional Security (NTS) issues and are defined as challenges to the survival and well being of people and states that arise primarily out of non-military sources, such as climate change, infectious diseases, natural disasters, irregular migration, smuggling of persons, drug trafficking, organised transnational crimes, etc. Thus non-traditional security challenges have taken as their point of reference, the concept of human security in order to promote a focus on security needs of individuals, groups and societies, and to encompass a wide range of chronic and complex insecurities confronting South Asia. This change in perception of security has given way to the idea of comprehensive security.

To millions of people of these underdeveloped and developing countries of South Asia, a feeling of insecurity arises from worries of daily life than from the fear of a cataclysmic world event. As long as these people are steeped in hunger, malnutrition, poverty, illiteracy and their physical surrounding threatened by environmental degradation, and ethnic and religious conflicts, the very idea of military security makes little sense to them. Thus non-traditional security issues are pushing their way to the top of international and regional security agenda. It pushes the security problematic a little beyond ensuring territorial security or sovereignty.

South Asia, an epitome of Third World, occupies juxtaposed problems with variance in social, economic, scientific, technological levels as well as factors accompanying development.

The region is more than ever confronted with 'transnational' threats and human security challenges. Though the socio-economic fibre of these South Asian countries (India, Pakistan, Bangladesh, Nepal, Bhutan, Sri Lanka, the Maldives, and Afghanistan) is very different, each of these states represents very similar kind of security issues. This can be attributed to their common history of prolonged period of exploitation resulting in low levels of development, which in turn generates rising expectation of the masses, putting the political structure of these countries under tremendous pressure. This situation is further aggravated by the challenges posed by globalisation.

Globalisation, however, is not a new phenomenon. But the speeding up of the process of globalisation in recent times has put traditional power and authority of the state under scrutiny. The 'openness' accompanied by globalisation has generated new prospects of learning and empowerment for the people of these South Asian counties. But it has also raised security concerns for nation-states—unhindered flow of technology and information has been a boon for terrorist groups operating in various parts of the world, the homogenisation of testes of people around the globe often leads to identity crisis resulting in the need to assert their indigenous identities through fundamentalist activities. Globalisation and trade liberalisation also exacerbate the existing poverty and inequality situation within and among countries.

Against this backdrop, the purpose of this paper will be to analyse some of the non-traditional security concerns of the countries of this region, these are: environmental degradation, human trafficking and drug abuse causing HIV/AIDS. These issues may not seem to be of immediate threat to the region but they surely are jeopardising the security environment of the region in a slow and steady manner. And the impact of these threats are analysed in the context of globalisation.

## Environmental Degradation

The process of globalisation is functioning around the world. It combines both the elements of international and multinational as a more advanced stages of integration among countries—more specifically economic integration which has its impact on the natural environment as well. In other words, globalisation alters the economic structure of developing countries which in turn puts pressure on the environment. Besides being an instrument of imperialism in the hands of the developed North, globalisation leads to unequal trade and transfer of dirty industry and low grade technology to the developing countries of the South because of their weak bargaining capacity. This in turn damages the environment of these low-regulation and often low-income countries. South Asia is also affected by the same trend of economic globalisation.

Environmental degradation plays a critical role in triggering major natural disasters and alters the way of living of the people. The underdeveloped and developing countries are more prone to such natural disasters. South Asian countries are very vulnerable so far as the affects of globalisation on environment are concerned. These societies, striving for a higher standard of living and a 'West'-like development often find themselves compromising conservation at the cost of economic growth. They cannot resist the opportunities that come with globalisation and gets trapped into the unfair global trading system which initially does lead to economic prosperity but ultimately affects the ecosystem of the developing countries, slowing the very pace of economic growth.

South Asian countries confront severe environmental degradation—rapid deforestation, soil erosion, over-cultivation and over-grazing, which can be attributed to increasing pressure of population on land and also rapid urbanisation. In order to keep pace with the global economic system, these countries embark on rapid industrialisation without adequate technological know-how, infrastructure, hazardous working conditions and clean industrial practices, which result in polluting of air and water.

Economies of most of the South Asian countries are driven by rapid industrialisation and an outward orientation strategy that lead to greater integration with the global economy. This has led to economic development and lifted millions of people out of poverty. But economic gains have come at a cost. South Asia has witnessed significant and worsening environmental problems as manifested by congested and polluted cities, increased greenhouse gas emission and less than optimal depletion of natural resources. Another feature of globalisation is the ecological interdependence of nations and the trans-boundary elements of much environmental harms. Thus the impact of greenhouse gas emission from any part of the world may have an impact on global warming which may in turn lead to environmental catastrophe around the world.

One of the major environmental problems faced by the countries of South Asia is increasing soil erosion in the hills of Nepal because of deforestation and construction activities, resulting in heavy siltation of river beds in India and Bangladesh, rising river bed levels and causing frequent flooding. Countries like India, Bangladesh and Nepal are prone to flood. In Bangladesh, as many as 80 million people are vulnerable to flood each year. Glacial Lake Outburst Floods (GLOFs) are another concern in the Himalayan region. Rising global temperature is an important cause of GLOFs, especially affecting countries like India, Nepal and Bhutan. Apart from these, countries of South Asia also suffer from drought, earthquake, land slide, etc. For example, because of man-made and natural factors, as many as 12,000 landslides occurs in Nepal. Another problem is of forest fire that has serious impact on health and global atmosphere. Again, in order to meet increasing demand for agricultural products for consumption and export purpose has resulted in over-cultivation of land, which in turn leads to infertility of land. Industrial disasters also have environmental implications. Exposure to toxic agents not only causes physical disabilities but also affects the natural environment, eg, Bhopal Gas Leak.

## Human Trafficking

One of globalisation's major contributions is 'openness', resulting in unhindered movement of goods and services indicating global economic integration and also a proxy for openness of borders to movement of people, that is, human trafficking. This very phenomenon results in 'commodification' of victims, as the trafficked person is sold at a particular price, to work as bonded labourers, maids, and more often than not as prostitutes.

In South Asia cross-border trafficking and transit is a big problem. The movement of young girls and women from Bangladesh and Nepal into Indian brothels is common. There is further movement of these girls to the Middle East as well as other destinations. Movement from Pakistan, Sri Lanka and the Maldives has also been observed. At times of hardship this starts out as illegal migration and ends up as trafficking. Trafficking thrives because it remains a low-risk; high-level reward enterprise for organised crime and with globalisation the demand for trafficked people has considerably increased.

South Asia comprises ountries which serve as high origin, transit and destination for women, men and children. Some of the countries also provide transit facilities for victims being sent to other parts of the world. South Asia is estimated to be home to the second largest number of internationally trafficked persons, estimated to be around 1,50,000 annually. People who are trafficked, especially women and children are often used for commercial sexual purposes, organ transplant and forced marriage. Trafficked women often end up in brothels working as prostitutes They also run the risk of suffering from sexually transmitted diseases and HIV/AIDS. This in turn threatens the very idea of human security. Trafficking for forced labour is another problem faced by the poverty-stricken people of South Asia. Unemployment, discrimination, corruption, conflict and some cultural practices—all exacerbate the vulnerability of men, women and children to trafficking. Problem of trafficking also increases the number of people living illegally within a country, for example-India.

Thus issues like human trafficking may not be considered as threatening the security of nation-states but they sure can inflict tremendous damage to human dignity and the socio-economic fibre of the society.

## Drug Abuse and HIV/AIDS

Deregulated and globalised markets have allowed the drug industry to spread its tentacles worldwide opening new trafficking routes and production zones and infiltrating the legal economy that becomes a major security concern for policy makers. Owing to the seamless world fostered by globalisation, no country tends to 'specialise': drugs of all kinds are produced in all parts of the world, catering to an estimated 200 million regular and casual users.

The capitalist unification of the world on neo-liberal ideals have opened new horizons for drug production and trafficking. Moreover, the dynamics of globalisation in the Third World regions like South Asia have created huge socio-economic disparities, unemployment and consequently illicit activities. The rural population of these regions, driven by poverty, often resorts to drug cultivation and use. South Asia has become one of the main regions for drug cultivation and trafficking. The Golden Crescent comprising Iran, Pakistan and Afghanistan are major producers of opium poppy. The population of the underdeveloped and developing countries of South Asia are more vulnerable to drug abuse. This is because these countries are unable to provide basic necessities to their people. Hence, the unemployed, poverty-stricken youths are more likely to resort to drug use.

This uncontrolled use of drugs among the youths of this region has also led to the spread of HIV/AIDS. South Asia is a heterogeneous and highly mobile region. Because of porous borders, human trafficking, especially trafficking in women and children is high within the region. These women are then forced into prostitution. Thus sex work is a critical driver of HIV transmission in the region. This is because of the fact that these sex workers often resort to the use of drugs in order to cope up with their situation. The HIV/AIDS scenario is almost same in all the countries of South Asia. The HIV/AIDS epidemic in these countries (India, Pakistan, Bangladesh, Nepal) occurs mainly within networks Injecting Drug Use (IDUs). IDUs are also growing in the Maldives. Estimation by the end of 2001 stated that there were 4.2 million people living with HIV/AIDS in South Asia.

Though the link between globalisation and these non-traditional security threats of environmental degradation, human trafficking and drug abuse and HIV/AIDS is still very much contested, it is however beyond doubt that the very process of globalisation has further complicated and helped the spread of the already existing non-traditional security threats in the South Asian region and beyond.

## References

1. Buzan, Barry. People, State and Fear: An Agenda for International Security Studies in the Post-Cold War Era.
2. Buzan, Barry. "New Patterns of Global Security in the Twenty-First Century". International Affairs (Royal Institute of International Affairs 1944) 67.3 (1991).
3. Baylis, John and S Smith: The Globalisation of World Politics: An Introduction to International Relations (Oxford University Press, New York 2005).
4. Khan, Abdur Rob, *Globalisation and Non-Traditional Security in South Asia*, Academic Press.
5. Chari, PR, *Security and Governance in South Asia*, Regional Centre for Strategic Studies.
6. Jasjit Singh, *Reshaping Asian Security*.
7. "South Asia: State of the Environment 2001", United Nations Environment Programme (UNEP), 2001.
8. Global Human Smuggling: Comparative Perspectives.
   David Kyle and Rey Koslowski. Baltimore: The Johns Hopkins University Press, 2001.

*Chapter 23*

# The India-Bangladesh Border: A Rising Threat to Human Security

*Subarna Bhattacharya*
Research Scholar
Department of International Relations
Jadavpur University, Kolkata

The concept of human security emerged during the post-Cold War period to link various social and economic issues in order to assure security. Some of the issues human security addresses are: organised crime and criminal violence, human rights, armed conflict and intervention, genocide, environment and resources, etc. It was first popularised by the United Nations Development Programme (UNDP) in early 1990s. Human security primarily focuses on protecting people and promoting peace and sustainable development in a broader way. Its main motto is to improve human conditions.[1] This article will highlight the extent to which human security in the Indo-Bangladesh border area is at stake and there will be an attempt to find out the possible wayouts of it.

India and Bangladesh share a border of approximately 2,429 miles. Besides, the Bangladeshi areas of Dhaka, Khulna, Rajshahi, Sylhet and Chittagong, the Indian states of West Bengal, Meghalaya, Tripura, Assam and Mizoram are situated along the border. Thousands of Bangladeshi people have been migrated to India by crossing these borders since the birth of Bangladesh. This made the border a tense area. More prominently, these illegal immigrants are affecting Indian economy, culture, politics, society and last but not the least, security for decades now.

The Bangladeshi people have been moving out of their own country and are migrated to India for diverse political, social, economic and environmental reasons. After 1971's Liberation War continuous political and economic turmoil forced some Bangladeshis to seek refuge in India. On the other hand, the population density of Bangladesh in 2011 was 964 per square kilometer, which was one of the highest in the world. It made the lives of Bangladeshi people vulnerable as there was a little scope of jobs for the vast population. Search for cultivable land and jobs are two major factors that are most likely to compel the Bangladeshis to migrate. Migration from Bangladesh to Assam and Tripura has been primarily for in search of better economic opportunities and livelihood. The impact of climate change and natural disaster also compelled them to migrate in India.[2]

Bangladeshis are the largest group of migrants in India. Illegal migration from Bangladesh mainly takes place into India in its Eastern and North-Eastern part. The highly affected states are West Bengal, Assam, Tripura, Nagaland, Meghalaya and Mizoram. These migrants have also spread too far off states like Kerala, Tamil Nadu, Gujarat, Rajasthan and Delhi. As per 2001 census, there are 3,084,826 people in India who migrated from Bangladesh.[3] In 2011 Census, the total number of Bangladeshi Migrants in India is 3,025,570.[4] Illegally migrated population from Bangladesh has already started to affect Indian social stability and economy in a great way. These migrants are so many in number that they are actually in position to influence the result of elections in the states of North East. They have also generated various political, social, ethnic, cultural tensions in the region. As a result of overpopulation, the pressure on land gravely increased in these states which resulted negatively indeed and also affected the economy of North East India. India is suffering from the issue of illegal migration since independence and it is a problem to India's social balance and human security. The issue of Bangladeshi migration has troubled the state of Assam mostly.

Assamese political and social discourses fear that, these migrations across the border may subvert their way of life and culture in near future.[5] Bangladeshi migrants drain out Indian resources as nearly 85 per cent of total encroached forest land in Assam was found out to be in the hands of Bangladeshi migrants. The demographic composition of the border makes it easier for Bangladeshis to sneak into India crossing the border. And due to similar body structure and features, they get assimilated into the local population quite easily. Being cheap labour migrated Bangladeshis find easy acceptance as domestic helps in Indian homes. Over the years, the illegal migration had reached such a proportion that it has started to threaten the socio-political life of the Border States. Often the migrants have settled down permanently, occupied Indian lands enjoying the rights of natural citizens of India. The issue rose to an alarming concern as the 1991 census showed the abnormal high growth rate of immigrants in Border States like West Bengal and Assam.[6] The increasing influence of religious fundamentalism in the border area is also a major factor of concern here. The Jihadi terrorist groups, who are taking shelter in the land of Bangladesh, are also entering the territory of India by crossing the border illegally. It is a severe threat to Indian national security and integrity.[7]

Not only migration, but illegal movement of people and goods are also a serious problem of India-Bangladesh border area. Cross-border trafficking has also become an issue of national and political concern that needs to be addressed in a more assertive way. Men, who are trafficked, are used and exploited for cheap labour or as bonded labour. Often they are forced to donate organs without any medical coverage or health benefits. It was clear that as women and children are weaker and have difficulties to understand the concept of human rights, they are the easy target to the traffickers. The victims of trafficking are usually taken to the brothels; they are threatened, beaten and often transformed into sex workers. Trafficked children are often used as bonded labours, street baggers and organ donors. Every year 5,000-7,000 women and children are trafficked from Bangladesh to India. From India, they are taken to Pakistan and the Middle Eastern countries for cheap labours and prostitution.[8] Not only are that, cross border smuggling, supplying of arms other notable problems are there in this context.

India has taken various initiatives to address these problems in a positive manner. These are erection of border fences next to the Zero Line, renovation and construction of border pillars, utilizing flood lights during the night and place more armed forces for more competent patrolling. But there are some border related issues between India and Bangladesh which are creating obstacles to the border security. There are yet to be solved. If the law enforcement agencies of both countries work together sincerely, and use cooperative strategic initiatives like Information and Intelligence sharing, Cooperation, Co-ordination and Trust Building, these problems can be dealt with properly. A clear border must be identified and clear rule of border crossing should be enforced by the both sides. On the Indian side, the regulation and registration of voters should be done in a strict administrative way. Only then it would be possible to identify the migrated people and they could be deported to their motherland.

Effective border management and maintenance of peace is only possible through mutual co-operation of both the countries. On humanitarian grounds, temporary work permits can be given to the migrants to minimise tension. Indian Ministry of External Affairs should take serious notice of this problem as it is one of the non-traditional security threats for India. However, the government of Bangladesh has repeatedly denied India's claims on illegal migration.[9] To deal with this problem systematic, concrete and time bound plans should be undertaken by the Indian Government. It's important to understand that illegal migration is no longer a humanitarian problem but transformed into a security threat now. India should strongly work on it without hampering the bilateral ties.[10] The Indian side has been constantly raising the issue of the presence of Indian insurgent groups like United Liberation Front of Assam (ULFA) in the lands of Bangladesh. Bangladesh government should address these issues in a prominent and positive way. It is important to sensitize the border population about the strategic importance of the area. Other than these, special photo identity cards can bring solution to the problem of identification near the border areas. If it is not entirely possible to stop illegal migrants from entering India, it can be minimised by a political will by both governments. On the other hand, India should expand the hands of co-operation and should develop better trade and economic relations with Bangladesh. If Bangladesh is economically strong and stable, these problems may reduce and India will get benefitted positively.

## Bibliography

**Primary Sources**

1. Human Development Report of United Nations Development Programme 1994.
2. Census of India 2001, Migration Tables.
3. Census of India 2011, Migration Tables.
4. "Fencing along India-Bangladesh Border", Press Release, Ministry of Home Affairs, Government of India, November 30, 2011.
5. Report on Illegal Migration into Assam, Submitted By The Governor of Assam, November 8, 1998.

**Secondary Sources**

1. Bauder, Harald, *Labor Movement: How Migration Regulates Labor Markets*, New York: Oxford University Press, 2006.
2. Bimal Pramanik, *"Illegal Migration from Bangladesh: A Case Study of West Bengal"*, in BB Kumar (ed), *"Illegal Migration from Bangladesh"*, Concept, New Delhi, 2006.
3. Sreeradha Datta, "Indo-Bangladesh Relations: An Overview of Limitations and Constraints", *Strategic Analysis*, Volume 26, No 3, 2002, p 430.
4. Saubhik Chakraborty, "Happy New Decade, India", *Indian Express*, January 1, 2010.
5. Jaithirth Rao, "Millennial Bharat, 2020 India", *Indian Express*, January 1, 2010.
6. "2 Cr Bangladeshis in India: George Fernandes", *The Tribune*, India, September 27, 2003.
7. "Stateless Misery on India-Bangladesh Border", *BBC News South Asia*, September 5, 2011.

8. Indo-Bangladesh border fence to speed up", *United Press International*, December 17, 2008.

**Online Sources**

1. http://www.humansecurityinitiative.org/definition-human-security Accessed on January 15, 2014.
2. http://www.idsa.in/system/files/IB_BangladeshiIllegalMigrationintoAssam.pdf? Accessed on December 26, 2013.
3. http://www.atsecindia.org/html/cross_border.html Accessed on January 4, 2014.
4. http://www.tribuneindia.com/2003/20030217/edit.htm#3 Accessed on January 3, 2014.
5. http://www.southasiaanalysis.org/paper632 Accessed on January 15, 2014.
6. http://www.satp.org/satporgtp/countries/india/states/assam/documents/papers/illegal_migration_in_assam.htm. Accessed on January 19, 2014.

## Notes

1. http://www.humansecurityinitiative.org/definition-human-security Accessed on January 15, 2014.
2. N Manoharan, "Illegal Migration from Bangladesh: Threat to India's Internal Security", *National Maritime Foundation*, September 18, 2013.
3. Census of India 2001. Data Highlights: Migration Tables. p19.
4. censusindia.gov.in/Tables_Published/D-Series/D-Series_link/D2_India.zip Accessed on January 22, 2014.
5. www.idsa.in/system/files/IB_BangladeshiIllegalMigrationintoAssam.pdf-Accessed on December 26, 2013.
6. http://web.archive.org/web/20120320024437/http://voi.org/books/tfst/appii1.htm Accessed on August 18, 2013.
7. Pushpita Das, 'The India-Bangladesh Border: A Problem Area for Tomorrow', Institute of Defense Studies and Analyses, New Delhi, December 8, 2006.
8. http://www.atsecindia.org/html/cross_border.html Accessed on January 4, 2014.
9. http://www.tribuneindia.com/2003/20030217/edit.htm#3. Accessed on January 3, 2014.
10. http://www.southasiaanalysis.org/paper632 Accessed on January 15, 2014.

*Chapter 24*

# Food Security and Human Development in South Asia

*Sharmita Bhattacharya*
Research Scholar
Department of International Relations
Jadavpur University, Kolkata

Food Security in developing countries of South Asia is a serious and multi-dimensional problem. It is a complex and complicated phenomenon which involves a number of factors ranging from availability to access and utilisation of food. Developing and low-income countries are amongst the most vulnerable in the world. As a result, food security will continue to be a major challenge for the South Asian region. Most of the populous countries of Asia which faced a serious food crisis during the early 60s and 70s were able to achieve significantly higher growth in domestic food production after the mid-seventies. This enabled many of these countries to considerably improve their performance in the matter of providing food to their people. This notwithstanding, with a few exceptions in most of the countries of Asia, where per capita availability of food and nutrition continues to remain far shorter than the required levels. The rapidly rising demand for food by the highly populated countries of Asia on the one hand, and the persistence of chronic food shortages and near famine conditions in some African countries on the other, has once again highlighted the need for providing food security to the teeming poor of the developing world. Whereas it is true that during the 20th century the world food production exceeded that of population by a comfortable margin, this has failed to solve the problem of shortages and famines in some parts of the world, due to highly skewed regional pattern of agricultural production. While all surpluses have emerged in the First World, it is the Third World which has faced food shortages and where the levels of calorie intake have remained inadequate.

Of the 1 billion food insecure people in the world, more than 30 per cent are in South Asia. The problem of food insecurity may be aggravated by the projected climate change, especially because of the water scarcity caused by rapid melting of the glaciers in the Himalayas, increase in variability in monsoonal rains and enhanced frequency of extreme events. The purpose of this paper is to examine the current state of food security and its future in the South Asian countries of Bangladesh, India, China, Pakistan, Nepal, Sri Lanka and Burma.

Food security is a complex issue and its definition has evolved over time. The question of food security has a number of dimensions that go beyond production, availability and demand for food. The initial focus on food security as a global concern was on the volume and stability of food supplies. In the 1974 World Food Summit, food security was defined as *"availability at all times of adequate world food supplies of basic foodstuffs to sustain a steady expansion of food consumption and to offset fluctuations in production and prices."* In 1983, FAO expanded its concept to include vulnerable people securing access to available supplies, stating that food security meant *"ensuring that all people at all times have both physical and economic access to the basic food that they need."* Later, the 1996 World Food Summit redefined food security to take demand, vulnerability and nutritional aspects into account. At the summit, countries agreed that *"food security exists when all people, at all times, have physical and economic access to sufficient, safe and nutritious food to meet their dietary needs and food preferences for an active and healthy lifestyle."*

In 2002, an FAO Expert Consultation on food security gave a working definition of food security: Food security exists when all people, at all times, have physical, social and economic access to sufficient, safe and nutritious food which meets their dietary needs and food preferences for an active and healthy life. Household food security is the application of this concept to the family level, with individuals within households as the focus of concern. Since then, several definitions have been provided by different organisations such as the World Bank, FAO and UNDP's Human Development Report.

## Major Causes of Food Insecurity in South Asia

The SAARC countries account for over 22 per cent of total population of the world with India alone contributing about 1.17 billion people (over 17 per cent) to it. The shares of Pakistan and Bangladesh in world's population stand at 2.5 per cent and 2.4 per cent respectively. The population growth rate has slowed down overtime in almost all the countries with Sri Lanka attaining a population growth rate of 1.3 per cent. Bangladesh, India, Nepal, and Pakistan also have moved in that direction though Pakistan still has a high rate of population growth (currently reported as slightly below 2 per cent). Though population growth has slowed down it is still high in relation to output growth and resulted in marginal improvements on per capita basis even than expansion in food production and general economic growth are somewhat satisfactory. The urban poor are generally more vulnerable to food insecurity resulting from shocks like high inflation. Despite high population growth in rural areas the reduction in the percentage of rural population in almost all the countries (except Sri Lanka during the period 1991-2006) points to an accelerated migration from rural to urban areas. This migration results from both pull and push factors working. Cities offer higher wage and better employment opportunities as well as greater availability of services like healthcare and education. The push factors that force migrants to leave rural areas include factors like displacement by conflict, disasters, droughts, landlessness, land degradation, and population pressures on land.

Thus the process of urbanisation is a potential threat to food security in the region. Agricultural production in South Asia is also prone to high risks resulting from high variations in weather. The future projections of climate change indicate that South Asia is very likely to be affected by warming during this century. The accessibility of freshwater is expected to decrease and coastal areas will face the greatest risk due to increased flood from the sea and rivers. It is predicted that an increase in temperature may reduce yields of rice, wheat, other cereals, and certain cash significantly (ICRIER et al 2009).

## Reasons for Persistent Food Insecurity

An important reason for the persistent food insecurity in the region is the low productivity of crops and livestock as compared to that in many developed countries. The investment made in agriculture research as a percentage of agricultural GDP has been declining in many of the South Asian countries from a very low base. India and Pakistan have badly neglected investment for maintaining their vital irrigation infrastructure which has led to its rapid deterioration. There is also great potential for improvement in poverty and food security by investing in development of improved technology and making it available to poor farmers. South Asian agriculture is also still highly dependent on weather (as India is currently witnessing with the failure of the recent monsoon in large parts of the country) and vulnerable to natural disasters. The total volume of food production fluctuates widely from year to year. The problem has been aggravated by factors such as rapidly growing population, skewed distribution of assets and income, degradation of the natural resource base and unsustainable management of land and water resources, which include increased and imbalance in the use of plant nutrient, loss of soil fertility and growing use of pesticides. Another important feature which has an important bearing on ensuring food security is that large areas in several of these countries are disaster prone. Incidence of natural calamities is more severe on the food insecure households. Cyclones and floods in Bangladesh and coastal parts of India are quite frequent. Recurring droughts are a common feature in the arid and semi-arid parts of India and Pakistan. The respective governments also have to devote large resources to cope with frequent natural disasters. These complex but inter-linked factors bring out the challenge faced by South Asian countries in ensuring food security. Some of the complexity also arises due to geographical location in terms of inaccessibility for trade because Afghanistan, Nepal and Bhutan are landlocked countries. The situation of food security also varies in SAARC countries due to heterogeneity in their physical and natural resources endowments, biodiversity, socio-economic conditions, climatic factors, and dominance of agricultural sector.

Given the enormity of the challenges faced, it is encouraging that the governments of SAARC countries are strongly committed to the goal of ensuring food security in the spirit of 1996 World Food Summit Declaration and the Millennium Development Goals (MDGs). All countries of the region have taken up food security as one of the important cross-cutting themes in their short, medium, and long-term plans. Moreover, despite the fact that States in the region are confronted with terrorism, bilateral conflicts, mutual mistrust, and intra-state tensions; the member-states of SAARC affirmed their resolve to ensure region-wide food security and make South Asia, once again, the granary of the world during the Fifteenth SAARC Summit held in Colombo on 2-3 August 2008. This underlines the commitment of all governments of SAARC countries to achieve some tangible outcomes in minimising the food insecurity situation in the region as a whole.

## Broad Trends in Factors Influencing Food Security

Agriculture is the dominant sector of economies of South Asia. Its contribution to gross domestic product (GDP) of respective countries during 1990s ranged from about 26 per cent in Pakistan and Sri Lanka to about 52 per cent in Nepal. The share of the sector has declined over the years but still accounts for about one-fifth of the GDP in Pakistan and Bangladesh. The contribution of the sector in India and Sri Lanka has declined to about 18 per cent and 15 per cent respectively while in Nepal about one-third of national GDP originates from agriculture sector. Majority of the people of South Asia reside in rural areas and directly or indirectly depends on agriculture for their livelihood. The rural population in Nepal, Sri Lanka and Bhutan accounts for more than 84 per cent of total population whereas over 70 per cent of the people of India, Bangladesh, and the Maldives live in rural areas. Since 1995, the agricultural sector has grown at an average rate of about three per cent or more in, Bangladesh, India, Nepal, and the Pakistan. However, average growth rate of agriculture was 2.6 per cent in case of Sri Lanka during the same period.

## Food Availability

With significant differences in fluctuations and trends in per capita production for cereals (wheat and rice) the overall per capita production index for SAARC shows no significant or sustained increase. Going to individual countries, during the past one decade per capita cereal production in Bangladesh showed a major increase after the year 1998. The index for per capita wheat production improved significantly during the 1990s attaining the highest level of 177 during 1999 and 2000. However, since 2001 it shows a declining trend. The rice production per capita fluctuated below the base year level of 100 during 1990s and started improving afterwards with some fluctuations. In India cereal production index showed notable improvement during 1990s except the year 1992. The index remained below 100 after the year 2001 mainly due to decline in per capita rice production in this period. The wheat production index for Nepal improved after mid-90s whereas growth in production of rice lagged behind the population growth rate throughout the last one and a half decade. The cereal production index is mostly discouraging showing wide fluctuations during the same period. The rice production index for Sri Lanka showed small improvements with wide fluctuations. In case of Pakistan, per capita food production index showed some improvements since 1990 with the exception of 1991, 1994, and 2002. The analysis shows that food production is prone to fluctuation in South Asia and the increase in food production has been mainly of set by high population growth in the region. The food production system of South Asia is generally characterised by a number of other constraints such as small size of landholdings, shrinking supplies of irrigation water, low productivity, poor marketing and transport infrastructure resulting in high post-harvest losses. This problematic situation gets further worsened in the wake of the fact that some areas are prone to a number of natural disasters like floods, droughts and cyclones.

## Accessibility

The real per capita GDP depicted a positive average growth rate since 1991 in almost all the countries of the region. The real per capita income grew at a relatively rapid rate in Bhutan, India, the Maldives, and Sri Lanka as compared to that in Bangladesh, Nepal, and Pakistan. The growth in per capita GDP picked up momentum after 2002 in all the countries of the region except Nepal. However, a slowdown in growth of GDP in countries of the region has taken place as a result of recent global financial crises. Over 1991-2004/5 the population living below the poverty line has overall declined for all countries except Pakistan based on estimates using the national poverty line or the World Bank new poverty line of US $ 1.25 a day. In Pakistan it rose in the 1990s after falling in the 1980s but again fell post-2001. In terms of relative poverty based on the US $1.25 per day, it is indicate that, Pakistan's poverty level is much lower than the other countries except Sri Lanka where the level has been consistently lower throughout the period. The recent global economic slowdown coupled with wide spread poverty in the region and recent hike in food prices would have adverse implications for food security situation in the region. High food prices result in reduced real incomes of the poor and decline in their food consumption. The real food prices index (measured as food price index divided by consumer price index expressed in percentage) remained below hundred in India and Nepal since 2000, showing that food prices increased less rapidly than the prices of other consumer items. While in Bangladesh, Pakistan and Sri Lanka an upsurge in real food prices was experienced during the same period.

The availability and accessibility to food fails to reduce food insecurity in the absence of proper food utilisation which is related to factors like nutrition education, health awareness, gender disparities, sanitation, access to safe drinking water, food preparation practices, eating habits, food safety, and health services and infrastructure. The indicators like immunisation coverage, infant mortality, child mortality, prevalence of undernourishment, life expectancy, access to safe drinking water and sanitation facilities, availability of doctors/ nurses, and public investment in health are the determinants of food absorption capacity of the population. The Maldives, Bhutan, and Sri Lanka spent relatively high percentage (over 1 per cent to 8 per cent) of their GDP on public health than the other countries of the region (1 per cent or less) during the years 2000-2008. In Sri Lanka access to improved sanitation has been enhanced from 69 per cent in 1990 to 91 per cent of the population in 2004. The access to improved sanitation in Bangladesh, India, and Nepal was respectively available to 39 per cent, 35 per cent, and 33 per cent of their population during 2004. One-fourth of the population of Bangladesh and one-fifth of the people in Sri Lanka lack access to improved water source during the same year whereas in Pakistan, India and Nepal respectively 10 per cent, 14 per cent and 10 per cent of the people didn't have access to an improved water source. A decline was observed in malnutrition in all the countries however it was observed among nearly 40 per cent of children (under 5 years) in India, Nepal and Bangladesh during 2005-2006.

A Food Security Index (FSI) has been developed for South Asia covering Bangladesh, India, Pakistan, Nepal and Sri Lanka based on the following four indicators: per capita food availability index (50 per cent weight); per capita food production index; self-sufficiency ratio index; and index of inverse relative food price (last three equally weighted for the remaining 50 per cent). The first two bring out availability, the third vulnerability in terms of import dependency and the last variable access in terms of rising food prices relative to other prices.

Achieving food security especially in the face of still high and fluctuating global food prices in the countries in South Asia is thus a multifaceted challenge. It also confirms that indicators of economic growth, increases in food production and availability and decline in overall poverty may have marginally improved the situation for South Asian countries; they still have a long and arduous task ahead. The lack of progress in terms of the rate of decline in reducing food insecurity, hunger and malnutrition in some countries also shows that their economic structure in terms of asset and income distribution, progress in HDI and gender disparities may be key factors in explaining their relative lack of progress.

Food security has always been of concern in developing countries of South Asia but of late a new concept of healthy food has slowly crept into the minds of economically well off and health conscious people. A further improvisation of organic foods—few industrialists and entrepreneurs who afford the means have started cultivating food items for their dining tables under their own strict vigil. With a whole new market of organic foods items emerging in cities, seriously conscious people feel that people engaged in commercial production of organics may sometimes ignore quality owing to their economics. In its first public statement on the WTO ministerial meeting on 30th November 2013, the Government of India said it will not compromise its position on food security even if subsidy limits are breached. This statement reiterated that there are issues which are of paramount importance to India and that India will secure and protect the right to food security of the poor people thereby defending its resource for poor and subsistence farmers. It further held that these are issues on which India shall never compromise.

## SAARC Collaboration in Ensuring Food Security: Possibilities and Constraints

Given the political realities in the region it may be important to distinguish between what may be desirable and what may be feasible for ensuring food security through regional collaboration both bilaterally and under SAARC. Trying to achieve the best may well be the enemy of the good. Liberalisation of regional trade, the intra-regional trade among SAARC countries is very low, at about 5.0 per cent of their total trade. Indeed as a recent study points out South Asia is the least integrated region in the world. This study identifies cross-country conflict as the most important reason for this very low level of integration. Intra-regional trade in South Asia is 0.8 per cent of GDP in contrast to East Asia's nearly 28 per cent. There are, however, sharp differences in the patterns of intra-regional trade among South Asian countries. The share of India in regional imports is quite low and increased only fractionally during 1985-2000. Similarly, the share of Pakistan shows only slight increase in imports from the region over time.

## SAARC Food Security Bank

The Food Security Reserve for SAARC was established in 1988 to address the problem of food insecurity in the region by building up a food buffer stock that could reduce food security risks, particularly after natural disasters. The working of the reserve achieved limited success in addressing the food security concerns of the region. However, due recognition of the importance of regional and sub-regional collective self-reliance with respect to food security by member-countries and realisation that the establishment of a regional food reserve based on the principle of collective self-reliance would improve their food security resulted in establishment of SAARC Food Security Bank in April 2007. The objectives were to meet the needs of food security in the region and to act as a regional food security reserve (of wheat and rice) for the SAARC member-countries during normal time food shortages and emergencies; and to provide regional support to national food security efforts; foster inter-country partnerships and regional integration, and solve regional food shortages through collective action. However, in the context of establishment of a SAARC Food Security Bank the development had been slow and attempts are in progress to make it operational. A number of reasons are believed to be responsible for the slow progress on the Food Security Bank.

In summary, it can be concluded that the chances of this dream being realised in an effective manner are a still some way off not least because no country would like to be in a situation where it finds itself vulnerable to a dependence on food supplies in an arrangement in which it does not have full confidence. Moreover, food security is a highly sensitive issue in all the countries of the region because of poverty and will be politically too risky to be left on the regional forums.

## Agriculture Pricing Policies

Intrinsically linked with trade in foodgrains is the issue of relative prices of foodgrains in the countries of the region. For if price differentials are high then even though legal trade may not be allowed porous borders lead to smuggling of foodgrains across countries. This illegal movement of foodgrains is not just among adjoining neighbours in South Asia but foodgrains may find their way to the Central Asian countries as was the case of Pakistan wheat in 2007 when low prices and a bumper crop resulted in domestic shortages. Again a strong school in economics supported by the IFIs postulates that governments should not be in the business of fixing food and commodity prices and these should be dictated by prevailing international prices as this would lead to the best allocation of resources. Yet again as discussed earlier SAARC countries have a long history of controlling or setting food prices of essential items to protect the perceived interest of vulnerable consumers including through food rationing. In the context of food security there is need for countries to exchange views on the whole issue of pricing of foodgrains and indeed also for essential inputs like fertilisers. This may gradually lead to a convergence of views and help foster reducing trade barriers as countries move to a system of encouraging prices to be set in line with global markets rather than being influenced by domestic political pressures.

## Conclusion

Many of the world's fastest growing economies today are located in Asia. Ironically, however, Asia still is home to two-thirds of the world's poor and more than 60 per cent of the world's undernourished population. Across the globe, poverty is the single-most common cause of food insecurity. Nevertheless, the progress in food security has been nearly stagnant since the mid-1990s and the absolute number of undernourished people in the region has increased as a result of rapid population growth. Adding to this, the global food and economic crises of 2007-2008 have pushed tens of millions more people into food insecurity. High and volatile food prices persist around the world, including in Asia and the Pacific. While food price spikes and volatility have adverse impacts on all segments of the population, these impacts are more acutely felt by the poor, who spend up to 70 per cent of their income on food items. Moreover, higher and more volatile food prices decrease poor people's ability to move out of poverty in the longer term as higher food bills crowd out expenditures on other basic needs such as healthcare and education.

The path to future food security in the region would require higher productivity in crops and livestock sub-sectors as well as conservation of water and land resources. The countries of the region are predicted to be the worst hit by climatic changes. With their limited resources all the countries of the region can address the new challenges through cooperation in agricultural research efforts, sharing research-based technologies and exchanging the experiences related to agricultural support services. The promising areas of cooperation include sharing of genetic materials and experiences in biotechnology, tissue culture, plant genetics, and hybrid seed technology. Collaborated research to combat threats of climate change; conservation of water and land resources; and control of trans-boundary livestock and poultry diseases offer the other promising area for regional cooperation. The introduction of new crops and adoption of uniform quality standards by the member states are yet other areas for collaboration. India has developed significantly its agricultural research and extension system. Pakistan has experimented with the Farmer Field School training programme under Integrated Pest Management (IPM). Other countries have also specialised in some crop or resource use.

All countries of the region can benefit through exchange of information and collaboration in organising relevant research activities. The states of the region should enhance allocations to agricultural research and should be open for exchange of experts and training of agricultural scientists. A combination of short- and long-term; economic and social; macro and structural; and global, regional, and national policies is required to promote food security and reduce both poverty and hunger. While a comprehensive policy framework is needed to ensure food security, some policy measures can deal with food security and poverty simultaneously. There are five basic policy strategies that could be considered:

(a) providing food-based safety nets and related social protection programmes,
(b) enhancing the productivity of agriculture,
(c) promoting rural development,
(d) supporting agricultural research, and
(e) investing in human capital and basic infrastructure.

Cash transfer programmes should be targeted only to the poor so programme costs are more sustainable, even given limited fiscal space. Governments could consider establishing a 'hunger alleviation fund', in which they set aside a reasonable amount—say, 1 per cent of GDP—as buffer in times of food crisis. Such a fund would provide a safety net for the poor and those most vulnerable to hunger, malnutrition, and starvation. Private corporations could also be offered incentives (such as tax deductions) to contribute to the fund, which could be run by the government in partnership with the private sector. Safety nets specific to farmers would include weather-based crop insurance and futures contracts. Weather is a key source of uncertainty for a farmer's projected incomes, and thus impacts investment and production decisions. Weather-based crop insurance can reduce a large part of this uncertainty, giving farmers the chance to engage in more productive (albeit possibly riskier) activities such as alternative crop selection and use of new technologies.

Future contracts, which assure farmers specified prices for output, can also help mitigate risks caused by price fluctuations. Futures help assure farmers a minimum income for their harvest. While crop insurance is meant to encourage greater production, futures contracts can encourage poverty reduction. Further, improving agricultural productivity is essential for ensuring long-term food security and promoting poverty reduction. Adequate food supply is a fundamental prerequisite for food security, especially as the global population is projected to reach 9 billion by 2050. Promoting rural development can contribute substantially to poverty reduction and food security. These policy measures, if given priority would go a long way in tackling food security issues and reducing poverty.

## Notes and References

1. Mahin Karim, "The future of South Asian Security: Prospects for a Non-traditional Regional Security Agriculture", NBR Project Report, April 2013.
2. Muhammad Iqbal and Rashid Amjad, " Food Security in South Asia: Strategies and Programmes for Regional Collaboration", http://www.pide.org.pk/pdf/foodsecurity/research/FS3.pdf (accessed on 24.01.2014 )
3. http://articles.timesofindia.indiatimes.com/2013-11-30/india-business/44595673_1_food-security-poor-and-subsistence-farmers-india (accessed on 24.01.2014 )
4. http://www.dawn.com/news/947239/food-security-a-major-concern (accessed on 24.01.2014 )
5. http://www.fao.org/economic/ess/ess-fs/en/ (accessed on 13.02.2014 )

*Chapter 25*

# The Maldives: Fighting for Life

*Deeplekha Sengupta and Devarati Mandal*
Research Scholars
Department of International Relations
Jadavpur University, Kolkata

The end of the Cold War and the reconfigured power equations, in tandem with the rising tide of globalisation, environmental degradation and international terrorism, have unleashed new dimensions of security. Against this context we need to define non-traditional security threats in a comprehensive manner. According to Mely Caballero-Anthony non-traditional security threats may be defined as "challenges to the survival and well-being of people and states that arise primarily out of non-military sources, such as climate change, cross-border environmental degradation and resource depletion, infectious diseases, natural disasters, irregular migration, food shortages, people smuggling, drug trafficking, and other forms of transnational crime."[1]

Our article figures out one such non-traditional problem which has hardly been able to draw the attention of the world, i e security threats emanating from environmental degradation. Primarily, the environmental degradation occurs due to two factors: industrialisation and urban development causing global warming, to such a large extent that its consequences could only be partly limited, not stopped.

According to the United Nation's Report, the world is on the way to a warmer climate and more extreme fluctuations of temperatures.[2] By the end of this century the icebergs will be disappearing and consequently the sea levels will rise at least by 28-58 cm. Although such dangers are threatening all the nations, irrespective of their size and geography, for some the threat is indeed grave.

It is the natural tendency of the scholars and researchers of South Asia, primarily to concentrate their attention to the happenings and issues of heavy weight countries like, India, Pakistan, Bangladesh, or at the most Nepal and Sri Lanka. But, we often forget to include a tiny littoral country named the Maldives, fighting a strange battle for life. And our article deals with the impact of enormous climate change and the environmental threats faced by the Maldives and other such littoral states across the globe.

Since childhood we were taught that 'water' is the other name of life. In case of the Maldives it is the other way round. Water is death for them. The Republic of Maldives comprises 1,190 islands in 20 atolls spread over 900 km in the Indian Ocean. Of these, just 199 islands are inhabited with a population of slightly over 3,00,000 people. The highest point of land is 2 meters or about 6 feet above sea level.[3] The Maldives is a country with a coastline even lower than that of Bangladesh, Andaman-Nicobar, and Lakshadweep with the lowest highest point in the world which is only 2.3 m.[4] The Himalayas often referred to as the third pole, is witnessing a severe meltdown which has a direct connection to the rising sea level thousands of miles south around the Maldives.[5] The small sizes of the islands coupled with increasing population pressure, force human settlements and infrastructure to be located near the coast and therefore at high risk from sea level rise.[6]

The sea had already tucked into its maritime territory—stretched over 1,68,000 sq kms of continental shelf—leading to the loss of its legal right over 20 nautical miles, under the UN convention on the law of the sea that the Maldives ratified in 2000.[7] Within 100 years the Maldives could become uninhabitable and the entire population would be forced to evacuate. But they lack necessary manoeuvring space, required for evacuating the population. Thus, the very survival of the country is at stake. In near future the globe will witness the slow but ineluctable death of a nation.

Climate change has direct bearings on its economy. Drawn by its pristine beaches, underwater coral reefs, and spectacular marine wildlife, this small island-nation attracts some 5,00,000 tourists annually.—all of them are being affected by, increased beach erosion, and stronger storms.[8] The rising temperature of sea is bringing the reef growth at an alarmingly poor status. The corals already growing in highest tolerable temperature have a grim possibility of survival, given the predicted rise in temperature. The marine eco-system is largely being affected. Historically fishing, one of the main occupations of the majority is also in danger as most of the species are no more available. Tourism and fishery, the two pillars of the Maldives' economy are on the verge of collapse. The Maldives, primarily an agrarian economy, also lacks adequate land for agriculture, habitation and other developments. Another particular concern of the Maldives is the unavailability of fresh groundwater. All these are leading to several associated problems. As the economy has almost been paralysed, there is hardly any scope for youth employment. Therefore, it is quite natural that eventually the Maldives would become a safe haven for terrorism and it might also become a training ground for future terrorists. Actually, all these problems are emanating from global warming and climate change.

The Maldives has been contemplating several utopian measures to find a way out of this crisis. It has been considering India, Sri Lanka and Australia as three prospective homelands for the Maldivians. This shows their desperation to move to a safer place and the lukewarm approach of the international community propelling the Maldives to ponder over many impracticable and daffy notions. However, the Maldives, a country with few natural resources but a growing population and energy demands, is on the forefront of nations attempting to take themselves off the grid.[9] The 'Safe Islands Programme' in the aftermath of the tsunami was aimed at the development of the larger islands with better economic opportunities, high environmental resilience, and incentives for voluntary migration to these islands.[10] The Maldives is also encouraging forestation to prevent beach erosion and is backing a plan to clean litter and debris from the country's coral reefs—a natural barrier against tidal surges.[11] They are engrossed in building dykes and raising the level of a new island near Male to make room for the Maldivian population.

The menace of climate change is not merely a Maldivian problem. It is a global problem, the only difference being that, the small island nations like the Maldives are going to be engulfed earlier owing to their geographical locations and low-lying landscape. The Maldives has been trying to get its voice heard alone and in group for over a period of time. Be it the astounding underwater cabinet meeting or the 2008 resolution on climate change and human rights...the Maldives has been ceaselessly illuminating the gravity of the trouble they are mired in.

UNDP is supporting the country in its efforts by helping to establish policies and frameworks that will guide the efficient management and protection of the country's environment and natural resources, including the wider use of renewable energy technologies, sustainable land management, solid waste management and reducing the impact of climate change on the tourism industry.[12] Through the 'Maldives Environment Management Project', a $13.5 million IDA credit, the World Bank is working with the Government of the Maldives to effectively manage environmental risks to fragile coral reefs and other marine habitats.[13]

However, according to the UNDP the most serious underlying driver of increasing vulnerability to climate change in the Maldives is the absence of systematic adaptation planning and practice. Climate change risks and long-term resilience are not adequately integrated into island's land use planning or into coastal development and protection policies and practice.[14]

The implementation of these programmes does require money, and this is where the problem lies. It is the lack of money that is hindering their leap to the epithet of the 'First carbon neutral country' on earth. It will cost more than USD 1 billion to switch to wind, solar and wave energy. Part of this money will come from a new green tax of USD 3 per day for every tourist as well as from grants from the governments of rich countries with guilty consciences.[15] But, it should be maintained that 'going green' is the only viable option that all of us have if we are to stave off our doom. The developed nations better realise that this is the high time that they did their bit. A flexible and uninterrupted flow of funds and technology is needed to help the Maldives and several other endangered nations to switch over to renewable sources energy. Initiatives are to be taken at the regional level as well. The SAARC countries should take an initiative in cajoling the developed countries to become alive to their faux pas and the hideous consequences it thrusts upon countries like the Maldives. It is not possible to go green overnight, but substantial cuts in the carbon emissions and phased transformation from fossil fed economy to a carbon neutral one can certainly pave the way out of this maze. If we do not wake up from our slumbers, all of us run the risk of complete inundation...today or tomorrow.

As Nasheed, the Ex-president of the Maldives once said in one of his interviews that, "Climate change isn't a vague and abstract danger but a real threat to our survival...if the world cannot save the Maldives today; it might be too late to save London, New York, or Hong Kong tomorrow." The country is fighting an uneven war with nature, with hardly any chance of winning the battle. Unless they can motivate the world forum in their favour, their immediate future is bleak. Since survival is the ultimate motivation of security, the Maldives is trying hard to keep itself above water.

## Notes and References

1. http://www.stanleyfoundation.org/publications/pab/pab07mely.pdf (for further details: NTS-Asia Web site *www.rsis-nts.org.)*
2. http://www.un.org/apps/news/story.asp?NewsID=40440 (accessed on 1st Feb 2012)
3. http://web.worldbank.org/WBSITE/EXTERNAL/COUNTRIES/

SOUTHASIAEXT/0, contentMDK:22413695~pagePK:146736~piPK:146830~theSitePK:223547,00.html (accessed on 29th Jan 2012)

4. http://www.guardian.co.uk.environment/2008/nov/11/
5. Kunda Dixit, "Charting Change", *Himal Southasian*, Oct-Nov 2009, Vol 22, No 10/11, pp 25-28.
6. http://www.adb.org/Documents/Assessments/Country-Environmental/MLD/Environment-Assessment.pdf
7. "Marine Assets", *Himal Southasian*, Sept 2010, p 10.
8. http://web.worldbank.org/WBSITE/EXTERNAL/COUNTRIES/SOUTHASIAEXT/0, contentMDK:22413695~pagePK:146736~piPK:146830~theSitePK:223547,00.html((accessed on 29th Jan 2012)
9. http://newswatch.nationalgeographic.com/2011/10/15/maldives-ground-zero-for-climate-change-impacts/(accessed on 30th Jan 2012)
10. http://www.preventionweb.net/globalplatform/2007/first-session/docs/info_docs/GP_2007_Inf5.pdf
11. http://news.bbc.co.uk/2/hi/south_asia/3930765.stm (accessed on 29th Jan 2012)
12. http://undp.org.mv/v2/?lid=72 (accessed on 1st Feb 2012)
13. http://web.worldbank.org/WBSITE/EXTERNAL/COUNTRIES/SOUTHASIAEXT/0, contentMDK:22413695~pagePK:146736~piPK:146830~theSitePK:223547,00.html (accessed on 29th Jan 2012).
14. http://undp.org.mv/v2/?lid=171
15. Kunda Dixit, "Charting Change", *Himal Southasian*, Oct-Nov 2009, Vol 22, No 10/11, pp 25-28.

*Chapter 26*

# Water Conflict between India and Bangladesh: A Threat to Human Security

*Utsa Sarmin*
Student
Indraprastha College for Women
University of Delhi, Delhi

India and Bangladesh, despite sharing a common colonial heritage, have many bones of contention. Among the most complicated problems that resulted in a deadlock situation between the two countries, is the sharing of the waters of the Ganges and the Farakka Barrage constructed by India. The recent denial of West Bengal Chief Minister Mamata Banerjee to go for a Bangladesh tour to discuss the issue of water sharing, took the conflict to a new level. What is happening between the two countries are having an adverse effect on the human security of both the countries, especially the people from Bangladesh is suffering because most of the people in that country depend on agriculture and if they are denied the water of the Ganges, the lands of Bangladesh won't receive any water for cultivation and the men will be deprived of their livelihood. This is a huge concern for the government of Bangladesh as their citizens' lives are in threat.

## Methodology

The relation between India and Bangladesh in the view of water security will be broadly discussed in this paper. As water security comes under the broad term 'non-traditional security', the latter will also be explained in order to make the further arguments clear. The relation between India and Bangladesh has a historical trajectory and is not new, so, a brief history of both the countries are required in order to understand the recent developments of the relation between the two neighbouring countries which share the same colonial and cultural heritage but still have enormous unresolved issues. The former Bangladesh Foreign Minister, Muhammad Shamsul Haq once talked about the big-country, small-country syndrome, which is often regarded as the reason for tension between the two countries and reveal the existence of power hierarchy in the International Politics which even leads to the threat of human security.

## Non-Traditional Security

Security means being free from threat or danger. Traditionally in the political sphere threat was considered as war or foreign aggression and nation-states meant security as being free from the threat of foreign aggression or securing the borders of that particular nation-state. This concept of security has changed with the emergence of globalisation, environmental degradation, international terrorism, etc. The earlier mentioned concept of security is known as traditional security and the nation-states' concerns have moved from a traditional dimension to a non-traditional dimension of security. The concept of security has gone beyond territorial and military issues of a state. With the change in global realities, new facets of security are emerging especially after the end of Cold War. This is mainly called non-traditional security. There is a definite sphere, concept and definition of traditional security but there are no concrete concepts of these contemporary security issues.

Some main non-traditional security concerns are international terrorism, human security, drug trafficking, water security etc. While international terrorism is mainly conducted by non-state actors and weaken the theory of ultimate state sovereignty and has a concrete sphere, theory and way to combat it, the other issues, mainly human security under which water security also falls, are abstract and don't have an easy way to achieve it. Often the power hierarchy in the international politics makes, this even more complicated for the less powerful countries because a powerful nation, rich in natural resources can use their resources to exert control over the other nations which in turn undermines the state sovereignty.

The recent historic gas sale purchase agreement (GSPA) among Turkmenistan, Afghanistan, Pakistan and India (TAPI Gas Pipeline) will bring in industrial and economic developments in these countries. It is believed that this agreement will change the politics of this region. Petroleum and Natural Gas Minister Jaipal Reddy said, "Hopefully, the spin-off benefits of this pipeline will encourage us to emphasise trade and investment issues over contentious political issues and enable us to build trust and confidence among ourselves as neighbours and partners in progress."[1]

This trust and confidence will ensure security. The security achieved through energy share is an example of non-traditional security. This will also help the neighbouring countries to fight against international terrorism jointly, which is a major non-traditional security threat to the whole world and especially in this region. The economic ties will ensure cultural and political ties and this will hopefully establish peace in this region.

Similarly, water sharing also comes under non-traditional security. Water, in the contemporary world, is used as weapon by many countries to control a neighbouring country or a way to interfere in the internal matters of a country. For example, if India wants, it can turn the fertile lands of Bangladesh into drought areas by not sharing the waters of the Ganga and the Teesta rivers. In this way the human security of Bangladesh will be endangered also because the affected agriculture will ruin the livelihoods of a large number of people.

India has disputes with its neighbouring countries, namely, Pakistan, China and Bangladesh in the matter of sharing water. Dams have been built on the river Indus and its tributaries like the Jhelum, etc, and it has been one of the main reasons of contention between India and Pakistan. Pakistani farmers are heavily dependent on the Indus and they fear that India will manipulate the flow of water from upstream by building dams on it. "Many in Pakistan accuse New Delhi of wantonly exacerbating the country's dire water shortages, choking its agricultural production and ruining livelihoods."[2] This dispute will endanger both the countries' security issues.

India has some similar problems with China on the basis of sharing of the water of the Brahmaputra river, which is a major source of water for both India and Bangladesh. China recently announced the plans of building a mega-dam on the Brahmaputra river. This will diverse the course of it and the diversion will terribly affect both India and Bangladesh. This will degrade the relations between China and its neighbouring countries and will also become a major security issue.

## A Brief History of India-Bangladesh Relation

In order to know the water conflicts between the two neighbouring countries, one needs to understand the India-Bangladesh relation. These two countries shared the same colonial heritage and were under British rule for a long time. After the partition of India, Bangladesh came under Pakistan and was known as East Pakistan. The continuous domination of West Pakistan on East Pakistan resulted dissent and war for independence in the later. India had helped Bangladesh in its liberation war of 1971. The then Prime Minister of recently formed independent Bangladesh, Sheikh Mujibur Rahman established a friendly relation with India. Bangladesh is surrounded by India and is also dependent on India. India on the other hand acted like a big brother and helped Bangladesh in many issues. The then Indian Prime Minister Indira Gandhi and Bangladesh's founding leader Sheikh Mujibur Rahman signed Indo-Bangladesh Treaty of Friendship, Cooperation and Peace on March 19, 1972. In the treaty it was mentioned that the two nations will establish a Joint River Commission to work for the common interests and sharing of water resources, irrigation, floods and cyclones control. But after the assassination of Sheikh Mujibur Rahman, Bangladesh fell in the hands of autocratic rulers. From 1975-1990 Bangladesh gradually became an Islamic Militant state and an autocratic state. In this period terrorist activities grew in Bangladesh and India faced security threats from its neighbouring country. This ruined the friendly relation between these two neighbours. India also stepped back from its promises of helping Bangladesh in development. The two countries faced a deadlock situation. Still now the situation has not improved though due to Sheikh Hasina, the new Prime Minister of Bangladesh, India-Bangladesh relation has some improvement but the deadlock situation still prevails.

## Water Conflict between the Two Countries

The water conflict between India and Bangladesh started after the assassination of Sheikh Mujibur Rahman and it is still a major issue between the two countries. This not only affects the relation between the two countries, but also the peace and security of this region.

The water conflict started with the debate over sharing the water of the Ganga. The sharing of the waters of the river Ganga is a long-standing issue between India and Bangladesh. The issue has remained a subject of conflict for almost 35 years, with several bilateral agreements and rounds of talks failing to produce results.

The Farakka barrage on the river Bhagirathi is situated in Murshidabad, a district of West Bengal, India. It is used to divert the water of the Ganga into the river Hoogly during the dry season, i e from January to June. Bangladesh claims that its rivers were drying up because of excess drawing of water by India. In May 1974 India and Bangladesh issued a joint declaration to resolve the water sharing issue. However, after the assassination of Sheikh Mujibur Rahman, India withdrew from the process of negotiations in September 1976. Bilateral relations had improved in 1977 when both countries signed a 5-year treaty. This duly expired in 1982 without being renewed. The formation of an

Awami League government under Sheikh Hasina Wajed, the daughter of Sheikh Mujib, in 1996 led to a fresh freindly relation. Both leaders met in the Indian capital on December 12, 1996 and signed a 30-year treaty. According to the treaty, the water of the river Ganga would be distributed from Farakka for the two countries between January 1 and May 31. This established a solution to the long term problems of water sharing between the two countries.

Recently many problems are arising due to the share of the water of Ganga.

Professor Subrata Bagchi of Political Science Department of Khidirpur College, Kolkata, West Bengal, India, has shared his view regarding the problems of this water sharing in an interview taken while this paper was being written. His view is mentioned here.

> "It is said that diversion of the Ganga water has caused the increase in the salinity levels, hampered fisheries, thwarted navigation and posed a threat to water quality and public health in Bangladesh. But the Ganga Water Treaty between India and Bangladesh, 1996 adversely affects the Hooghly river and the Kolkata Port too. It is alleged that Bangladesh was supposed to receive 35,000 cusec water during the dry season in terms of the water agreement between the two neighbouring countries in terms of the Treaty, signed in 1996. But the country is actually getting 82,801 cusec water due to the drainage of water through the gates of the Farakka barrage. It has been pointed out that the excess outflow of water from Farakka barrage through two damaged sluice gates has reduced the Ganga's water level by three metres and is posing a threat of erosion at Jangipur area of Murshidabad district. The water level at the barrage, which should remain 21.90 metres, has come down by three metres as gate numbers 13 and 16 have broken down as a result of which the excess outflow was causing scarcity of water at NTPC's Farakka plant. So, India and particularly West Bengal face this adverse situation and any further review of the treaty in

favour of Bangladesh would destabilize the economy and living of the flora and fauna in the whole Bengal delta in India."

So it is seen that if this situation continues to exit, India's, especially West Bengal's people will face problems. The human security will also be in danger as the lower level of water will destroy the livelihoods of people, ie agricultural activities.

The river Teesta is also a river of contention between the two neighbouring countries.

The Teesta is the fourth major river after the Ganga, Brahmaputra and Meghna in the eastern region. It originates in Sikkim and after traversing 172 km in the hilly region, runs for 97 Km in the plains of India and another 124 km in Bangladesh. Sharing of Teesta water between India and Bangladesh is multi-dimensional. The Northwest region of Bangladesh is known as the granary of the country and the adequate water of the Teesta helps this region for cultivation. But due to India's larger share of water retained through the Gazoldoba Dam in Jalpaiguri district, the north-west region of Bangladesh faces drought in most part of the year. So this treaty is very important to Bangladesh. It would ensure food security. This will cause a threat to human lives also. This will cause degradation in flora and fauna and also cause illegal labour migration, also an enormous size of population would one day be without their traditional livelihood opportunities and means for survival. So if this treaty is signed, a vast number of Bangladesh's population can be saved. But India's North Bengal region is under-developed. There is no trade or industries, etc, the people are dependent on agriculture. So the agro-based industry of this region will receive a severe jolt if India gives away its water. West Bengal's food security also depends much on adequate monsoon and irrigation system in which the Teesta plays a pivotal role. "The argument then boils down to the fact that poverty in one part of Bangladesh cannot be dealt with by aggravating poverty among the population of another country, ie population of North Bengal in India," said Prof. Subrata Bagchi.

I asked Prof. Subrata Bagchi about India's suffering, if it shares the water of the Teesta as demanded by Bangladesh. His opinion:

> "The first one is that India's interest when conceived from the point of view of local interest would be affected if water is shared between these two countries, even though Bangladesh has her own right to region's natural resources as a member of the SAARC and as per the international norms for mutual friendship and cooperation. But India's perception of interest, conceived from the practical understanding of the geo-political factors relevant to the situation in South Asia and all over the world particularly after the collapse of the socialist Soviet Union suggests that Bangladesh's request for water share for her economic growth needs to be addressed with adequate diplomatic skill, political sagacity and acumen by taking into cognizance of Bangladesh's critical need to get tangible help from India. With this objective in mind water governance of these two countries should thrive on mutual respect to each other's needs. This is also necessary for India as well as for the present regime of Awami league, headed by Sheikh Hasina Wajed in view of the rising tide of Islamic fundamentalism in Bangladesh and Pakistan's persistent policy of hostility against India and China's military supremacy and her ambition for super power status in the changed international political scenario when she seems to be readying for taking on the US in the power game for control over Asia. So, domestic politics has to be dovetailed with South Asian perspective as well as international politics by keeping in mind India's military security, obviously food security and concerns for eco-system and water needs of the North Bengal region in mind".

Mir Mahmudul Hasan Astak, reporter of *Prothom Alo*, leading newspaper of Bangladesh, commented on this issue while discussing India-Bangladesh relation with me. He said, "Bangladesh will suffer if India won't share the water of the Teesta. As consequence of the situation, giant Teesta barrage and

Teesta Irrigation Project will be ineffe ctive. Production of paddy and other crops will fail in northern region of Bangladesh resulting in famine like situation. Desertification will be accelerated, birds and fishes will loss habitat and people living in the Teesta basin will be compelled to migrate to different place."

The Tipaimukh Dam is also playing a major role in the decline of the relation between India and Bangladesh.

The Tipaimukh dam, the 'Multipurpose Hydroelectric Project' over Barak river in Manipur has now turned into a major dispute between India and Bangladesh. This project is the bone of contention between the two countries. It is said that the damming of Barak river, seriously limiting free flowing of the Surma and Kushyara rivers will cause huge damage to agriculture, irrigation, drinking water supply, navigation, etc, and will reduce recharge of ground water during lean season. The dam would also leave millions jobless with the drying up of the two rivers. There is no international law which can prevent India from building up the dam. The issue may turn into a major hitch between these two countries in future.

Mir Mahmudul Hasan Astak said, "Tipaimukh dam project is a blockade to India-Bangladesh friendly relation. As impact of the dam, major rivers of Sylhet region will be dried up causing disaster to our people and economy. If a big country like India wants to get benefit hampering Bangladesh's interest then how can India-Bangladesh friendly relation sustain?"

"Any bilateral issue will seriously concern a nation's key and uncompromisable interest, if not resolved to the extent of satisfaction of the countries as the stakeholders might slip into major reasons for dispute between them. On this count Bangladesh and India are no exceptions. The sense of political realism might induce them battle for national interest. But an understanding of the relation between the two countries in the backdrop post-1971 period in the aftermath of Bangladesh Liberation Movement presents the view that although the issues are extremely important for them, they should not pursue them to the extent of producing a permanent hostility since both Pakistan and China intend to dominate India and Bangladesh in South Asia. Therefore, they need to draw a baseline of common interest in the perspective of South Asian politics upon which the other major issues of bilateral interest must be resolved. Moreover, both the societies resemble each other in terms of many linguistic and cultural traditions. So, political and economic interests need to be pursued by keeping in mind the whole set of political scenario/ factors and also cultural and political affinities. The foundation of non-traditional security aspects involving the eco-system, bio-diversity, and food security, security of employment and retention of workforce needs to be addressed with proper attention and timely intervention from the governments of both the neighbouring states," said Prof. Subrata Bagchi.

Mir Mahmudul Hasan Astak said, "Indian Government, again and again is promising that the treaty will be signed but every time they failed to live up to their promises. Bangladesh Government is finding this very insulting." He also said that, "Economic relation is the root of developing all other ties like cultural ties and political ties. If Bangladesh is economically hampered then the other ties will also be affected. It will also weaken non-traditional security issues."

Prof. Samad of Political Science Department of Presidency University gave his opinion in this matter. He said that, "As a big brother, India should look beyond political issues. It should look at the side of humanity and help Bangladesh to have adequate water. India should work out plans that will store water in rainy season so in lean seasons both the countries can use the stored water."

After listening to all the opinions, it is clear that the bilateral relation between India and Pakistan is in stakes. To improve this relation India should take some steps because Bangladesh is deprived because of the former one. Also India has greater power than Bangladesh and India can make a difference in international politics by adopting humanitarian way to solve this water issue. This will ensure peace and friendly relation in this region and hence the non-traditional security will not be hampered.

## Bibliography

1. *TAPI pipeline gas sale agreement signed,* The Hindu; Access date:3/02/2014, Available from: http://www.thehindu.com/business/Economy/article3449588.ece
2. Mandhana, N Water Wars: *Why India and Pakistan Are Squaring Off Over Their Rivers;* Access date: 3/02/2014, Available From: http://www.time.com/time/world/article/0,8599,2111601,00.html

*Chapter 27*

# A Journey from Present to Future Perfect Through the Prism of Health Security

*Dr Ranjit Chakrabarti*
Consultant Gynaecologist and
Laparoscopic Surgeon, Kolkata

Security is most commonly defined and explained by academicians, security experts, bureaucrats, foreign policy experts and politicians. However, security is mostly analyzed from an academic perspective and very rarely from a medical viewpoint. Medical security is an essential factor for the growth of any nation. Hence, the health of the state is the wealth of a good state.

This paper aims to put forward the concept of security from a medical practitioner's perspective, a unique outlook. As a gynaecologist, it is a privilege to treat women from different parts of the world—developed and developing world. When we're talking about the urban population, there is a similarity with the western developed world, while in case of the rural population; it is in contrast with the western developed regions. This paper deals with the challenges and probable remedies in the health sector—rural and urban in India, Nepal, Bhutan and Bangladesh based on my personal experiences. In case of India, my experience revolves around both rural and urban people, while in case of Bangladesh; my experience is of treating mainly economically privileged classes apart from the fewer number of economically backward people. It is also the case in Nepal and Bhutan. As per the HDI 2012, India ranks 136th, Nepal ranks 157th, Bhutan ranks 140th, and Bangladesh ranks 146th.

Health refers to the state of the body and mind that leads to a healthy person. It is the state of being well or ill. However, the primary cause behind health problem is ignorance. Ignorance about being healthy leads to a host of physical and mental disorders and diseases. However, ignorance emanates from gross illiteracy. Lack of adequate knowledge about health issues and lack of awareness creates massive ignorance which consequently gives birth to a series of health hazards.

It is often found that among the population, the general concept of health revolves around sickness. Health concerns only start when we fall sick which basically keeps us far away from a healthy nation. The people in this region feel concerned about health when they are affected, rather than being conscious about their health all throughout, in order to have a better and hazard free region.

As mentioned everywhere, India's majority population lives in the village and a good chunk of them at below poverty line. This rural population is hardly, rather not at all aware about health issues. They don't have any knowledge about keeping their basic health proper and fit; they are only concerned when they fall sick and are suffering. In fact, once they are out of the suffering, they barely follow-up with the doctor or go for routine check-up.

In this context, it needs to be mentioned, that anemia is the biggest sickness in India that has affected most rural girls and women. To check this major health hazard, young girls, who are the easily affected, should to be taught about hygiene and health. In fact, these girls along with their mothers needs to be educated about hygiene even before the young girls start menstruating. These females should also be provided with proper nutritional foods and supplements, so that various deficiency diseases can't distress the female population of rural India. In fact, once a year a health check-up is also a worthy step towards combating any health problem, but unfortunately no such facilities are available in the rural part of the country. Shockingly, most rural population, irrespective of men and women are barely aware through the medium of primary health centres, which ought to be the biggest lifeline for them.

Awareness is a big zone of stress in rural India. Awareness about teenage marriage and pregnancy needs to be adequately meted out to the rural women. Moreover, lot needs to be done since early teenage as that is the time when the body of a girl metamorphoses. In case of rural India, the fight against these health hazards needs to be channelized through the following stages:

- School level
- Puberty level
- Marriage level

This fight can be dealt out through two broad categories—

- **Preventive Medicines**: Efforts has to be put in for availability of personal hygiene, availability of toilets and proper utilization of the toilets and availability of drinking water. Efforts should be also put in to cure anemia through awareness, access to adequate nutritional supplements and access to vitamin tablets. In rural India, people are affected by worms, which causes serious hazard; efforts should be put in to aware people about it and also to prevent it. Health centres for young girls should be erected for their regular check-up.

  Married and aged people must be kept under surveillance as they are susceptible to sickness. In the rural areas, there are no mechanisms for cancer screening programmes to aware them about the killing disease. Hence, screening programmes should be organized for senior citizens and women in the rural areas of India.

  Since, women are worst affected by breast and cervical cancer and therefore screenings and awareness programmes for women should be arranged. Proper check-up for pre and post-menstruation should be conducted to avoid further risks.

- Fighting diseases and pregnancy: For pregnant women, proper nutritional intake is essential. Adequate nutritional quotient would eventually prevent different deficiency diseases. Thus, sufficient amount of vitamin, iron and other minerals are required.

  Child delivery is a crucial issue in rural areas. Delivery at primary health centres should be done even more professionally and carefully. In fact, trained mid-wife should be roped in for preventing major catastrophe. However, government initiatives already have been taken like ASHA, but more of such efforts are required to meet the needs.

So far the Indian government is alert and concerned about women health. Government have put in efforts to cure deficiency diseases affecting women, preventing HIV among mothers and children, creating awareness about HIV, preventing early marriage and pregnancy, etc.

Though door to door workers are there in rural areas, but they should be more in numbers, campaigns should be done to promote overall health awareness, alongside HIV and pregnancy.

Now, cervical cancer vaccines are available in India, but they are quite expensive which is beyond the reach of the rural people. Government should take the initiative to make the vaccines available, if possible at a cheaper rate in the rural areas.

However, the problem in urban India is reverse, but not less in impact. The problems in urban India are increasing manifold, and the problems are:

- **Late marriage**: This leads to infertility and pregnancy disorder. This is a rampant problem in the Indian cities.
- **Lifestyle disorder**: This is commonly considered as a western impact to the Indian society. This disorder has made teenagers suffer from PCOD (Poly-cystic Ovary Disorder), which is a serious problem with a good number of Indian young women. In fact, according to studies, PCOD is turning out to be a turbulent disease. Regular

USG, light food and avoidance of junk foods help prevent these problems.

- For most Indian urban women, career has taken the front seat. Career becomes priority than family and children.
- **Stress:** Personal and professional stress leads to disturbing conjugal life, adjustment problem and eventually leading to the rise of divorce rate.
- Young generations are gradually losing trust on the institution of marriage due to a liberal society. Due to this liberal society, there has been a growth in sexually transmitted diseases, unwanted pregnancy and growth of abortion. Another serious concern is the growth of multiple sexual partners, which prevalent amongst young girls and women.
- **Safety:** The idea of safety has to be considered. Use of condoms and contraceptive pills is essential. Though, the Indian urban society has incorporated western liberal social lifestyle, yet it has to build up efforts for sex education like the West.

Hence, lack of exercise and bad food habit leads to a bad lifestyle which is equal to rural hazards regarding health.

In case of Bangladesh, the two societies are completely different. There are only two classes in Bangladesh—rich and poor. Though, in economically privileged sections, there are two categories—one, claim to be orthodox and other is comparatively open and modern. For these two categories, even the challenges are different in nature. Though the idea of family planning in the Bangladesh society has not been completely gloomy, yet there is no consideration of women's wishes in most cases of procreation.

Unfortunately, infertility is also rising in Bangladesh with growing aspirations and needs. In the villages of Bangladesh, the problems are mostly like ours. However, the urban society in Bangladesh is covered up; they don't open up. This is a serious problem as it prone to risk and hence such a risk-affected society cannot come for help.

Thus, to conclude it can be asserted that the societies in India and Bangladesh are highly affected by cross-cultural impact. Lot of efforts and initiatives has to be taken up by the government and private health organizations to prevent serious health hazards that affect women and girls and consequently harm the growth and development of the nation as well as the South Asian region. The healthier a state, a region and a continent lives, the maximum will be its scope and development.

# Contributors

- **MK Narayanan** is the Governor of West Bengal. He was formerly the country's third National Security Advisor (2005-2010). He headed the Intelligence Bureau (IB) from 1987 to 1990, before heading the Joint Intelligence Committee. He became Chief of the IB again in 1991, before retiring in 1992. He was the Special Advisor for Internal Security to the Prime Minister of India beginning in May 2004.
- **Shakti Sinha**, a former civil servant, worked with the Government of National Capital Territory of Delhi as Principal Secretary (Power and Industry) and other important departments. Earlier, he was with the Andaman and Nicobar Administration as Chief Secretary. Earlier with the UN Mission in Afghanistan for three years coordinating international support to the Government on National Development Strategy, and on governance issues. Spent about two years with think tanks in Delhi (Observer Research Foundation) and Singapore (Institute of South Asian Studies) working on development issues and Afghanistan respectively. Authored a number of chapters and papers on the Afghan situation including for international publications plus various articles for newspapers and journals on Governance, Political Economy of Reforms and on the Chinese economy.
- **Krishnan Srinivasan** is a retired Indian diplomat, scholar, author, former Indian Foreign Secretary, and Deputy Secretary-General of the Commonwealth of Nations. He was

appointed to the Indian Foreign Service in May 1959. His early postings included Oslo, Beirut, Tripoli. He was India's Ambassador/High Commissioner to Zambia and Botswana, Nigeria, Benin and Cameroun, the Netherlands and Bangladesh. He was appointed Secretary and finally Foreign Secretary and retired in 1995. In 1995, he was appointed Commonwealth Deputy Secretary-General for Political Affairs in London where he served until 2002. He was the Fellow of Wolfson College Cambridge (2002-05), Fellow of the Centre for International Studies Cambridge (2002-05), Fellow of the Institute of Commonwealth Studies London (2002-08), Fellow of the Netherlands Institute of Advanced Studies (2003-04), Fellow of the Maulana Abul Kalam Azad Institute of Asian Studies, Kolkata from 2006, and Fellow of the Swedish Collegium for Advanced Study at Uppsala in (2008 and 2012-13). He is a regular columnist and book reviewer on international affairs for the two Kolkata based English newspapers—*The Telegraph* and *The Statesman*.

- **Alok Bansal** is Senior Fellow at the Centre for Land Warfare Studies (CLAWS), New Delhi and the Executive Director of South Asian Institute for Strategic Affairs (SAISA). He has been a Visiting Professor at the Pakistan Studies Programme of Maulana Mohammed Ali Jauhar Academy of International Studies at Jamia Millia Islamia. He has been the Executive Director of the National Maritime Foundation (NMF) and has worked with the Institute for Defence Studies and Analyses (IDSA), New Delhi for over five years. He has authored a book titled; Balochistan in Turmoil: Pakistan at Cross Roads; in 2009 and has co-edited three books titled *South Asian Security: 21st Century Discourses*, *Pakistan Occupied Kashmir: The Untold Story* and *Sri Lanka: Search for Peace*. He has written extensively in International and Indian professional journals as well as for Indian, Pakistani and international newspapers. He has presented Research Papers at Seminars and Round Tables and has lectured extensively at Military and Academic Institutions, both in India and abroad. He was part of the

Indian Team at Indo-Australian and Indo-Malaysian Strategic Dialogues and has been a participant in various Track II Dialogues between India and Pakistan.

- **Sanjay Bhardwaj** is Assistant Professor at South Asian Studies Division, School of International Studies, Jawaharlal Nehru University, New Delhi. His academic interests include Politics, identity, Water and energy Security, socio-economic development and foreign policy issues of Bangladesh in particular and South Asian countries in general. He has been the ASIA Fellow 2010-11 (ASIA Scholarship Foundation, Bangkok), at the University of Dhaka, Bangladesh to pursue his research on 'Bangladeshi Perspective on Water Sharing Issue vis-à-vis India and Sir Ratan Tata Fellow 2009-10 at London School of Economics and Political Science, London, UK for the research on 'Contesting Identities in Bangladesh'. He has also been Chinese Academy of Social Science-ICSSR Visiting Fellow-2013 at Beijing and conducted his research on China's South Asia Policy. He has authored over three dozen articles and research papers on contemporary socio-political issues including water and energy security issues in South Asia.
- **Biswanath Chakraborty** is Associate Professor at Department of Political Science, Rabindra Bharati University, Kolkata. He is a distinguished political analyst and often takes part in political discussions aired on electronic media. He is also a regular contributor to daily newspapers. Apart from contributing several articles in reputed journals, he has also authored 13 books on Local Government and Politics, International Relations, Voting Behaviour and Rural Development. He was also involved in different research projects funded by the Government of India, Government of Netherlands, University Grants Commission (UGC), etc.
- **Anindya Jyoti Majumdar** is an Associate Professor at Department of International Relations, Jadavpur University, Kolkata. His area of specialisation is Security and Disarmament Studies; Conflict and Peace Studies, Forced

Migration, Foreign Policy. He had been a Research Consultant with the Indian Council for Research on International Economic Relations, New Delhi. He visited University of South Carolina, USA, under a Fulbright Program and attended various other international schedules including Regional Defence and Cooperative Security workshops in Shanghai and Colombo. Apart from contributing to various compendiums, he has authored a book, Lethal Games on India-Pakistan nuclear relations and edited or co-edited a few others on nuclearisation, forced migration, global politics and foreign policy issues.

- **Partha Pratim Basu** is Associate Professor, Department of International Relations, Jadavpur University, Kolkata. His publications include *Press and Foreign Policy in India, North-South Relations: A Postcolonial Research Agenda* (co-author), *Revisiting Rammohun Roy's Political Agenda, Democracy and Democratization in the 21st Century* (co-editor), *Locating Cultural Change* (co-editor) apart from several book chapters and articles contributed to edited volumes and national and international journals of repute.
- **Shounak Set** is a post-graduate student in the Department of International Relations, Jadavpur University. A critical observer of current affairs and international developments, he has presented papers at several seminars and contributed to student journals and news bulletins. He has been awarded the SYLFF Fellowship (Sasakawa Young Leaders Fellowship Fund) 2013-14 for multi-disciplinary research and leadership potential. He has presented papers in various national and international seminars.
- **Pratyay Dutta** is a Research Scholar at Department of International Relations, Jadavpur University, Kolkata.
- **Shubhodeep Chakrabarti**, Assistant Professor, Department of Political Science, Scottish Church College (University of Calcutta), Kolkata.
- **Amartya Ray**, Research Scholar, Jadavpur University, Kolkata and Fellow, Global India Foundation.

- **Somali Mukherjee** is Assistant Professor at Gurudas College (University of Calcutta), Kolkata.
- **Suranjan Das** presently holds the position of Vice-Chancellor, University of Calcutta and Honorary Director, Netaji Institute for Asian Studies, Kolkata. He is a Professor of History (currently on lien) in the University of Calcutta. He earned DPhil from the University of Oxford in 1987. He has authored several books on communal riots, food movement and electoral politics in South Asia etc. He has authored many articles in international and national journals. He has also attended international seminars/workshops/conferences in the UK, Germany, France, Italy, the Netherlands, Sweden, the USA, Vietnam, China, Uzbekistan, Pakistan, Bangladesh, Nepal, and Sri Lanka. He has received several international and national awards, scholarships and prizes.
- **Pradip Bhattacharjee** is currently the Member of Parliament, India and a veteran Indian politician. He has also served the Government of India as a minister. Earlier, He was a Professor at a city based college under University of Calcutta.
- **Ashwini K Roy** is a retired Professor of Jawaharlal Nehru University, New Delhi from 1974-2004. He had held visiting assignments in several universities in India and internationally including ones at the London School of Economics, Cambridge University, Sorbonne, and many more. His latest published work in 2004 is titled *Western Realism and International Relations: A Non-Western View*.
- **Aloke Sen** is a retired Indian diplomat. He holds extensive diplomatic experience spanning 34 years and especially covering Central Asia, Turkey, South East Asia and South Asian regions. He was India's Ambassador to Turkey, Cambodia and Myanmar from 2001-10. He has also served as Ambassador-at-Residence at Calcutta University's Institute of Foreign Policy Studies. He currently speaks and writes on foreign policy issues.
- **Saswati Ghosh** is a feminist economist and activist with aptitude and training in macro and meso data handling and

analysis, also at dissemination of information at popular and specifically vernacular (Bengali) level. Her interests include gender-based quality of life—with respect to survival and health, education and work participation, especially of the marginal groups. She has been actively engaged in feminist activism in Kolkata and has been a founder-member of first-ever autonomous women's group, Nari Nirjatan Pratirodh Mancha and its fight against rights' violation by state and non-state agencies. She is also a founder-member of Maitree network, a post-Beijing network of women's groups, NGO's and individual women. She is a volunteer with Jabala Action Research Organisation, working for the rights of deprived children. She has a number of books and articles in edited collections in her areas of interest, both academic and popular.

- **Sanghamitra Sarker** is Associate Professor at Department of Political Science, Surendranath College for Women, Kolkata. She has been working on a host of research projects ranging from women issues, foreign policy and conflict studies funded by the Government of India, Indian Council for Social Science Research (ICSSR) and University Grants Commission (UGC). She has made several foreign visits for paper presentations and film screenings at Paris, France; Berlin, Germany; Dhaka, Bangladesh and Yangon. (She has also contributed several articles in journals and newspapers. She has won international accolades for a documentary feature 'Anwesha' on Hindustani classical music.)
- **Satabdi Das** is a Research Scholar at the Department of International Relations, Jadavpur University, Kolkata. She has presented papers at various national and international seminars on Environmental Security, Water Resources, Climate Change, etc.
- **Shankhamala Ray** is a journalist with the ABP Group, Kolkata. She is a Doctoral Scholar at the Department of International Relations, Jadavpur University. She works on political connotations in post-2000 films from Muslim-majority countries of South Asia and West Asia. She is a

Faculty member at Surendranath College for Women. She has worked as a UNICEF project fellow on representation of child issues in the print media. She is an independent documentary and short film maker. She has made a documentary (Right To Joy) on child's rights, produced by UNICEF; a political animation on India-Pakistan relations, which was screened in Kolkata film festival 2011, etc. Shankhamala is a member of Jadavpur Association of International Relations (JAIR). She has two publications—*Films as Ushers of Democracy* and *Islamic Women in Films: Turning the Voyeurs into Spectators*.

- **Moutusi Paul Choudhury** is a Research Scholar at the Department of International Relations, Jadavpur University, Kolkata.
- **Subarna Bhattacharya is a** Research Scholar at the Department of International Relations, Jadavpur University, Kolkata and a Faculty member at Surendranath College for Women. Earlier, she had worked as a sub-editor (*Desh Magazine*, ABP Group).
- **Sharmita Bhattacharya** is a Research Scholar at the Department of International Relations, Jadavpur University, Kolkata.
- **Devarati Mandal** and **Deeplekha Sengupta** are Research Scholars at the Department of International Relations, Jadavpur University, Kolkata.
- **Utsa Sarmin** is an undergraduate student of Political Science at Indraprastha College for Women, University of Delhi. She has a keen interest in feminist politics, world politics and International Relations. A lover of debate, she has participated in various national and international levels Model United Nations Conferences. She has presented papers in various seminars. Her published works include "Legal Security of Women: A Comparative Study of India and Bangladesh", "Beauty Women and the Market", "Chalo Bandh Bhangi" Britter Baire Andarer Galpo" (A Collection of Short Stories on problems of Muslim Women in Bengali)and "Fire Dekha".

- **Dr Ranjit Chakrabarti** is a Consultant Gynaecologist and Laparoscopic Surgeon practicing as a senior consultant in Kolkata's leading hospitals for 15 years. His area of specialisation is treating ovarian cyst, breast cancer and management of infertility. He had also worked as a Registrar at the Princes Margaret Hospital. He participates and conducts regular CME's in Kolkata as well as in different parts of West Bengal.

# Index